GOVERNING MOTIONS

Vote required?	Applies to what motions?	Motions can have what applied to it (in addition to withdraw)?	Can be renewed?
majority	no other motion	no other motion	yes [2]
majority	no other motion	amend [1]	yes [2]
no vote	no other motion	no other motion	no
majority	main, amend, appeal	no other motion	yes [2]
two-thirds	debatable motions	no other motion	yes [2]
two-thirds	debatable motions	amend [1]	yes [2]
majority	main motion	amend,[1] vote immediately, limit debate	yes [2]
majority	main, amend	vote immediately, limit debate	yes [2]
majority	variable in form	subsidiary motions, reconsider	no
majority	main motion	vote immediately, limit debate	no
majority	no motion	specific main, subsidiary, object to consideration	no
majority	main, amend, appeal	vote immediately, limit debate, postpone definitely	no
majority	main motion	all subsidiary motions	no
majority	main, amend, appeal	no other motion	yes [2]
majority	main motion	amend	yes [2]
tie or majority	decisions of chair	limit debate, vote immediately, postpone temporarily or definitely	no
no vote	any error	no other motion	no
no vote	no motion	no other motion	no
no vote	all motions	none	yes [2]
two-thirds	no motion	no other motion	yes [2]
two-thirds negative	main motion	no other motion	no
no vote	main, amend	no other motion	no
no vote	voice votes	no other motion	no

[1] Restricted.   [2] After change in parliamentary situation.

LEARNING PARLIAMENTARY PROCEDURE

LEARNING

illustrated by ALAN ATKINS

1953 NEW YORK TORONTO LONDON

PARLIAMENTARY PROCEDURE

ALICE F. STURGIS

AUTHOR OF *Sturgis Standard Code
of Parliamentary Procedure*

with verses by RICHARD ARMOUR
and cartoons by LEO HERSHFIELD

McGRAW-HILL BOOK COMPANY, INC.

LEARNING PARLIAMENTARY PROCEDURE

FOREWORD

Parliamentary law is applied not only by legislatures, executives, and courts but by many others. Parliamentary procedure is to legislation what court procedure is to litigation. It is essential to competent self-government. It also can help any group make up its mind. It leads, as promptly, fairly, and intelligently as possible, to the discovery of high common factors of agreement.

Free people will do well to learn its elements with their alphabets and use them in every policy-forming group—from a troop of Scouts to the Parliament of Man. It requires the wishes of a deliberative body to be ascertained with justice to each member, and when so ascertained, it expects each member to abide by them.

This book explains how diverse views in any group may be brought to an issue by orderly discussion and converted into majority action. Such procedure enables free people to take united action and yet retain the greatest individual freedom consistent with the interests of all. It is a precious passkey to peace and good will.

Associate Justice
Supreme Court of the United States

v

ACKNOWLEDGMENTS

This book absorbs and reflects the judgment, wisdom, and varied experience of hundreds of individuals and organizations. It is truly a cooperative effort. Try as I may, I shall probably fail to make my bow to many who deserve my thanks.

Among those who read the manuscript and made constructive suggestions were: Clarence T. Simon, Professor of Speech, Northwestern University; A. Craig Baird, Professor of Speech, State University of Iowa; James Gordon Emerson, Professor of Speech at Stanford University; Fred S. Stripp, Associate Professor of Speech at the University of California; and Paul Mason, author of the *Manual of Legislative Procedure.*

Among those who advised on the bibliography and other material were Leland Chapin, Professor of Speech at Stanford University; Gordon Hearn, Professor of Education, University of California; Thomas Reed, Municipal Consultant; Marguerite Vanderworker, Social Group Worker, University of California; George Kyte, Professor of Education at the University of California; Richard T. LaPiere, Professor of Sociology, Stanford University.

Valued advice on the importance and relationship of voluntary organizations to democracy was given by Paul Gray Hoffman, of the Ford Foundation. I was helped in developing the subject of conventions by the vast practical experience of James A. Farley, now Chairman of the Board of the Coca-Cola Export Company; by J. S. Turner, Secretary-Treasurer of the International Association of Convention Bureaus; and by the following bureau managers: Clarence A. Arata, Washington, D.C.; Royal W. Ryan, New York City; Chester A. Wilkins, Chicago; and Walter Swanson, San Francisco.

To the many leaders and executive secretaries of national organizations who made available records, explained procedures, and invited me to attend their committee sessions, their meetings and their conventions, I am deeply appreciative.

A few of the verses by Richard Armour first appeared in *The Saturday Evening Post, The Christian Science Monitor,* and the *Wall Street Journal,* and I am grateful to the editors of these publications for permission to include them in the present volume. I also appreciate the courtesy of Erwin D. C. Canham and Herbert E. Thorson, of *The Christian Science Monitor,* for permitting me to use portions of my own column, "Mr. Chairman," which appeared weekly in that newspaper, and the permission of William I. Nichols, editor of *This Week Magazine* to use part of an article of mine, "Don't Let Them Push You Around," which that magazine first published.

I thank Ellen J. Cornish, reference librarian, who has done research for me in libraries, from Stanford University to the Library of Congress and Robert English, teacher and parliamentarian, who has furnished valuable material.

Special gratitude for their encouragement, counsel and help goes to Cody Fowler, former President of the American Bar Association; Captain James E. Brenner, who has accomplished many missions for the American Bar Association; Roy E. Willey, former Chairman, House of Delegates, American Bar Association; and David Maxwell, Chairman, House of Delegates of the American Bar Association.

For friendly advice and guidance I express my deep appreciation to Joseph Henry Jackson, Book Editor of the *San Francisco Chronicle,* Irita Van Doren, Book Editor of the *New York Herald Tribune,* and Samuel Hayakawa, Editor of *ETC.*

I shall always be grateful for the wide vision of the importance of meeting procedures to a free people, given me by Harold H. Burton, Associate Justice of the Supreme Court of the United States, who wrote the inspiring foreword.

To Owen J. Roberts, former Associate Justice of the Supreme Court of the United States, who leads in organizations that are world-wide in scope, yet who has time to help in village community projects, I pay tribute for warm and practical cooperation.

ALICE F. STURGIS

CONTENTS

PART ONE: PROCEDURE
Its Principles and General Rules

PART TWO: MOTIONS

PART THREE: ORGANIZATIONS
Their Structure and Functions

INTRODUCTION

PURPOSE OF THIS BOOK

This book is intended to help anyone to learn parliamentary procedure and to participate more effectively in the work of various types of organizations. Beyond this, it attempts to explain the reasoning and the fundamental principles underlying group functioning and the relation between voluntary organizations and our self-government in a democratic society. It is based upon the *Sturgis Standard Code of Parliamentary Procedure,* a manual of principles and rules based in turn upon common practice and law and intended for adoption by organizations.

Because the Code is primarily a book of reference, it has seemed desirable to prepare a book more directly aimed at the learning process—a book arranged for convenience of study and containing an informal and extensive discussion of subjects which could not be included in a code of rules.

Such a book is the present one. Here will be found a presentation of such subjects as voluntary organizations, the history of procedure, the uses and characteristics of motions, and the work of committees, conferences, and conventions. Here too are such teaching and learning aids as a glossary of parliamentary terms, extensive practice projects, offering a wide variety of experience in the application of rules to actual situations, and tests by which the reader may check his progress and comprehension of the subject. An additional feature is the presentation of meeting procedures, not in the form of abstract rules, but in application to specific situations.

SOURCES OF RESEARCH

Until embarking on the present study, I had what I considered a respectable familiarity with the procedures of our outstanding voluntary organizations. For some years, as a consultant on organizational problems to a score or more of national groups, I had studied group methods. But my knowledge gained from this experience was more broad than deep. What was needed was the incentive and the opportunity to make a thoroughgoing analysis of a representative selection of outstanding voluntary organizations.

The good fortune of receiving a fellowship from the John Simon Guggenheim Memorial Foundation enabled me to make analyses which play a large part in the present book. Working as a research fellow, I began an intensive study, still continuing, of the methods and procedures of six national organizations: The American Farm Bureau Federation, the National Congress of Parents and Teachers, the Chamber of Commerce of the United States, the American Federation of Labor, the American Medical Association, and the American Bar Association. Greater familiarity with the working of these groups has more than ever impressed me, not only with their efficiency of effort, but also with the democratic nature of that operation and its significant part in the free, cooperative endeavor of our nation.

ARRANGEMENT OF MATERIAL

There are numerous effective ways of teaching parliamentary procedure.

In arranging this text I faced a choice; one alternative was to present a chapter on some general subject and then a chapter on motions, and to continue this alternation. This plan would leave no leeway for the instructor to choose his own order to meet his needs. The second plan was to group similar subjects together and leave the instructor free to select his order of study, or the reader to go through the book in whatever way he finds most profitable. The latter plan seemed more logical, and the text was therefore divided into the following three parts:

1. Procedure: Its Principles and General Rules
2. Motions
3. Organizations: Their Structure and Functions

Most of the successful instructors whom I have observed alternately take up chapters on general subjects and chapters on motions. For example, Chapter 1 of Part One, "Our Voluntary Organizations," would be the first assignment, and it would be followed by Chapter 11 of Part

Two, "The Main Motion"—then Chapter 2 would be followed by Chapter 12.

This method gives a sustained and cumulative period of practice with motions and brief, immediate practice with other subjects, such as constitutions, committees, and conventions, as each is studied.

PRACTICE PROJECTS

The practice projects are suggestive only. Every teacher has his own methods of testing and reviewing which he may prefer to use.

The projects are, in the main, based on situations.

Experience in applying general principles and rules to specific situations is the direct way of training for effective participation in actual organizations. Learning rules and forms is useless unless the student develops the ability to reason out the answer to a situation from his knowledge of fundamental principles.

Emphasis should be placed on the form and phraseology of motions and suitability of their discussion, rather than on the facts of either the motions or the discussion. To this end, it is helpful to hold meetings of a type of organization completely different from the kind of organizations to which you actually belong.

If your study group is composed of college students, assume the roles of members of the Society for the Prevention of Cruelty to Animals, or the Boilermakers' Union, or the Board of Directors of the Standard Oil Company. This role-playing is fun. It exercises the imagination, fosters an understanding of the problems and points of view of other groups, and saves the participant from becoming absorbed in his own ideas and convictions to the neglect of the rules.

If your group is made up of practicing lawyers, pretend to be any type of organization except one of lawyers. It is also well to change the type of organization several times during the practice period, so that the members will not become too concerned with the problems of the organization that they are representing, but, again, will concentrate on the rules. The danger of conducting practice within the framework of a familiar organization is that the attention soon centers upon the material being discussed, rather than on the rules. In an unfamiliar situation the rules stand out more clearly.

PARLIAMENTARY CONTESTS

The first class in Parliamentary Law that I taught was at a summer session of the University of California. The session closed with a parliamentary contest that drew a large audience.

The class was divided into two groups: the Republicans and the Democrats. The Republicans were given half an hour to try to put through a motion, and the Democrats opposed them by proposing innumerable motions, by using dilatory tactics in debate, and by utilizing every trick and stratagem they could devise. Judged by the wild enthusiasm and the intense interest, the contest was a huge success.

Some weeks later two of the students who were active in the contest were delegates to a convention. There they disrupted the convention session through the very tactics they had used as contestants. They made complete nuisances of themselves. They proved that they were expert in parliamentary knowledge, but that they lacked a comprehension of the fundamental philosophy and intent of parliamentary procedure. The fault, of course, was mine. Despite my warnings, they were using a constructive tool as a destructive weapon. I had evidently failed to convince them that trickery does not pay in the long run, and that it is a misapplication of a constructive art.

However, there is no reason why such a contest should not be held to illustrate the possibilities of sharp practices and filibustering in opposition. Parliamentary law is a subject that lends itself to contests. Numerous stimulating types of competitions can be devised to illustrate the constructive use of parliamentary procedure.

An occasional contest of this type is enjoyable, but it should be labeled what it is—a contest in obstructive tactics, an illustration of what-not-to-do in actual organization work. The only time such tactics are justified is when they are used first by others. Sometimes it is necessary to meet fire with fire.

This is not to say that students should fail to understand all the many little tricks of parliamentary procedure. If they do not understand them, they may be defeated by them.

On page 326 will be found several contests that have been used with good results and which test the student's ability in constructive, cooperative participation in a group.

BIBLIOGRAPHY

Since parliamentary law deals with working together in groups, it interests persons in many fields and professions. In colleges, the departments which are using the *Standard Code of Parliamentary Procedure* at present are: English, Speech, Law, Social Science, Political Science, Sociology, Education.

The author has attempted, in compiling the reading bibliography in the back of this book, to reflect the broad needs of these departments, which are already teaching parliamentary law, as well as the varied interests of individual readers. The suggested bibliography has been checked with authorities in each of the general fields.

VERSES, CARTOONS AND ILLUSTRATIONS

Even Shakespeare's tragedies have their lighter scenes. Comic relief, the literary critics call it. This book is hardly Shakespearean, and I hope it is not tragedy. But I think the reader will be relaxed and refreshed by the gay verses by Richard Armour and the accompanying drawings by Leo Hershfield that pop up here and there. The student's understanding of the themes will be clarified by the illustrations of Alan Atkins. It is also fitting that a book about a cooperative subject should itself be a cooperative endeavor, and in this enterprise Richard Armour, Leo Hershfield, Alan Atkins and I have worked together with the same friendly spirit that in this book has been urged upon those who participate in organizations. This book is, in effect, the report of a committee of four—a writer of light verse, a cartoonist, an illustrator and a parliamentarian.

Richard Armour is one of the most proficient and widely read light verse writers in America, and Leo Hershfield is the "Leo" whose name appears below witty drawings in numerous national magazines. Alan Atkins has gained a high place as a designer of *Fortune* covers and an illustrator.

What Richard Armour has done for (or to) parliamentary procedure and the work of organizations, he has done, in his deftly playful way, for many other subjects in his verses in magazines ranging from *The Saturday Evening Post* to *The New Yorker,* from *Better Homes and Gardens* to *Esquire*. In his serious moments Dr. Armour heads the Department of English at Scripps College. His is the technique of the social satirist. In the verses included in this book, he has fun with us and with himself, and in a good-natured but meaningful way helps us to see our shortcomings.

I hope you are amused, as I am, with the verses and drawings. May you laugh as you learn.

PART ONE: PROCEDURE

Its Principles and General Rules

CHAPTER 1

OUR VOLUNTARY ORGANIZATIONS

THE SEED IS PLANTED

In that long-ago time when thirteen sparsely settled colonies, strung along the lonely Atlantic shore, were repairing the ravages of the founding war, our countrymen in their wisdom and foresight conceived an idea that shocked the great powers of Europe.

This idea is the theme and spirit of our Constitution and Bill of Rights. It is this:

The sovereign power of the United States rests with the people; and the people, as free individuals working together, create, control, and conduct the life of this country.

Are you wondering what this important moment of history has to do with parliamentary law?

Just this—out of this new concept of the people's function came a whole structure of formal government operated by the people through their representatives, and a vast parallel structure of informal government by voluntary organizations through which the people themselves speak and act. In these democratic structures, both the formal and the informal, we need the basic tools with which people work together in groups. These tools we call "parliamentary procedure."

IT GROWS AND GROWS

When you realize that there are in the United States today at least 200,000 organizations, probably more, for they won't stand still long enough to be counted; when you realize that almost every man, woman, and child, from the kindergarten class to the centenarians' club, participates in organized groups; when you realize that these voluntary organizations spend two and one-half *billion* dollars each year on conventions alone—when you realize all this, you begin to see the vastness of voluntary organizations and their vitalizing role in the life of the nation.

All the free democracies have voluntary organizations, but they are stronger and more numerous in America. In fact they are so numerous as to lead to the charge that America is "overorganized." To a degree this is true but, thank Heaven, we are not "underorganized"! We are free to associate ourselves with others. We are free to encourage "the human individual, by his own free will toward his own ideals."

VOLUNTARY ORGANIZATIONS AND DICTATORSHIPS

Dictatorships have been quick to realize that voluntary groups are dangerous to totalitarian rule. Not long after seizing power in Czechoslovakia, the Communists found themselves threatened—as authoritarian

regimes in their first stages inevitably are—by the existence of clubs, churches, and fraternal organizations. Within the shelter of these groups, the individual could still speak his mind, voice his discontent, perhaps find a rallying ground for effective resistance to his iron-fisted masters. The Communists, accordingly, brusquely and summarily banned all volunteer organizations and abolished the right of voluntary assembly.

If the Czechs had any doubt that their conquerors were bent on smashing every vestige of democratic life, this decree dispelled that doubt. The Communists knew that these voluntary organizations provided the life breath of democracy and must be strangled to insure the death of Czech democracy.

THE GREATEST PHENOMENON

To assure that American democracy should live, our forefathers guaranteed to Americans the right to join together in organizations, to speak their minds without fear of reprisal, and to chart their own course of action. They did this by means of the Bill of Rights. These constitutional rights undergird the great body of American volunteer groups freely meeting and freely voicing their opinions.

From generation to generation we have passed on our belief in the importance of group action. Now it is a feeling so deep and so ingrained as to have become almost instinctive. Perhaps this is why we are not aware of it as a unique national characteristic. We join organizations; we form new organizations; we act by means of organizations in our businesses, our philanthropies, our social life, our recreations, our personal crusades; and we take it all for granted.

To us there is nothing remarkable in little Mary's membership in the Brownies or the Children's Theater, in her big brother Jim's presidency of the Sailing Club and chairmanship of Homecoming Week; in her mother's participation in the PTA, the Woman's Club, the Red Cross Motor Corps, and the League of Women Voters; or her father's activities in the Chamber of Commerce, the Rotary Club, the Community Church, the American Legion, and half a dozen other local and national organizations.

The truth is that Americans are just about as busy with their un-

ORGANIZED EFFORT

Father has his business group,
Mother has her clubs,
Sister's in a Brownie troop,
Brother's in the Cubs.

Everyone is organized,
Everyone belongs.
Badge and card and pin are prized,
So are grips and songs.

Here's the basis of my rhyme,
Burden of my pome:
Try to find a single time
Everybody's home!

official, unremunerated, voluntary activities as they are with their business and official duties. What is more, as pointed out in an article in *Fortune,* the "unpaid, unofficial off-duty activities have a deeper and more lasting effect upon American life than do the official ones."

The true significance of this intermingling of voluntary organizations with our lives is best observed at the community level. With little experience and no pattern, groups of citizens all over America unite to build hospitals, beautify their towns, plan entertainment for teen-agers, establish nursery schools, build community churches or swimming pools, form mosquito-abatement districts or school districts, develop parks, zoos, or any of the hundreds of facilities which make their communities finer places in which to live.

This interweaving of our lives with groups is so commonplace to us that we do not even think about it. We are startled by Paul Hoffman's characterization of America's voluntary organizations as the "greatest phenomenon of American democracy."

Perhaps we are too close to our voluntary organizations, or too busy working in them, to see their power, their value, their remarkable achievements.

WE ARE THE GOVERNMENT

Most of us, when we mention our government, speak of it as "they." "They" are raising our taxes; "they" won't fix the street in front of our house; "they" sit in Washington or the state capital or the city hall and run our lives. "They" are the elected or appointed officers who constitute the formal authority of our government.

Actually "we" raise our own taxes. "We" fail to fix our street. That's what democracy means. In our formal government it seems difficult to think in terms of "we." But in the informal part of our government, through voluntary organizations, the "we" comes naturally. Here is the "we" of government in America—"we, the people."

To Americans, self-government is not something that is carried on only at the polls on election day. Americans believe that self-government is every citizen's daily business. The more successful a man, the more numerous and far-reaching are his obligations toward the voluntary organizations to which he gives his time. This belief has resulted in what seems to Europeans the basic paradox of American politics and

government: that a people, on the one hand so historically devoted to the principle that each man shall think and speak and act for himself, should, on the other hand, voluntarily choose to express their thoughts and translate them into action through mutual association in groups— the voluntary organizations of America.

This paradox, of course, is no real contradiction but an expression of our national awareness of the power of group action—of our well-founded faith in the creative magic of cooperation. Free, individualistic Americans, from this country's beginning to the present day, have banded together in thousands upon thousands of voluntary organizations for every conceivable purpose, to get something done. Through these organizations the people's will, in which our sovereign power eternally rests, finds its day-to-day expression.

ORGANIZATIONS ARE GOVERNMENT

The extraordinary thing, the unique thing, about the voluntary organizations of America is that they are so inextricably interwoven in the fiber of American government that they have actually become a part of government itself. Just as the political party system and the President's cabinet—neither of which was written into our original constitution—have evolved of necessity as basic operating forces in the nation's government, even so in the course of history have the voluntary organizations of America emerged as a means of the people's self-government.

Thus the formal authority of government harkens to the opinions and will of the people as expressed through the informal, unofficial government which consists of our voluntary organizations. This is democracy in action, American style, and there is no other government quite like it in all the world.

ORGANIZATIONS HAVE POWER

Wise politicians have always recognized the importance of voluntary organizations. Throughout our country's history the professional politicians have paid the organizations of America the tribute of respectful attention and prompt action. When the American Farm Bureau Federation, the AFL, the CIO, or the Chamber of Commerce of the United States speaks, congressmen and state legislators listen carefully.

Do you yourself understand the immeasurable power of these great, energetic organizations? Do you hear the voice of a free people speaking through them? Those voices can begin as a whisper, in a tiny town on the Iowa plains, and sweep across the mountains and prairies until their roar fills the halls of Congress.

In the little country community of Rockwell, Iowa, the farmers used to "go visiting" at neighboring farms on Sundays. While the women chatted in the parlor or exchanged recipes in the kitchen, the men sat around the barns and whittled and talked about crops or better days for the farmer. On Saturday nights they gathered about the stove in Emerson's General Merchandise Store chewing tobacco, and arguing, and planning.

Around those Iowa barns and general-store stoves, the powerful farmers' cooperatives were born at the beginning of this century. Local farmers, like Edward Dunn and Clifford Gregory, led their neighbors in the great farm movement which is represented today by the mighty farmers' cooperatives. What happened in Iowa was duplicated in other parts of the country. In the productive farm region of upper New York State, meetings of small groups of farmers developed into the powerful and efficient American Farm Bureau Federation.

These are two examples of the cumulative force of a people dedicated to the faith of individual dignity and joined in cooperative endeavor.

The people speak through their organizations and make their voices heard—in legislation, in taxation, in our social and economic culture pattern, in the ethics and standards of professional and trade organizations, in the appropriation of public funds. These groups are politics at the neighborhood level, which is where all political action originates and where power lies.

EACH HAS A FRANCHISE

When a group becomes so well established that people look to it as entitled to speak for the trade or profession, it has in effect obtained a franchise to represent America in that field. The American Bar Association speaks for the United States in the sphere of law, and the Carpenters' Union in the field of carpentry. The American Bowling Congress is the voice of the bowlers of this country. Each group has the responsibility of honorably and honestly representing its members, but it has a greater responsibility to set standards, to develop ethics, to educate the public, and to advise on legislation in its field.

To be more specific, take the work of one of these organizations—the American Bar Association. This group watches and largely controls the standards of training in law schools, studies and regulates the ethics of legal practice, keeps the public informed concerning its legal system, provides public defenders for persons who are without funds, advises and gives approval on the appointment of judges, and furnishes the public with analyses of current legislation.

If there were no American Bar Association, all these functions would have to be performed by the government, in all probability less effectively, and certainly at great cost to the taxpayer.

STRENGTH FROM THESE ROOTS

The core of the strength of our voluntary organizations lies in two basic elements. The first is that they are voluntary. Americans are not drafted into this country's multitude of clubs and organizations. We join voluntarily in order to speak and act  effectively. We contribute to the boys' clubs of America because we want to do something concrete to lessen juvenile delinquency. We campaign for the city-manager plan of government because we believe in its efficiency. We join the alumni drive to build a new law-school dormitory because we think one is needed. No one compels us to do these things—we do them because we want to.

A dictatorship is weaker than a free democracy because it is only as strong as the man at the top. A free democracy draws endless vitality from its millions of members at the local-organization level. The millions who have joined such groups believe with Daniel Webster that "there are many objects of great value to man, which can only be attained by association."

The second source of the strength of voluntary organizations is that they consist of individuals who have joined together for a common purpose. The power of any group is far greater than the sum of the power of its individual members. Individuals organized as a group have a strength and a stature far exceeding those of the same individuals unorganized. The interaction and harmonizing of personalities in a group generates inspiration and new power which knows few limitations.

One voice can easily be lost in the thunder of voices over this wide and articulate land of ours. Speak alone and you may never be heard. Speak through a group and your voice is magnified hundreds of times.

JOINERS AND DOERS

You don't start out with the intention of joining a large number of groups. Your life leads you into them.

Is this because we are just naturally a nation of "joiners"? Perhaps, to some degree. But isn't it rather that we are joiners because we are a nation of *doers?* We join groups that give us the power to translate our urgent desires into deeds.

We develop strong loyalties to the organizations to which we belong. We become skilled practitioners in the art of working together in groups.

Our long experience in cooperation is our best defense in time of emergency. As Arthur Schlesinger points out, "In times of war impromptu organizations spring up as if by spontaneous generation to invigorate the national will and to supplement the government's military

efforts in a thousand ways. This instinctive recourse to collective action is one of the taproots of the nation's well-being."

When American citizens, in 1950, were stirred by the threat of a Communist-dominated world, by the hundreds of thousands they pledged their support to the "Crusade for Freedom." All over the nation, when Americans want to get something done, they form a "citizens' committee." They organize, they meet, they discuss, they *act*.

WE HAVE TO KNOW THE RULES

Perhaps you hadn't thought about parliamentary procedure as having a close relation either to the life you live or to the life you plan to live. Perhaps you are like the student, a forestry major, who wrote to his instructor the year after he graduated:

I never thought I would use my parliamentary procedure, but I needed an extra unit. I pictured myself up on a mountaintop, miles from civilization and meetings.

But I developed some new ideas on fire fighting and I wanted to get them tried out. First I got them through our County Foresters' meeting. Now I am appearing before clubs here in the county to get their support for a larger state appropriation. Next week I will be down from my mountaintop and on my way to Washington as a delegate to our national convention.

Do you begin to see why parliamentary procedure is a necessary, basic tool of the twentieth-century citizen? When organizations play so important a role in our lives, when they are so involved in the continuing life of our country, officially and unofficially, we must have some knowledge of how to work well in them. Parliamentary law gives us that knowledge.

Practice Projects

1. If there were no group such as the International Association of Machinists to represent the machinists of the United States, how would the ethics and standards of that trade probably be controlled?

2. Describe the functions of some voluntary organization with which you are familiar.

3. What are some of the services performed for the general public, as distinguished from services for its members, by the following organizations?

1. Chamber of Commerce of the United States
2. American Medical Association
3. American Farm Bureau Federation

4. Explain and comment upon some of the common personal aims which lead people to join voluntary organizations.

CHAPTER 2

WHAT IS PARLIAMENTARY LAW?

SOURCES OF OUR PARLIAMENTARY PROCEDURE

Parliamentary procedure is the code of rules for working together in groups. It has evolved through centuries out of the experience of individuals working together for a common purpose. It is logic and common sense crystallized into rules of law.

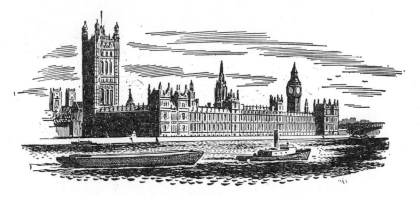

Parliamentary procedure is fundamentally alike in all democratic countries of the world. One who knows our American principles and rules would have no difficulty in applying them in Canada, France, or India.

Our procedure is founded principally upon processes developed in the British Parliament, elements of which can be traced back to Roman law.

The procedure in Parliament was the direct development of procedure in the king's council going back without a break to the earliest Saxon kings. Many of the elements appeared to be universal in their application to democratic bodies and were found in Rome and Greece. The rules of procedure as used in Parliament were transplanted to America with the first colonists and flourished in the free atmosphere of this country.

15

GETTING STARTED

Some people,
A purpose,
A place
To meet,
A name,
A few rules,
Maybe light
And heat.

A chairman,
A charter,
A gavel,
A goal,
A hope,
A desire,
And you're ready
To roll!

DEVELOPMENT OF AMERICAN PARLIAMENTARY PROCEDURE

The first great parliamentarian of this country was Thomas Jefferson, outstanding president and able lawyer. As the second presiding officer of the Senate of the United States, he compiled a set of principles and rules to guide the Senate in its deliberations. Clear, simple, logical, the principles and rules interpreted by Jefferson have roots that strike deep into the subsoil of freedom and equality which underlies our democracy. Jefferson understood and stated the principle of adherence to majority decision.

Excellent as were the specific rules of the British Parliament and of the United States Congress for these particular bodies, they were not suitable for ordinary deliberative groups—for the thousands of clubs, societies, churches, associations, and fraternal organizations which were rapidly developing into a pervasive force of American life.

As Clarence Cannon, famous parliamentarian of the House of Representatives, later pointed out:

These rules of Parliament and of Congress are designed for bicameral bodies, generally with paid memberships, meeting in continuous session, requiring a majority for a quorum, and delegating their duties largely to committees. Their special requirements and the constantly increasing pressure of their business have produced highly complex and remarkably efficient systems peculiar to their respective bodies, but which are, as a whole, unsuited to the needs of the ordinary assembly.

Luther Cushing, after Jefferson the second great parliamentarian in America, realized the need for a manual containing Jefferson's principles, but with rules which would be suited to the voluntary organizations of a democracy. Cushing, like Jefferson, was an experienced lawyer, and devoted his life to a study of parliamentary law. In 1845 he published a manual which coordinated the fundamental principles of Jefferson's work in this field with the common practices and procedures which groups had developed through their own experience. Cushing's manual emphasized principles rather than rules and was adapted to the needs of deliberative assemblies of that day.

In 1876, Major Henry Robert, an Army engineer, wrote a set of detailed rules for the conduct of meetings, which he advocated for adoption by clubs. In part he relied upon the peculiar and specialized rules of Congress of the 1870's. In part he invented his own rules and did not base them upon court decisions. The result was a book which emphasized technicalities rather than principles and, in the words of Samuel Hayakawa, internationally recognized expert on language, had a "ritualistic tendency." Joseph Henry Jackson wrote recently of Robert's book:

> Unlike a more recent code of parliamentary procedure, which was written to enable people to agree, Robert's book specialized in techniques of obstruction and disagreement; you could use the rules, if you were smart about it, to block practically anything you didn't want to see happen.

Such was Robert's genius for promotion, however, that his book was widely adopted and meticulously followed. It has never been substantially revised. Robert made a great contribution by enlisting the interest of many people and groups in the subject of parliamentary procedure.

For a long time many organization leaders and parliamentarians have felt a need for a simplification and modernization of the rules of procedure. The *Sturgis Standard Code of Parliamentary Procedure,* published in 1951, represents a cooperative attempt to meet this need. This code emphasizes principles rather than technicalities and is based upon court decisions.

WHEN PARLIAMENTARY PROCEDURE IS NEEDED

The courts hold that every deliberative body conducts its business subject to the rules of parliamentary procedure. Almost every detail of parliamentary law has, in the course of our nation's lifetime, been ruled upon by the courts. Parliamentary procedure actually constitutes a portion of our common law.

There are, of course, many meetings where almost no rules of procedure are necessary. Observance of a few principles of procedure is sufficient. A small group, for example, gathered to receive instructions or explanations, a meeting to listen to a program, people who have come together informally to talk over some matter—in none of these situations, nor in similar ones, is there need for the more detailed rules of parliamentary procedure.

Whenever a group, however, meets for the purpose of presenting proposals, discussing them, and arriving at decisions, parliamentary procedure is not only helpful but indispensable. In all organizations the rules of procedure must be observed if the actions of the assembly are to be legal. When decisions are to be made by groups, the time-tested processes of parliamentary procedure will always be necessary.

PARLIAMENTARY PROCEDURE IS NOT RITUALISTIC

The first purpose of parliamentary procedure is to make it easier for people to work together effectively. Its aim is not to emphasize or to multiply technicalities, but rather to supply the essential rules which will aid a group in reaching its goal and carrying out its purposes. Its object is always constructive. Its rules are not intended to confuse the uninitiated, to trick the unwary, nor to discourage those who do not know them.

In carrying on the business of a meeting there are few exact, precise, indispensable phrases. Some texts require students to memorize definite formulas and responses. While it may be good discipline, in a class in parliamentary drill, to insist upon exact phrasing, it is misleading to assume that this exact phraseology is of great importance in actual meetings. This is emphasizing ritual rather than principles. There is no sacred formula which must always be repeated. There are usual ways of saying things in a meeting, but these ways may differ and still be correct.

For example, a member has a right at all times to know what the group is discussing so that he may vote intelligently. The precisely correct way to request information is to rise and announce to the presiding officer:

"I rise to a parliamentary inquiry."

If an inexperienced member should, however, stand up and say, "I would like some information," or "Can you please answer a question for me?" it is as much the duty of the presiding officer to give the information as though the inquiry had been phrased in the formally correct language.

The celebrated British parliamentarian John Hatsell wrote, in 1776, that "motives ought to outweigh objections of form." He also wrote of a rule: "It is rather to be kept in *substance* than in *words,* and the good sense of the House must decide upon every question how far it comes within the meaning of the rule."

The interpretations of the courts make it clear that the intent and good faith of the members of a group are of more importance than the particular phraseology used in a given instance.

HOW PARLIAMENTARY LAW GROWS

The courts have held that every organization is presumed to be operating under parliamentary procedure when it meets to transact business. Most organizations have a few special rules which are particularly suited to their own use and then adopt the parliamentary code which they consider most satisfactory to them.

An organization has the power to adopt for its own use any rule it wishes, which does not conflict with public policy. It can adopt any rule as a special or standing rule of the group, or it can include such rules in its bylaws. Such rules rank above any adopted parliamentary authority.

Parliamentary law has no authorized legislative body to enact changes enabling it to keep pace with changing conditions. Instead it is dependent on general usage and court decisions for sanction of new procedures. Its principles do not change, but its rules must develop with changing conditions.

A parliamentary writer who prepares a book for adoption by organizations should never presume to create a new rule and state it as a rule of parliamentary law. Should he propose some new and ideal rule not sanctioned by custom and by law, he should be subject to censure, for he would lead organizations astray. However, a writer who is not preparing a code of rules for adoption may suggest a new idea so long as he makes it plain that it is his own idea. It is possible that the idea may be widely adopted and in time become a precedent—that is, a way of doing something which has been followed over a substantial period of time. Gradually a precedent may become a custom which is generally recognized and observed.

Parliamentary law is also altered and extended by important court decisions, supporting or overruling some action of an organization.

DEMOCRACY AND PARLIAMENTARY LAW HAVE
THE SAME PHILOSOPHY

The philosophy and aims of democratic government and of parliamentary law are identical. The philosophy of each is based on freedom of the group and of the individual, on equality of opportunities and responsibilities for all, and on the right of the majority to decide.

The aim of democracy in our world today is clearly expressed by Paul Hoffman when he writes:

> We want to unite people, cooperate with them, help them to gain and keep freedom. Hence, we inevitably will continue to use our own democratic tools of free choice, open debate, and voluntary decision.

The aim of parliamentary law is to facilitate and foster the use of these tools—to make free choice, open debate, and voluntary decision realities in every group.

The philosophy of parliamentary procedure ensures freedom and equality to the group and to its members. The common liberties provided by parliamentary procedure include the freedom of individuals to form themselves into an organization, to devise their own rules and regulations, and to determine their course of action; freedom to administer their own internal affairs; freedom to choose their leaders without fear of coercion; freedom to propose propositions; freedom to discuss them, to decide by a vote of at least a majority what actions shall be taken, and to carry out those decisions.

The members of the group also have freedom to disagree, to protest and to oppose, and even to replace their leaders through orderly processes whenever they fail to carry out their proper functions.

In the exercise of these freedoms there is an equality of rights and duties which is common to all individuals of the group. Each member has the right to propose motions or candidates for office, to discuss freely and to persuade, to ask questions, to oppose, to protest, and—most important of all—the right to vote.

These rights of free speech and free action are shared equally by every member. This equality of individual rights and privileges has a corollary of equality of individual obligations and duties.

Both democracy and parliamentary procedure have an underlying philosophy which is more important than is the structure. This philosophy is based on a faith in the ability of a free people to deliberate together and to make their own decisions. Parliamentary rules are the mechanical means for translating this philosophy into group action.

A few misguided individuals, who emphasize technicalities, strategy, and trickery rather than the use of simple, forthright principles, are responsible for a misconception regarding parliamentary procedure. They have caused many people to think of it as a hair-splitting device to hinder straightforward persons from reaching an honest decision.

The fault lies not with the rules themselves—for they are only tools—but with the trickster who misuses them. Parliamentary procedure is not a bag of tricks; it is democracy at work. Its philosophy and its principles must remain the guiding force behind the application of its rules. Whenever the philosophy underlying the rules of democracy or of parliamentary law is neglected or forgotten, discord and difficulties follow.

It is, in fact, through the use of parliamentary law in meetings that the average citizen comes in closest contact with the principles of democracy. It is in the meetings of his church, his union, his service club, that he learns its possibilities and how to use them to fulfill his needs and the needs of his organization.

In thousands of voluntary groups, as citizens apply the principles of parliamentary procedure in their meetings, democracy takes on concrete meaning. The national government and the complex mechanisms of congressional lawmaking are remote from the average citizen, but his everyday, working relations with clubs and organizations are a constant experience in *living* democracy.

PARLIAMENTARY LAW PREPARES FOR LEADERSHIP AND MEMBERSHIP

Probably at some time you will be called upon to take the lead in some group activity. Good leaders are in unceasing demand. Group leadership involves many skills and abilities. It requires the confidence which comes from a knowledge of the rules of working together. It requires an understanding appreciation of people as individuals and of how they behave in groups. It requires an ability to lead the group confidently, and with recognized effectiveness, directly toward a common goal.

You should qualify yourself to take your place as a leader and equip yourself to serve as an officer of the organizations with which you work. This is an obligation you owe to the democratic institutions under which you live. It can also be a deeply satisfying experience to you personally.

But some people say, "I don't want to lead—I just want to be a member." Good members, it is true, are quite as necessary to the functioning of the group as are good leaders. But to be a good member, in the full sense of the term, one likewise needs an understanding of parliamentary procedure and skill in its use. Moreover, to participate in the choice of an effective leader, which is one of the responsibilities of a good member, one must have some knowledge of what will be demanded of such a leader.

Each member of an organization makes important decisions every time he votes. The vote of the most inexperienced and silent member is just as decisive as the vote of the leader of the organization. No member of a group can vote intelligently, or work effectively as a member, without a knowledge of the rules of the game.

The study of parliamentary procedure is not a career in itself. It is an aid to any career you may choose. Whatever your life work, you will find yourself involved in group effort and consequently will need to know the principles of parliamentary law.

COST OF YOUR INVESTMENT

Your investment in the study of parliamentary law is modest in terms of the time and energy required. Parliamentary law is a small and well-defined subject. It is logical and easy to understand and apply. Many years of effort are required to become an astronomer, a physicist, or a doctor, but anyone who has learned the rules of football or bridge, or who can turn out a hand-knit sweater, can master parliamentary law in a short period of study and practice. With concentration and practice, you can easily become a skilled parliamentarian.

Practice Projects

1. List the organized groups of which you are a member and state the purpose of each.

2. Interview two professional men or women, two businessmen, and two union members and secure a list of the organized groups to which each belongs.

3. Discuss the contribution to community welfare which is being made by some voluntary group in your home district.

4. What groups will you probably join as a result of the career which you have chosen?

5. Scan a copy of a daily newspaper and clip out items in which organizations, either voluntary or governmental, are prominently mentioned. What proportion of the total news space do these articles represent?

6. In 50 B.C., Cicero wrote (*De Finibus,* Part IV): "We were born to unite with our fellow men—and to join in community with the human race." Discuss this statement in relation to our American organizations.

7. Why do you think Thomas Jefferson adapted the rules of the British Parliament instead of writing rules of his own?

8. If certain rules as stated by a particular author are generally disregarded by organizations, what does this indicate?

9. Why cannot an author create a new rule of parliamentary procedure if he thinks it would be helpful?

10. Cite several examples of meetings which have no need for parliamentary procedure.

11. Have you observed any meetings which would have benefited by more knowledge and application of procedural rules? Describe them.

12. What general types of situations give rise to rulings by the courts on parliamentary procedure?

13. What important fact is overlooked by the person who uses parliamentary procedure as trickery to confuse and outwit those who do not understand it?

14. Do you believe that an organization profits as a whole when its members are trained in meeting procedures? Give examples to support your answer.

CHAPTER 3

FUNDAMENTAL PRINCIPLES OF PARLIAMENTARY LAW

RULES ARE BASED ON PRINCIPLES

A few fundamental principles underlie parliamentary procedure, and most of its rules are based upon these principles. If you have a thorough understanding of the principles, you rarely have need to memorize rules. They are largely self-evident. If you are in doubt as to a rule, it is usually not difficult to reason it out from the principle from which it derives. For example, it is a principle that there is a logical order in which motions must be considered. Therefore an obvious rule deriving from this principle would be that a motion to postpone a  matter to another time would have to be decided before voting upon the motion which it is suggested be postponed.

Lawyers rely upon an understanding of legal principles and their ability to apply them rather than upon a knowledge of specific detailed laws. Parliamentary law is best learned and practiced in the same way. If a person has a knowledge of the principles of procedure, the problems which arise in the course of a meeting can be decided more easily and satisfactorily by reason than by reference to an authority.

The following are the most important principles of parliamentary procedure:

1. *Parliamentary rules exist to facilitate the transaction of business and to promote cooperation and harmony.* Parliamentary law is intended to help organizations conduct their business and carry out their aims. It has only one great purpose—to facilitate getting things done. It is not intended to confuse or to confound individuals or to obstruct the carrying out of the majority's will.

The principles of procedure are often more important than the minutiae of rules. A too technical insistence on the observance of every small point is a misuse of procedure. Technicalities should not be used merely for their own sake. Some meetings require the strict application of technical rules. Others can proceed quite informally. Some situations, likewise, require strictness of application, while others do not. The presiding officer should be the best judge of these varying needs.

The structure of parliamentary law has been developed to expedite business and to make it easier for the members of a group to work harmoniously together and to take action after reaching substantial agreement.

2. *The vote of the majority decides.* Democracies are founded upon decision by majority vote. The power of an organization, or a democracy, rests with the majority of its members. No group can tolerate control by a minority.

On the other hand, true unanimous agreement is seldom possible. Almost every great decision of our democracy has been made by majority vote rather than by unanimous agreement. Declarations of war by the United States in 1917 and in 1941 were by majority vote and were not unanimous. The decision of the states to send delegates to the Constitutional Convention, in 1787, to save themselves from anarchy and possible civil conflict under the Confederation, was not a unanimous decision; Rhode Island declined even to send delegates. The constitution was ratified by only eleven of the thirteen states, but was, in the end, adopted and supported by all.

Recognition that decisions by a majority are an integral and vital element of democracy was forcefully and clearly stated by Thomas Jefferson in a letter to Baron von Humboldt, written in 1817. Jefferson wrote:

> The first principle of republicanism is that the *lex-majoris partis* is the fundamental law of every society of individuals of equal rights; to consider the will of the society enounced by the majority of a single

vote, as sacred as if unanimous, is the first of all lessons in importance, yet the last which is thoroughly learnt. This law once disregarded, there is no other but that of force, which ends necessarily in military despotism.

Requirement of a unanimous vote runs counter to the spirit of democratic organizations. Only in certain social groups, such as sororities and fraternal orders, where such a vote is the rule for admitting members, can it be justified. Otherwise a decision by the majority is usual and proper.

Strange as it may seem at first glance, whenever more than a majority vote is required, control passes from the majority to the minority. For example, if a two-thirds vote is required to take an action, one-third of the members of the organization make the decision as to whether the measure is to pass or to be lost. Each of the members of the one-third minority, therefore, has twice as much power of decision as each of the members of the majority. Similarly, if a unanimous vote is required, control is taken away from the majority and given to one member.

The United Nations is an example of an organization which is frequently thwarted by the requirement of a unanimous vote to act. The charter requires a unanimous vote of all five members of the Security Council to take any action. This requirement places in the hands of one member the power to defeat the will of the majority.

The will of the group is determined by the vote of the majority of its members. When a person joins an organization, there is a tacit understanding that he will abide by the decisions of the majority. Indeed, he agrees that he will not only abide by them but cooperate with them.

3. *All members have equal rights, privileges, and obligations.* Every member possesses the same rights as every other member. He has the right to propose motions, to discuss them, to oppose, to persuade, to nominate and be nominated, and to vote.

He has the right to do anything that other members of the organization can do. Even more than this, it is the right of every member to insist on the protection of his rights and the rights of other members.

Since each member has equal rights, it follows necessarily that he has equal duties and obligations. It is the responsibility of the presiding officer to see that equality of rights and obligations and duties is maintained among members.

4. *The minority has rights which must be protected.* There are certain

SWINE

As alike as a pig
 And its brother, the hog,
Are the two kinds of rollers—
 The steam and the log.

basic rights of minorities which democracies always protect. The right to be heard, to protest, to seek to convince, to understand fully the questions which are to be decided, are all rights which should never be infringed upon. These rights are protected by parliamentary law.

Majorities and minorities are not static—they are constantly changing. Members of the majority on one question may be part of the minority on the next. Protection of minority rights is therefore of importance to every member of a group. If you, as a member of a majority, ignore the rights of the minority, you may expect to find the same methods used against you when you are a member of the minority.

5. *Full and free discussion of every proposition presented for decision is an established right.* This is the right of free speech. It is the right to hear and to be heard. It is almost as fundamental as a member's right to vote. The right to discuss a question fully and freely without interruption, subject only to the rules applicable to all other members, belongs to each member. The right "to speak his piece," "to have his chance to be heard," and "to say his say" are phrases which express the fundamental democratic concept of each member's right to discuss propositions on which the assembly is to vote.

6. *The simplest and most direct procedure for accomplishing a purpose should be used.* As Thomas Jefferson long ago pointed out, the use of confusing technicalities or devious approaches to accomplish an object should be ruled out of order by the chairman when "the same result may be had more simply."

Members frequently take a roundabout method of attaining their object. For example, they may attack a motion by attaching unfavorable amendments to it instead of opposing it directly. Whenever there is a simple way to accomplish a purpose, the presiding officer should insist that the simple and direct procedure be followed.

Even presiding officers sometimes complicate procedure unnecessarily. As far back as 1620, the Speaker of the House of Commons was blamed because "sometimes he neglects his duty to the House in that . . . he intricates the question and hath made many plausible questions abortive." A presiding officer sometimes complicates a motion by stating it in a needlessly long and technical way.

7. *A definite and logical order of precedence governs the introduction and disposition of all motions.* Since there are many motions, it is necessary to give the more important ones a definite priority or precedence in

GENTLEMAN'S AGREEMENT

You vote for my motion
And I, by-and-by,
Will vote for your motion—
An aye for an aye.

which they must be proposed and acted upon. This proper sequence prevents motions from piling up in confusion. Each motion has its particular rank and if this sequence is followed, the proceedings of the organization will be clear.

8. *Only one question can be considered at a time.* This principle protects the organization against the chaos which would arise if several motions were simultaneously under consideration. If each motion is considered separately and individually and in its proper order, confusion will be prevented and business expedited.

9. *Every member has the right to know what the question before the assembly means before he votes.* The presiding officer should keep the pending motion clearly before the assembly at all times. If any member does not understand what the pending motion is, or what it means, or what its effect will be, he has the right to request that information from the presiding officer. It is this principle which underlies the right of a member to rise to a parliamentary inquiry or to ask questions of the presiding officer.

Members are called upon to exercise their best judgments when they vote. In order to do this, a member is entitled to a reasonable knowledge of the facts of the question. Every member has the right to ask an explanation of any pending question which he does not understand, in order that he may vote intelligently.

10. *The membership may delegate duties and authority but retains the right of final decision.* Each member of an organization cannot work personally on every project of the group. In democratic governments and in democratic organizations, many duties are delegated to officers and to committees. They act as representatives of all the members and may be given the authority and the power to carry out our decisions. However, when a committee submits a report the organization has the final authority to accept or to reject it.

The members of an organization also retain the right to withdraw this delegated authority or make the final decision on any matter.

11. *Parliamentary rules must be administered impartially.* A presiding officer serves his organization best when he remains strictly impartial. He does not take part in discussion while he is presiding. In larger organizations he usually does not vote unless there is a tie. He should not favor his friends by giving them more than their share of opportunities nor take revenge upon his opponents by denying them

privileges. One of the greatest assets of any presiding officer is his ability to show no favoritism, to keep out of disagreements among the members, and to treat all members alike. This attitude is certain to win respect and confidence.

Impartiality, be it added, is highly desirable not only in a presiding officer but in every officer and indeed in every member of an organization.

Practice Projects

1. Can you recall instances in which parliamentary tactics were misused in a legislative body to block or delay the carrying out of the majority's will?

2. Can you give an illustration of how the rights of a minority group, faction, or party, might be safeguarded by parliamentary procedure?

3. Why is the requirement of a unanimous decision upon a candidate, policy, or course of action essentially antidemocratic in character?

4. Explain how an increase in the proportion of affirmative votes required for an action—for example, from a simple majority to a three-fourths vote—reduces the power of the majority.

5. When a unanimous vote is required, where does the power of decision lie?

6. What fundamental principles are involved in the following situations, and how would you apply these principles if you were presiding?

1. The Fruitvale Parlor of the Native Sons of the Golden West was discussing a motion that "A stone marker commemorating the first Pony Express station be erected at Emigrant Gap."

Mr. West rose and said, "Mr. Chairman, I'm not clear about this motion. I wish you would explain the cost more fully."

The presiding officer replied, "We haven't time to stop for that now. I'll explain it to you after the meeting."

2. At a meeting of the Riverdale Humane Society, members were considering a motion to enlarge the boarding quarters for dogs. Three members opposed the motion, and forty-five members favored it. The three members all spoke against the motion. A member arose and said, "Mr. Chairman, why do we have to waste all this time listening to three members, when it is perfectly obvious that a majority of us are in favor of the motion?"

3. At a Chamber of Commerce meeting a measure for rezoning an area to permit apartments was being discussed. One group favored complete rezoning; a second group favored partial rezoning; and some members opposed any rezoning. It was voted to refer the question to a committee of three for investigation and recommendation. The chairman knowingly appointed three members from the group who opposed rezoning.

4. The committee of the United College Fund was holding a meeting to determine how more money could be raised. Nine of the members favored personal solicitation. Three of the members advocated a dinner at which former contributors would be asked to renew their subscriptions. The plan for personal solicitation carried, the vote being 9 to 3. The three members refused to take any part in the solicitation, stating they had voted against the motion and so were not bound by it.

5. At a convention of the North Counties Fruit Growers' Association, most of the members favored an increase in salary for elementary school teachers. While one delegate was making a speech opposing the raise, some members called out, "Shut him up!" "Throw him out!" "Sit down! Sit down!" The speaker was embarrassed and sat down in confusion, and the chairman hastily recognized another member.

6. At a meeting of the Hillside Tennis Club, the members were considering a motion to hire an additional coach. During the discussion, one of the members insisted that the subject of raising the dues be considered at the same time.

7. At a meeting of the Lynnville Window Washers' Union, the group voted to allow one-half hour only for discussion of the motion that apprentices be given a five-cent hourly raise. The president favored the raise, so when several members asked for recognition at the same time, in each instance he recognized one of his friends who believed as he did. At the end of the half-hour, only three minutes' time had been given to opponents of the measure.

8. The Milk Drivers' Local 446 appointed a committee to draft a pension plan. After six months, since the committee had not yet agreed upon any plan, the local voted to turn the matter over to its executive committee for study and recommendations. The pension committee protested that it had been given the authority to submit a plan and that that authority could not be withdrawn and given to the executive committee without its consent.

9. The City College Student Council had a membership of twelve. The council adopted a rule that ten members must vote in favor of any important motion in order to pass it.

10. Miss Hobson was a member of the Hayward Art Association. She only occasionally attended meetings, and suggested that since she was absent so much, she should have her dues reduced.

11. At a meeting of the student body of Washington Junior College, which was scheduled for a free period from eleven to twelve o'clock, a small group of students were against a motion to increase the price of student-body dues. The motion was proposed at 11:30, and each of the opposing students made a long speech and asked numerous unnecessary questions. At twelve, when the meeting was forced to adjourn, there had been no opportunity to take a vote on the motion.

CHAPTER 4

THE PATTERN OF MEETINGS

USUAL ORDER OF BUSINESS

Organizations usually follow a fixed pattern in conducting their meetings. This order is arranged for convenience and enables members to know in advance when each type of business will be considered. The order of business should be provided for in the organization's by-laws or standing rules.

If the bylaws do not contain an order of business, parliamentary law has established the following pattern for a meeting:

1. Call to order
2. Reading or disposition of minutes of the previous meeting
3. Reports of boards and standing committees
4. Reports of special committees
5. Unfinished business
6. New business
7. Announcements
8. Adjournment

If there is an invocation or roll call, this usually follows the call to order.

Flexibility in the Order of Business

The purpose of an order of business is to provide a blueprint for a smoothly running meeting. There should be flexibility, however, in any order of business. Too rigid adherence to the accustomed pattern should not be permitted to hamper the actual progress of a meeting. For example, if for some reason the organization wishes to take up im-

HOW'S BUSINESS?

Business comes,
        One quickly finds,
In many flavors,
        Sorts, and kinds.

There's old, there's new
        (They all occur there),
And let us not
        Forget "no further."

portant new business, the reports of committees can be deferred until later.

There may be deviation from the order of business by a motion to suspend the rules or by general consent. To secure general consent the chairman states that there will be a change in the order of business if no member objects. The presiding officer may say:

"According to our order of business, the Committee on Membership should now report. This committee needs more time to prepare its report, so unless there is objection, we will listen to the report of the Ways and Means Committee."

If anyone objects, a member may make a motion to suspend the order of business to permit the assembly to take up business out of its proper order.

Not only should an order of business be flexible but it may also need to be individualized. Labor unions, for example, have expanded and changed the general order of business into an order which is highly particularized to meet their own needs. One of the most interesting and effective adaptations is the insertion, in their order of business, of an item called "Good and Welfare." When "Good and Welfare" is called for, members may discuss anything from a "gripe" to a new idea for getting more members out to meetings. Members are not allowed to present motions, however, during this period. This item in the order of business offers an opportunity for members to "get things off their chests" and to speak informally, without introducing their remarks by a motion.

Call to Order

Meetings should be called to order promptly at the appointed time, provided a quorum is present. The presiding officer calls the meeting to order by rapping with his gavel and announcing:

"The meeting will please come to order,"

or

"The Thirty-third Annual Convention of the Mississippi Teachers' Association is now convened."

Reading of Minutes

Unless there is an invocation or roll call, the reading of the minutes of the previous meeting or meetings is the first item of business.

The presiding officer may say:

"The secretary will please read the minutes of the last meeting."

Or, if the meeting is a busy one, the presiding officer may say:

"If there is no objection, we will dispense with the reading of the minutes of the last meeting." This has the effect of postponing the reading of the minutes, but the minutes must nevertheless be read at some future time.

If the organization has postponed the reading of the minutes of several previous meetings, the secretary should be directed to read all previous unread minutes. When the minutes have been read they are corrected, if necessary, and approved.

If the organization wishes, it may postpone the reading of the minutes to another meeting by majority vote or by unanimous consent, unless some member objects.

Reports of Committees

The presiding officer next calls upon the chairman of each board or standing committee and asks if he has a report. The usual order is: (1) the chairman of the executive board or board of governors, if there is such a board; (2) the chairmen of standing committees in the order in which the committees are named in the bylaws; (3) the chairmen of special committees in the order of their appointment.

Usually in conventions, and frequently in other meetings, the order of committee reports is necessarily determined by the order in which committees are ready to report.

Unfinished Business

Following the committee reports, the presiding officer calls for unfinished business. He may say:

"Unfinished business is now in order."

or

"Is there any unfinished business?"

Unfinished business consists of all business which was pending and undisposed of at the last meeting, as well as any matters which may have been postponed to this particular meeting.

It is the duty of the presiding officer to present any item of unfinished business which some other member does not present. For example, he may say:

"We will now consider the motion, proposed at our last meeting by Mr. Kennedy and postponed to this meeting, that this organization elect three representatives to the Central Council of Civic Clubs. The secretary will please read this motion."

After the secretary has read the motion, the chairman continues:

"You have heard the reading of the motion that this organization elect three representatives to the Central Council of Civic Clubs. Is there any discussion?"

Discussion and a vote on the motion follow.

New Business

When the unfinished business has been completed, the presiding officer announces:

"New business is now in order."

or

"Is there any new business to come before the assembly?"

This offers an opportunity for members to bring up any motions which they wish to have considered by the organization. If no new business is presented, and the chairman knows of matters which should be considered, he informs the assembly of these matters and asks if any member wishes to propose a motion covering them.

Announcements

When all members who wish to present motions have done so, the presiding officer calls for announcements.

If it is possible to confine all announcements to the period set aside for them, rather than to have them presented at various times throughout the meeting, business will be expedited. The chairman first calls upon members who have previously indicated to him that they wish to make announcements. He then asks if there are any other members who have announcements and concludes with his own.

Adjournment

When the business of a meeting appears to be completed, some member should move to adjourn. As soon as a motion to adjourn is proposed, the chairman should put the motion to a vote, and if the motion carries, he announces that the meeting is adjourned. The meeting is not adjourned until formal announcement of its adjournment is made by the chairman.

If no member moves to adjourn, the chairman may suggest that if there is no further business, some member should move to adjourn.

CHAIRMAN'S MEMORANDUM ON ORDER OF BUSINESS

In addition to the blueprint of plans for a building, the contractor who is directing the job needs drawings of important details. Similarly, the presiding officer of a meeting needs a memorandum of the items to be dealt with under each heading of the order of business. This detailed list helps to ensure that nothing is omitted and that the meeting moves ahead smoothly. An efficient secretary can prepare or help the presiding officer prepare this list. The following is an example of a detailed list under various sections of the order of business, to guide and prompt the presiding officer:

Chairman's Memorandum—Meeting, Feb. 15

1. *Call to order*—promptly at 8:00
   Appoint Mrs. Henes to serve as temporary secretary in absence of Mr. Davis, who is in hospital.
   Call attention to fact that meetings will start exactly at 8:00.
2. *Minutes*
   Call attention to the error in listing the date of the June conference which appears as June 16 instead of June 18.
   Suggest change of wording in motion creating a committee on Revision of Bylaws from "to study and report on" to "to study, rewrite, and report on," since that was the way Mrs. Brewster proposed the motion.
   Call for other corrections.
3. *Standing Committees to Report*
   a. Executive board
      Mr. Hoffman will read report in absence of Mr. Davis
   b. Membership—Mr. Philips, Chairman
   c. Ways and Means—Mr. May, Chairman
   d. Program—Ask Chairman Rhodes to tell of preliminary plans for convention

4. *Special Committees*

Call on:

a. Mr. Archer to report on the cost of printing the yearbook

b. Mr. Murphy to report on progress being made by his committee on the establishment of a club library

c. Mr. Brandt, to give final report from Committee on Loud-speaker

5. *Unfinished Business*

Motion made by Mr. Knowles, which was under discussion when last meeting adjourned, to increase the salary of janitor by $20.

Motion made by Mr. Eckman, postponed from last meeting, to give scholarship to Brighton College.

6. *New Business*

Ask what club wishes to do about invitation to meet with Cosmos Club next month.

Call attention to request of executive secretary for more chairs in auditorium.

7. *Announcements*

a. Call on Mr. Beebe to announce plans for new classes

b. Mrs. Arnold on cooperation with Public Forum Series

c. Announce meeting of City Council on March 1 to which all civic clubs have been invited to send representatives

d. Remind members of change in date of next meeting

Practice Projects

1. Let each student prepare a memorandum of an order of business for the chairman of a hypothetical organization which he selects and names. Another student, as presiding officer, can take this memorandum and lead the group in a brief meeting of the suggested organization. Students may suggest need for deviations in usual order of business so that the chairman and group may practice making changes by general consent and by motions authorizing the change.

2. Report on any order of business you know that differs from the usual order, and explain why the differences are suited to the needs of the particular organization.

CHAPTER 5

HOW MOTIONS ARE HANDLED

PRODUCTION LINE OF MOTIONS

The business of a meeting is carried on by means of motions. In a broad sense a motion is a formal statement of a proposal for an assembly to consider and vote upon.

To propose a motion is equivalent to announcing to the group: "Here is something which I think we ought to do. I'd like to have your ideas on it, and then we'll decide what to do about it."

When a member proposes an idea for the group to consider, he introduces it by a phrase which, during the centuries, has made the proposal a formal motion:

"I move . . . ."

A motion is sometimes referred to as a "question," a "proposition," or a "proposal."

To save time and keep proceedings clear, motions progress through a series of identical steps. These form a production line, or process, which presents a motion, states it to the assembly, opens it to discussion, and submits it to a vote.

It is well to develop a facility with these steps and with their phraseology. Only after these mechanics of a motion become second nature can one concentrate on the content of the motion.

42

THE COURSE OF A MOTION

The following are the steps in handling a motion:

1. A member rises and addresses the presiding officer.
2. The presiding officer recognizes the member.
3. The member states his motion.
4. Another member seconds the motion.
5. Presiding officer states the motion to the assembly.
6. Members may discuss the motion, if debatable.
7. Presiding officer takes the vote.
8. Presiding officer announces the result.

Addressing the Presiding Officer

Any member, except the presiding officer, may propose a motion. He may do this at any appropriate time whenever there is no business before the assembly.

To present a motion, a member rises and addresses the presiding officer by his official title; for example: "Mr. Chairman," "Mr. President," "Mr. Moderator," or "Madam Chairman."

If the presiding officer has no distinctive official title, he may always be addressed as "Mr. Chairman," or if the presiding officer is a woman, as "Madam Chairman."

Addressing the chairman is equivalent to requesting permission to present a motion or to discuss a motion already presented.

Recognition by the Presiding Officer

The presiding officer recognizes a member by calling his name, or by nodding to him if he does not know the member's name, or by addressing him as "Mr. Member," or by designating him in some other way, such as, "the gentleman in the third row."

In conventions or in large meetings where it is impossible for the presiding officer to know the names of all the members, the delegate usually addresses the chairman by saying, "Mr. Chairman—Mr. Lewis, delegate from Memphis." The chairman may reply, "Mr. Lewis has the floor," or "The chair recognizes the delegate from Memphis."

As soon as the chairman recognizes a member, that member is entitled to the undivided attention of the assembly while he proposes or discusses a motion.

Proposing a Motion or Resolution

A motion is a proposal that the assembly take certain action or express certain sentiments. It is always stated in the form:

"I move . . . ," followed by the proposal to be considered.

This is the correct form for proposing a motion because it definitely establishes, as a motion, the proposal which follows. Such introductory phrases as "I suggest," or "I think we should," or "I propose that," or "I make a motion," or "I move you," or "I so move" may get the desired result, but are not good form.

An occasional brief introductory remark may preface a motion, but discussion or debate is usually not permissible until a motion has been stated by the chairman and is before the assembly for discussion. If it is desirable to have discussion before a motion can be formulated, this may be done by moving that the subject be considered informally.

When a motion is complicated, or when it must be very accurately stated, or when the details may be controversial, the proposal should be written and handed to the secretary at the time the motion is proposed.

When the proposer wishes to express a sentiment or a conviction, or to be sure that a motion is meticulously stated, or to phrase a motion for publication or for transmittal to another body, it is customary to offer his idea in the form of a resolution.

The earlier practice was to propose resolutions with a number of clauses, each introduced by "whereas," which explain or present the background or reasons for the resolution. These introductory clauses are not always necessary and often detract from the effectiveness of the resolution. They should be used only when it is important for the resolution to include the arguments as to its necessity or to explain its purpose.

The following are examples of typical resolutions:

"Resolved, by the Kiwanis Club of Reno, Nevada,

1. That the club extend its hearty congratulations to our honored brother on his nomination to the office of Lieutenant Governor by the Democratic Party of Nevada.
2. That a copy of this resolution be sent to Mr. John Gordon; that copies be sent to all newspapers in Reno; and that a copy be inserted in the minutes of this organization.

"*Resolved,* That the Association of the Bar of the City of New York request the President of the United States to submit names of proposed judicial appointees to the Federal District Courts and to the Circuit Courts of appeal located within the City of New York, for investigation and approval by the Association before final appointments are made, and be it further

"*Resolved,* That a copy of this resolution be sent to the President of the United States."

Seconding Motions

When a member has proposed a motion, he should take his seat. As some wag once said, "You never know that a man is a finished speaker until he sits down." It is then in order for another member to second the motion. The seconding member, without rising, says:

"I second the motion."

If the chairman does not hear a second to a motion, he should ask, "Is there a second to the motion that . . . ." and repeat the motion, since it may be that some of the members have not understood its meaning. If no second is forthcoming, the chairman declares the motion "lost for want of a second."

Seconding a motion means that the seconder wishes to have the motion presented to the assembly for consideration. It does not necessarily imply that the seconder favors the motion or intends to vote for it, although this is usually true. Requirement of a motion and a second is based on the belief that at least two members should be interested in the discussion of a proposition before a motion is presented to the assembly. Some organizations, by special rule, require no seconds.

Routine motions, such as approving the minutes, are frequently stated by the chairman without waiting for a second, unless some member objects. If a member does object, the chairman must call for a second.

In committees and boards or in small organizations, no seconds are required. If a second were required in a board of, say, five members, it would mean that 40 per cent of the membership would have to favor a motion before it could be brought before the board. This requirement would obviously be illogical and unreasonable. There is another instance in which seconds are not required. That is in legislative and governmental bodies, from Congress on down through local boards. The reason for this is that such bodies are composed of representatives

AFTER A LONG PAUSE

In meetings, I love
*   With a special devotion*
The person who finally
*   Seconds my motion.*

who are acting for others, who are, in a sense, the seconders of their proposals.

Statement of Motion by Presiding Officer

As soon as a motion has been properly moved and seconded, it is the duty of the presiding officer to state the motion promptly to the assembly. Until he has done so, the motion is under the control of its maker and can be withdrawn or modified by him as he wishes. Once the motion has been stated to the assembly, it is in the possession of the body to do with it as it chooses.

If a motion is proposed in a form which is misleading, vague, or overly complicated, it is the duty of the chairman either to request the member to rephrase his motion or to rephrase it himself. If the chairman rephrases the motion, he should make sure that he does not change its meaning. He should ask the member whether the rephrased motion, as stated to the assembly, expresses his proposal correctly.

If a motion proposes action which is contrary to law, or to the by-laws or rules of the organization, or if it is obviously dilatory (that is, made for the purpose of delaying business), or is completely unsuitable for the consideration of the assembly, the chairman should rule it out of order. He may say, "The chair rules your motion out of order," and state the reason for so doing.

Form of Stating Motions

The presiding officer states a motion in the following form:

"It has been moved and seconded that Mask and Dagger pay the expenses of its delegate to the National Convention of Dramatic Societies in Chicago on January third. Is there any discussion?"

or

"It has been moved and seconded that the following resolution be adopted:

"*Resolved,* by the San Francisco Chapter of the American Society of Mechanical Engineers,

1. That a cordial invitation be extended to the national organization to hold the next annual convention in San Francisco; and
2. That the San Francisco Chapter of the American Society of Me-

chanical Engineers include in its invitation an offer of $15,000 to help defray the expenses of entertaining delegates."

As soon as the motion has been stated to the assembly and discussion is called for, it is open to discussion and debate. The motion then becomes the "pending question."

Discussing a Motion

A member obtains the floor to discuss a motion in the same manner as he does to propose a motion.

Once a member has been recognized for the purpose of discussing a motion, he must be protected in his right to speak, so long as he observes the rules of decorum and confines his remarks to the subject.

Debate is restricted to the measure under consideration, and neither its proposer nor his motives can be discussed. The rules of debate require that all discussion be impersonal and that it be addressed to the presiding officer. During debate, members must be referred to in a respectful manner. The older practice was to refer to members by such phrases as "the last speaker," "the lady who preceded me," or "my colleague from New York." Modern practice, particularly in small bodies, is to refer to members by name, as "Mrs. Smith" or "Mr. Jones."

Voting on a Motion

When it appears that all members who wish to discuss the question have done so, the presiding officer may inquire:

"Is there any further discussion?"

or

"Are you ready for the vote?"

This query gives notice that debate is about to close, and that if any member wishes to claim the floor, he should so do immediately.

The chairman should ignore calls of "Question!" from the floor, for no member has a right to try to force an immediate vote in this manner.

If no one rises to claim the floor, the chairman, after a pause, puts the question to vote.

"Those in favor of the motion that this association join the League of County Clubs, say 'Aye.' . . .

"Those opposed, 'No.' . . ."

If there is no doubt in the mind of the chairman as to the results of the vote, he announces:

"The motion is carried."

or

"The motion is lost."

If the chairman is in doubt, he should call for another vote, even though no member requests it.

The announcement of the vote by the presiding officer is the last step in the production line which has carried the motion from its introduction by an individual member to its disposal by vote of the assembly.

Practice Projects

1. Do you believe that requiring a second to a motion serves any useful purpose?

2. Why is the demand "Question! Question!" out of line with the usual character of parliamentary procedure?

3. Can you give examples of motions which should be ruled out of order on the ground that they are:

1. Contrary to law?
2. Contrary to the bylaws?
3. Dilatory?
4. Unsuitable for consideration?

4. Why do you think a rule developed that, after a member has proposed a motion to the assembly, even if it is clear, it must be repeated by the presiding officer?

5. Prepare a resolution endorsing the candidacy of Jeff Karen for governor which will be suitable for publication in a newspaper.

6. Which of the following statements are true:

1. To introduce a motion by the phrase, "I move you" or "I so move" is just as good form as to say "I move."
2. A motion is often called a "query" or "demand."
3. A presiding officer cannot recognize a member unless he knows his name.
4. The presiding officer may usually be addressed as "Mr. Chairman" or "Madam Chairman."

5. If the presiding officer does not hear a second to a motion, he should second it himself.

6. A member must always rise and address the presiding officer when he wishes to second a motion.

7. The best way to state a vote is by saying, "As many as are in favor of the proposition will signify by the usual sign."

8. Members must confine their discussion to the motion itself.

9. If the chairman is in doubt about the result of a vote he should say, "The motion is carried."

CHAPTER 6

THE PRECEDENCE AND CLASSIFICATION OF MOTIONS

WHAT IS PRECEDENCE?

The nightmare of a railroad engineer is a vision of two oncoming trains smashing together in a head-on collision. Fortunately, this nightmare very seldom comes true, because trains are routed and scheduled according to a strict rating of their importance and urgency. The special train may outrank all others. The milk train is shuttled onto a siding so that the streamliner can go through. The fast freight gets priority over the commuters' local. And in a smooth, orderly manner all the trains speed to their destinations.

Sometimes there may be so many motions on the floor of the meeting that they, too, threaten to pile up in a tangle of wreckage. But motions, like trains, are ranked according to a fixed and definite order in which they may be proposed, considered, and disposed of. The rank of motions, which is called "precedence," keeps the business of the meeting going with easy efficiency, and every motion is attended to in its proper turn. The order of precedence of motions is based on the degree of their urgency; and it is logical and easy to understand. The following is a list of the more important motions, arranged in the order of their precedence:

51

IT'S AN ORDER

To this, good friends, give credence,
  For it's life or death, methinks:
It's as bad to mix precedence
  As it is to mix your drinks.

Order of Precedence

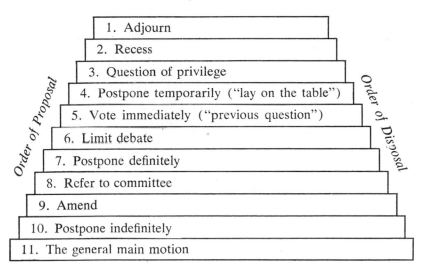

Number 11 is the main motion.
Numbers 10–4 are subsidiary motions.
Numbers 3–1 are privileged motions.

THE FOUR CLASSES OF MOTIONS

For convenience and for determining their precedence, motions are classified loosely into four groups. Each group has certain general characteristics. These four groups are:

1. Main motions
2. Subsidiary motions
3. Incidental motions
4. Privileged motions

Main Motions

This group is made up of motions which bring subjects (as contrasted with procedural questions) before the assembly for decision. These motions constitute the principal business of a meeting. They are the most important of all motions because they bring the main business before the meeting.

Main motions are divided into two groups.

1. *General* main motions are motions which have no specific name and deal with any subject which a member may properly bring before

an assembly. "The main motion" is the term applied to any general main motion.

2. *Specific* main motions have been given specific names and may have some individual characteristics and rules differing from those of the main motion. The more common specific main motions are: reconsider, rescind, and resume consideration. Examples of less frequently used specific main motions are the motions to concur, ratify, reject, repeal, annul, and adopt.

Subsidiary Motions

This group is made up of seven motions which are alternative methods of changing or disposing of the main motion. Their name derives from the fact that they are subsidiary to the main motion and therefore can be proposed only when a main motion is before the assembly.

If a main motion is pending and some members do not wish to vote on it directly at the time, they have several choices as to how the motion may be modified or disposed of. For example, one member may believe that it is an unsuitable motion for the assembly to consider and may move to postpone it indefinitely. Another may think that the motion should be changed so that it conforms more nearly to the ideas of the assembly and may move to amend it.

Incidental Motions

The motions of this group arise incidentally out of the business which is before the assembly. In general, they are concerned with the rights and privileges of members. They have only a few characteristics in common.

The purpose of this group of motions is to handle procedural problems which arise out of the consideration of other questions. These problems, naturally, must be settled before consideration can be given to the question out of which they arise.

Incidental motions are not included in the list of precedence because they may be proposed at any time and must be decided whenever they arise. Therefore, they present no problem of precedence. They have no precedence in relation to each other and, as a group, rank between subsidiary and privileged motions. They take precedence over motions to which they are incidental. The important incidental motions are:

Appeal   Withdraw a motion

Point of order   Object to consideration

Parliamentary inquiry   Division of a question

Suspend rules   Division of the assembly

Many additional motions may arise incidentally during the discussion of another motion. For example, if an assembly were considering a main motion, some member might move that it be voted upon by ballot. This would be an incidental motion and would be voted upon immediately.

If, however, no main motion were pending and someone moved that hereafter votes be taken by ballot, this would be a main motion and not an incidental motion. This is an example of how motions may vary in their classification according to the situation out of which they arise. Further examples of motions which may arise incidentally are: motion to excuse a member from voting; to consider a resolution paragraph by paragraph; to take a vote by roll call; to close nominations.

Some of the incidental group are demands or requests, which are decided by the presiding officer. They are not true motions and therefore do not require a vote. If the same demand or request is phrased as a motion, however, it follows the usual rules applying to main motions, except that it must be considered and voted upon as soon as it is proposed.

Privileged Motions

This small group is composed of motions which are so important that they are given privileges not accorded to other motions. They are, in effect, main motions which, because of their urgency, must be decided before the pending question. They relate to the members and to the assembly rather than to the main motion.

RULES OF PRECEDENCE

The chief purpose of dividing motions into the four groups is to determine their rank or precedence. This rank is fixed and definite and is based on logical reasoning. It is simple to understand and to apply.

It is not necessary to memorize the precedence of the eleven important motions. Practice in using them will soon fix their rank in your mind because their order is so logical that they could not be effectively arranged in any radically different way.

There are two important rules of precedence:

1. *When a motion is pending, any motion of higher rank may be proposed, but no motion of lower rank is in order.* The motion to adjourn (No. 1) has the highest rank, and a main motion (No. 11) has the lowest. If a main motion, No. 11, is pending, any motion of higher rank (No. 10 to 1) can be proposed. If No. 8 is pending, No. 7 to 1 can all be proposed, but No. 9 or 10 cannot.

2. *Motions are considered and voted upon in inverse order to the order of their proposal,* the last one proposed being considered and disposed of first. For example, if motions No. 11, 10, 7, and 2 were proposed in that order, they would be considered and voted upon in the following order: No. 2, 7, 10, and 11.

HOW PRECEDENCE WORKS

Now let us see how precedence works. Suppose that discussion is in progress on a motion to refurnish the student union. Someone moves to amend the motion by adding "and repaint" after the word "refurnish." Is this new motion in order? Yes, because the motion to amend takes precedence of the main motion.

Here is a more complicated problem of precedence: At a meeting of the Village Choral Society, a motion was pending "That $50 be set aside to purchase some new robes for the society." During discussion of this main motion (No. 11), Jim Murdock moved to amend (No. 9) it by striking out the "$50" and substituting the words "a sum not to exceed $80."

While this amendment was being discussed, Dolores Angelo said she did not think the matter could be decided by the members without further information, and moved that the matter be referred to a committee (No. 8). While this motion was under consideration, Gene Johnson moved that the matter be postponed indefinitely (No. 10).

Ken Young immediately rose to a point of order (incidental) calling the attention of the chairman to the fact that the motion to postpone indefinitely (No. 10) was of lower rank than the motion to refer the matter to a committee (No. 8) and was therefore out of order.

The chairman ruled that the point of order was well taken and the members returned to consideration of the motion to refer to a committee (No. 8).

Wayne Jefferson then moved to postpone the matter temporarily (No. 4). When this motion had been stated, Lee Rideout, who opposed the purchase of new robes and was tired of the discussion, moved that the meeting adjourn (No. 1).

All these motions, with the exception of the motion to postpone indefinitely, which was ruled out of order, were then pending before the meeting in the following order of precedence:

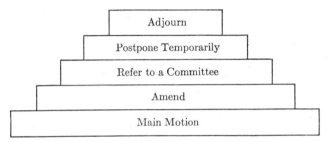

The assembly first voted on the motion to adjourn. This was lost. The chairman then called for a vote on the motion to postpone temporarily. The vote was close, and Ken Young called for a division of the assembly (incidental). The chairman took a rising vote and announced that the motion to postpone temporarily (No. 4) was lost.

Next the question to refer to a committee (No. 8) was voted on, and it, too, lost. Then the motion to amend (No. 9) was discussed and voted upon. The amendment carried, so that the main motion (No. 11) then read, "That a sum not to exceed $80 be set aside to purchase new robes for the society." After some discussion the amended main motion was voted upon and carried.

Practice Projects

1. Into which of the four groups would you classify the following motions:

1. "I move that we select a committee to study the problem of fund raising."

2. "I move that we repeal the ordinance making it illegal to park on the north side of Oak Street."

3. "I move that we vote by roll call on the pending motion."

4. "I move that we vote by roll call on all important questions."

5. "I move we adjourn."

6. "I move that we always adjourn our regular meetings at three o'clock sharp."

7. "I move to refer the motion to a committee of three."

8. "I move that we choose a committee for building a new tennis court and authorize them to begin this project immediately."

2. If you were presiding, and the following motions were presented in the following order, each without any of the preceding having been voted upon, which ones would you rule out of order; which incidental motions would you yourself decide immediately; and in what order would you present the remaining motions to the assembly for consideration and vote? For practice purposes assume that each motion voted upon is lost.

1. Main motion
   Postpone indefinitely
   Point of order
   Limit debate
   Amend
   Parliamentary inquiry
   Suspend rules
   Vote immediately

2. Main motion
   Withdraw a motion
   Point of order
   Amend
   Postpone definitely
   Refer to committee
   Point of order
   Postpone indefinitely
   Recess

3. Main motion
   Refer to committee
   Point of order
   Appeal
   Amend
   Limit debate
   Adjourn

CHAPTER 7

DISCUSSION

THE PRINCIPLES OF DEMOCRATIC DISCUSSION

In August of 1789, the members of the House of Representatives were discussing the Bill of Rights and amendments to the Constitution of the United States. Some members were impatient and wanted to railroad the proposed legislation into law.

One hot afternoon Elbridge Gerry, Representative from Massachusetts, rose and said:

"The gentlemen seem in a great hurry to get this business through. I think, Mr. Chairman, it requires further discussion; for my part, I had rather do less business and do it well, than precipitate measures before they are fully understood."

Then James Madison, Representative from Virginia, and future president, spoke: "Is not the report before us *for* deliberation, and to obtain the sense of the House upon it?"

This early and forthright assertion of the importance of free and open discussion, of the right of every member to understand fully the question on which he is to vote, forecast the fundamental role which discussion was to play in our democracy.

Organizations meet to deliberate, and the original meaning of deliberate is to "weigh fully." Deliberation is based on the belief that consideration by many minds is better than consideration by one. That is not merely an axiom—it is a principle of democratic society.

In parliamentary language, the terms "discussion" and "debate" are interchangeable. To say that a motion is "debatable," then, means that it may be discussed.

SOUND PRINCIPLE

Some talk twice as much as others,
Twice their silent sisters, brothers,
Some make twice as many motions,
Some have twice as many notions.
This however's well worth noting:
All are equal in the voting.

The right of a member to take part in discussion is as important as his right to vote. It is through discussion and the interchange of opinions that members become familiar with the problems which come before the assembly and are able to decide them intelligently. It is through listening to discussion or participating in it that agreement on ideas is reached. Intelligent discussion can harmonize many discordant wills into just and wise decisions.

The right of every member to participate in discussion is equal to that of every other member, and it is the duty of the chairman of the meeting to see that this equality of privilege is maintained.

In any group which is working under democratic processes, it is important that as many members as wish participate in the discussion. It is one of the duties of the presiding officer to guide and stimulate discussion in such a manner that it will arouse the interest of members and cause them to participate.

A capable presiding officer will draw out the ideas and reactions of individual members. He will see to it that there are opportunities to speak and will encourage members to use those opportunities. He will seek to create a climate which is favorable to free, frank, and thoughtful discussion; an atmosphere in which members will find every encouragement to express their opinions. He will subscribe to the conviction of Macaulay that "men are never so likely to settle a question rightly as when they discuss it freely."

THE SILENT MAJORITY

There is usually a rather large proportion of members in almost every organization who do not enjoy speaking in meetings. They are sometimes referred to as the "silent majority." Organization leaders worry about these members and seek constantly to devise means by which they may be forced to speak in order that "everyone may be heard from."

It is doubtful whether any benefit results from coercive methods to force members to take part in discussion. To point out that "it is your *duty* as a member to speak," or to call on a member directly by saying, "Mr. Smith, what is *your* opinion on this?" sometimes drives those who do not like to speak in public away from meetings. Organizations need these silent members and could increase attendance by making them feel comfortable in meetings.

Though agreeable in theory, universal participation in discussion is impractical, except in small meetings. Those who do take an active part in discussion generally reflect all the varied views which can be brought to bear on the subject at issue. There is little left for many to say except "me, too," or "me, neither."

The "silent majority" serves its own important purposes. Its members are usually in a better position to weigh arguments and make decisions than the vocal few; they exercise their own highly effective type of eloquence when they vote. In so doing, they emphatically and effectively speak their minds on the proposal at hand.

The speakers have already gone on record as holding a certain belief and are usually more concerned with advancing that belief than in judging the pros and cons of what is being said.

The listeners frequently are better able to size up facts and arguments calmly and dispassionately and therefore to decide wisely. Can you perhaps recall a meeting where most of the speakers favored an idea and it seemed certain to pass, but when the vote was taken it was overwhelmingly defeated?

Such incidents indicate that the listeners are thinking objectively and independently.

Democracy works by delegating power to chosen representatives and does not require every citizen to participate in every function of government. Similarly, in large meetings, the vocal few serve as representatives for the silent majority. It is unlikely that the meetings or ordinary assemblies would be improved if every member felt obliged to speak on every question. Meetings can profit by listeners as well as speakers. It is important that the listeners realize that they also are contributing to the meeting. Thus they will feel at ease in meetings and will attend in greater numbers.

DISCUSSION SITUATIONS VARY

Constructive discussion places the facts of a problem before the group. It stimulates an interest in these facts and in reaching the best decision as to a solution.

The great bulk of discussion in meetings is amicable and clarifying. It is entered into for the purpose of reaching agreement about the questions which come before the group for decision. Even where there appears to be substantial agreement, discussion is necessary to ensure that each member understands the exact meaning of the question on which he is to vote.

There are times when a sharp diversity of opinion arises. One group holds one conviction while other groups champion opposing beliefs. The discussion in such a situation has a purpose beyond that of explanation or clarification: it seeks to persuade, to influence, and to convince. A disagreement often helps to clarify ideas and if entered into in friendly fashion is highly constructive. If arguments become too heated, however, the common good of the organization is sometimes forgotten. Opponents may strive to win a decisive vote, not only through their arguments, but by parliamentary tricks and maneuvering. Bickering and quarreling may replace intelligent discussion.

Whenever such a situation develops, parliamentary principles and rules governing discussion must be applied strictly. The principles of equal right to discuss, of rigid adherence to the question, and of the speaker's right to protection from interruption must be vigilantly maintained. A tense situation also demands that no reference to personalities be permitted and that strict rules of decorum be observed. If correct principles of parliamentary discussion are followed, even heated debate can be kept on a constructive and dignified level.

The nature of discussion is sometimes misunderstood. A person who is inexperienced in the ways of meetings may misinterpret the vigorous and forthright manner in which members sometimes support or oppose ideas of their fellow members. This clash of ideas usually is basically friendly and serves to clear the air, so that the facts become evident. Just as two lawyers will oppose each other spiritedly in the court room and then go out to lunch in most comradely fashion, so members may challenge, defend, and attack the ideas of fellow members entirely without enmity toward their sponsors.

Agreement in a group is a desirable goal. This is sometimes best reached, however, by examination of divergent opinions and elimination of the least desirable, until a consensus is reached. Agreement without discussion might indicate a lack of interest. Friendly, impersonal, flexible discussion and disagreement are normally beneficial to any group.

TYPES OF DISCUSSION VARY

Just as discussion situations vary, so do the types of discussion. A member's discussion may consist of a brief remark such as, "I think

ETIQUETTE OF DISCUSSION

Denounce the motion, if you will,
In voice that quivers, voice that's shrill.

Protest that it is ill-advised
And underdone or oversized.

Deplore, with all your heart and soul,
Its wisdom, wording, good, and goal.

Demand, in mighty burst of breath,
The motion's sure and sudden death.

But while you rip it, inch and acre,
Don't mention once the motion's maker!

that's a fine idea," or a question, "Have we the money to finance this?" or a long explanatory speech. Discussion varies in type from a simple remark to a speech which, on occasion, may reach the peak of high oratory.

The following is a list of the different forms of speaking heard during the actual consideration of one motion in a convention. They are arranged in the order in which they occurred:

Explanation of the motion
Suggested changes in the motion
Detailed explanation of the motion
Question as to the meaning of a term used in the motion
Explanation of the intended meaning
A speech to arouse to action
Correction of factual errors
Demonstration that certain ideas are not mutually exclusive
Challenge of need for proposed action and answer to challenge
Humorous reference to ease tensions
Presentation of alternative plan
Pointing out of fallacies in alternative plan
Plea to return discussion to main issue
Testimony for the proposition
Citation of authorities
Summary of discussion up to this point
Merger of similar ideas already advanced
Analysis of opposing arguments
Resolving conflicts of attitude
Contrast of points favoring and disagreeing with motion
Modification of original motion

This example is somewhat more complicated and varied than the average discussion but it is typical of many situations. Discussion is a slow, steady, but sometimes uneven progress to a decision.

DISCUSSION MUST BE GERMANE

The most important principle governing discussion and debate is that it must be relevant to the subject before the assembly. Any member who has the floor during discussion has been given it for the purpose of discussing the pending question. If he departs from the subject, he is out of order. In discussing a motion, a member may tell a story, use illustrations, read short extracts from an article or book, or quote an authority—unless there is objection. But if he digresses noticeably from the main topic, he is out of order. It is the duty of the presiding officer to see that the speaker does not wander from the subject.

If the speaker is talking "off the point," the presiding officer should courteously interrupt him and request that he confine his remarks to the motion before the assembly. If the presiding officer fails to do this, any member may rise to a point of order and call the attention of the chairman to the fact that the speaker's remarks are not relevant. The chairman, if he agrees, should request the speaker to confine his remarks to the question under discussion.

If several motions are "before the house," discussion is confined to the "immediately pending motion." For example, if a motion and an amendment are pending, debate is limited to the immediately pending amendment, until it is disposed of.

NO PERSONALITIES IN DISCUSSION

Discussion must not involve personalities. It must be impersonal at all times. For instance, a member can call a measure "obnoxious," or "infamous," or a "menace to our club," but he cannot say of its proposer that he is "stupid," "stubborn," or "just looking out for himself." It is measures, not men, that must be the subjects of discussion. If a member attacks the motives of another member, he should be immediately interrupted by the chairman. To preserve impersonality, all discussion is directed to the presiding officer and not to an individual member. Officers are referred to by their official titles and members are referred to respectfully by name.

DECORUM DURING DISCUSSION

During discussion, a member's attitude toward the presiding officer and toward other members should be uniformly courteous and considerate. Even if this were not a requirement of procedure, it would be a requisite of an effective speaker.

If a member should so far forget himself as to lose his self-control and use improper language or become disorderly, personal, or rude, he should immediately be called to order by the chairman or by some member rising to a point of order. When the speaker is called to order by another member, he must immediately take his seat until the point of order is decided by the chairman.

If a member refuses to conduct his discussion in an orderly and courteous manner, he may be denied the right to further discussion. If necessary, he may be ejected from the room by order of the presiding officer or by vote of the assembly.

DEBATABILITY OF MOTIONS

Motions divide into three groups, according to their debatability:

1. Motions which are undebatable
2. Motions which permit limited debate
3. Motions which are fully debatable

The motions which permit no discussion are mostly procedural motions which can be decided by a "yes" or "no," or are motions restricting or cutting off debate. The motions to object to consideration and to vote immediately are examples.

The motions which permit limited discussion are procedural motions which may require brief, restricted discussion before they can be decided. The discussion is limited to those points which can be varied in the motion. The motion to postpone definitely is an example. It may be varied by changing the time of postponement, and consequently it is open to discussion as to the desirability or time of postponement.

The motions which are debatable are all motions which present a subject for discussion and decision. These are substantive motions as opposed to procedural motions. An example of a fully debatable motion is the main motion.

BRIEF COMMENTS ARE NOT DISCUSSION

An inquiry or a brief suggestion is not considered discussion or debate and is not subject to the rules limiting debate. Inquiries are permitted because a member has the right to know at any time exactly what the question before the assembly is and what its effect will be. He is entitled to have motions restated whenever he is uncertain about them. He has the right to ask for an explanation or to raise a parliamentary inquiry. Even on undebatable motions, it is permissible for the chairman to allow an occasional brief suggestion or query or comment.

PRESIDING OFFICER'S RESPONSIBILITIES DURING DISCUSSION

It is the duty of the presiding officer to expedite discussion, to see that its principles and its rules are observed, and to see that all of the rights and privileges of the members are maintained. When a member has been granted the floor, he is entitled to discuss a question without interruption. He has a right to the respectful attention of the assembly so long as he conducts his discussion properly.

It is the duty of the presiding officer to prevent whispering and walking about, to suppress disorder, and to avert heckling, annoyance, or improper interruptions.

It is also his duty to keep the question under discussion clearly before the assembly, to repeat it when necessary, and to rule out irrelevant discussion. When there is a difference of opinion, the presiding officer should see that equal opportunity is given to proponents and opponents of a measure. When one viewpoint has been presented, the presiding officer may say, "Does anyone wish to continue the discussion for the opposing side?" or "Now let's hear from the other side." The chairman creates the atmosphere and mood which invite and encourage free discussion. He keeps this discussion moving steadily and progressively toward the goal of decision.

LIMITS ON DISCUSSION

Parliamentary law fixes no arbitrary time limits on discussion and debate. Some organizations include in their bylaws provisions limiting the length of speeches. These limitations vary greatly according to the needs of each organization. The chairman's insistence that speakers confine their remarks to the subject will ordinarily keep discussion within reasonable limits.

Although the motion to vote immediately is designed to cut off all discussion, it is unwise to make a practice of cutting off debate on debatable motions or of bringing motions to a vote without allowing adequate opportunity for discussion.

When it appears to the chairman that all of the members who wish to speak have done so, he may say:

"Are you ready for the vote?"

or

"Is there any further discussion?"

These queries give notice to members that if they desire to speak, they must claim the floor immediately. The proper response is to be silent unless one wishes to discuss the motion. The chairman should never hurry the vote and should pause for a moment before putting the question to a vote of the members.

Putting the question to vote prematurely does not necessarily cut off the right of a member to speak. A member, if reasonably prompt in claiming the privilege, can assert his right to discuss at any time before the announcement of the final vote. If discussion interrupts the taking of a vote, the whole vote must be retaken, since members may have changed their opinions during discussion. The announcement of the vote, however, completely closes any opportunity for further discussion.

INFORMAL DISCUSSION

In a small and orderly group discussion can be quite informal. In many large organizations, also, there are times when it is desirable to suspend temporarily the formal rules of discussion and debate in order to allow informal discussion.

There are situations in which it is almost impossible to follow the general rule that no discussion can be entered into until a motion has been proposed, seconded, and stated to the assembly. It is sometimes extremely difficult to phrase a main motion if the problem it seeks to cover is not defined or understood. An understanding of the problem can come only through a presentation of facts and through discussion.

Let us suppose that an organization needs to increase its membership. No one member knows exactly what the problem is or how it should be solved. Discussion is necessary before a formal motion can be offered that will meet the problem. In such a situation some member may rise and say:

"Mr. Chairman, we realize we must increase our membership. We know some action must be taken, but we don't know how much increase we need or how to go about it. I move that we consider this matter informally."

If this motion carries, the chairman opens the meeting to informal discussion. During this period, a member may discuss a motion and its amendments as a whole, and there is no limit to the length of speeches or the number of times a member may speak. The chief advantage is that there is no fixed restriction on the range of the discussion. As soon as the problem has been settled or disposed of, permanently or temporarily, informal discussion ceases. No motion or vote to resume the regular rules of debate is necessary.

Some legislative bodies secure informal discussion by a motion to resolve the assembly into a "committee of the whole." This procedure necessitates the appointment of a chairman in place of the usual presiding officer and is therefore not as simple and practical as a motion to discuss a matter informally.

Practice Projects

1. Do you recall any instance where a presiding officer was particularly successful in stimulating discussion? Describe the situation and the methods used.

2. Give examples from your own experience or observation on the problem of the "silent majority."

3. Why is it difficult to plan a formal speech that can be used effectively during the discussion of a question?

4. When tensions arise and discussion becomes heated, what are some of the ways in which an experienced chairman can help the members to relax?

5. What type of discussion has annoyed or bored you in meetings you have attended? Give examples.

6. Comment on the following quotations from actual discussions:

1. "This proposal greatly endangers the fundamental purpose of our association. Therefore it is misleading and vicious. Mr. Jones is trying to use our club for his own personal gain. We shouldn't permit anyone to take advantage of us like that."

2. "I think we should all relax and take more time to study this question calmly before we vote on it. I, personally, don't understand the financial outlay it involves, and there must be other members who are confused also."

3. "The member who was offering this motion is a traitor to our club. He is selfish and obstinate and therefore we should all vote against his motion."

4. "So far our discussion seems to boil down to this: Those favoring the motion assert that building conditions are good now and we should go ahead and build our clubhouse. Those who oppose the motion contend that building conditions will be much better next year than this, and therefore we should wait. I suggest that we consult several contractors on this, since the motion seems to hinge on building conditions, of which we know little."

5. "Anyone who votes against a motion like this is just a plain fool. Anybody with any sense can see that this is a good motion."

6. "I want to speak on this question of dues. This motion reminds me of when I was a boy back in Kansas. We had a little country school and the schoolhouse was painted red and we had one of those old maid school marms. Which reminds me that William Allen White once wrote an editorial entitled 'What's Wrong With Kansas' and ever since he has been known as the Sage of Emporia, etc., etc."

7. "Ladies and gentlemen of this noble organization: I rise to discuss a question that is foremost in the minds of every alert American citizen today. A question that involves the sacrifices and blood of our forefathers on the altar of liberty and justice. This is the time for every patriotic citizen to rise in defense of our noble principles and . . . ."

8. "Could you please explain more clearly the result of the motion?"

9. "It seems evident that much of the difference of opinion on the motion is caused by the fact that members are interpreting the term 'nonresident member' in different ways. May I read the definition of a nonresident member from our bylaws? 'A nonresident member is one who resides outside the county of Kentfield.'

"If we understand this definition, we see that a member who is traveling temporarily and still is a resident of this county is not a nonresident member."

10. "Are not Mr. Elliott and Mr. Stanhope closer together in their ideas than they realize? Mr. Elliott believes in levying an assessment to

pay off the club's note, and Mr. Stanhope argues that any tax on members to meet the note should be spread over a year's period. If Mr. Elliott would agree to an assessment to be paid on the first of each month for a year, both ideas would seem to be in agreement."

11. "I think that we should all be for any motion Mr. Sproul suggests. He has done so much for our club that I think we would be most ungrateful if we do not back him in anything he wants to do."

12. "Mr. Alexander has been arguing strongly for this motion: 'that Colorado should reduce the number of her state militia.' I suggest that we amend Mr. Alexander's motion by adding 'and that since our militia is to be reduced in numbers, there can be no more riots or disasters or floods in Colorado for ten years.' "

CHAPTER 8

QUORUM

DEFINITION OF A QUORUM

A quorum is one necessary ingredient for a meeting. What is a quorum? A quorum is the minimum number of the members of an organization which must be present at a meeting in order to transact business legally. Before a presiding officer calls a meeting to order, he should be reasonably sure that a quorum is present. If a quorum is not present, all the group can do is to fix a time for another meeting and adjourn.

VARIATION IN QUORUM REQUIREMENTS

Every organization has a right to fix its own quorum, and this number is usually stated in the bylaws. If the organization does not have a provision establishing a quorum, common parliamentary law fixes the quorum as "a majority of the members."

This number is far too high for practical operation. Quorum requirements usually range downward all the way from a majority of the membership to one-twentieth of the membership, depending upon the needs and requirements of the group. As a practical consideration the quorum requirement should ordinarily be somewhat less than the usual attendance at meetings.

Organizations having a *fixed* number of members usually specify a *definite* number as a quorum. Organizations having a *fluctuating* number of members usually select a *percentage* as a quorum, so that the quorum adjusts itself to the varying size of the membership.

In a *convention,* unless there is a contrary provision in the bylaws, a quorum is always a *majority* of the qualified delegates in attendance.

A *committee* requires a *majority* of its members for a quorum.

At a *mass-meeting* the *number* of persons present, no matter what the number may be, is a quorum.

73

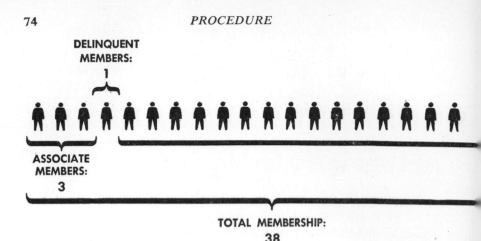

Organizations which meet only annually or biennially and whose members seldom attend often provide that the number present at any regular meeting shall constitute a quorum.

HOW QUORUMS ARE COUNTED

In computing a quorum, only active members in good standing are counted. For example, the quorum of an organization with a total membership list of thirty-eight and a quorum defined as "one-eighth of the total active members" might be computed as follows:

Total membership list	38
Associate members	3
Delinquent members	1
Active members in good standing	34
Required for a quorum	5

A quorum always refers to the number of members who are present and not to the number of members voting. In this instance, if only five or even one member voted on a motion, the vote would be legal, providing a quorum of five or more active members in good standing were present.

An interesting court decision makes this point clear. A school board in Indiana consisted of six members. Its rules fixed a quorum at four members. At a meeting, attended by all six members, three were trying to elect one candidate for superintendent of schools, while the other three were supporting another candidate. Vote after vote resulted the

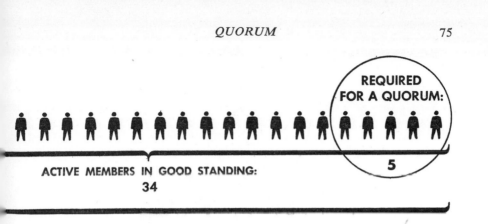

REQUIRED FOR A QUORUM: 5

ACTIVE MEMBERS IN GOOD STANDING: 34

same—3 to 3. Large groups of citizens, including friends and relatives of the board members, were excitedly cheering their respective candidates.

The board was meeting around a table at the front of the room. Finally, the three members supporting candidate B left the table and sat down with the spectators. They assumed that this move would "break the quorum" and also end the meeting. The three members remaining at the table, who were better versed in parliamentary law, proceeded to vote for their man.

The vote was now three for Mr. A, and the chairman declared him elected. He took office as the new superintendent. The defeated candidate and his supporters went to court, challenging the election.

The court ruled that the three members who left the board table were still present at the meeting and so there was still a quorum, all members being present. The vote for the candidate was 3 to 0, or a majority of the members voting, and consequently the new superintendent of schools was declared legally elected and entitled to the office.

A member who is disqualified because of personal interest or benefit in a motion cannot be counted in computing a quorum for a vote on that question. For example, if a vote is being taken on a motion awarding one of the members a contract for a new club building, the member who expects to receive the contract cannot vote upon the question, nor can he be counted in computing a quorum.

The presiding officer, if he is a member of the organization, is counted as a member of the quorum.

NUMBERS GAME

The followers, the silent folk,
    Don't snoot them, don't ignore 'em.
You may be glad to have them when
    You're scraping up a quorum.

RAISING THE QUESTION OF QUORUM

At any time during the meeting, a member who doubts that there is a quorum present has the right to request that the presence or absence of a quorum be determined. He may do this by asking:

"Mr. Chairman, is a quorum present?"

The chairman should then direct that the members be counted or the roll be called to determine whether a quorum is present. If it appears that a member is raising the question of a quorum simply to delay progress in a meeting, the chairman should rule the member out of order.

THE DISAPPEARING QUORUM

Sometimes, when a quorum is present at the beginning of a meeting, members gradually leave until there is no quorum. This is frequently called "a disappearing quorum."

One of the most interesting and misunderstood facts about parliamentary law is the question of the "disappearing quorum." This problem has twice come before the Supreme Court of the United States in recent years, and in each case serious questions of liability for prosecution hinged partly upon it.

In the case of the *United States v. Bryan* (1950) 339 U.S. 323, the executive secretary of the Joint Anti-Fascist Refugee Committee refused to appear before a congressional committee and bring the records of the organization. When she was prosecuted for her refusal, her attorneys argued that there was not a quorum of the committee present at the particular time when she refused, and so the committee could not legally function.

At the opening of the committee meeting, a quorum was present, but several of the members had been called out temporarily. No one had raised the question as to whether a quorum was or was not present at the particular time when the witness refused to produce her records.

The Supreme Court ruled that, where a quorum had been present, and there was no objection by anyone that a quorum was no longer present, the question of "no quorum" could not be raised later. This decision followed the common-law rule on the disappearing quorum.

If the minutes show that there was a quorum present at a certain time during a meeting, and if the minutes do not show that there was an adjournment or a recess meanwhile, it is presumed that a quorum continued to be present. Since any member can raise at any time the question as to whether or not a quorum is present, if this question is not raised, it is reasonable to presume that a quorum continued to be present.

If an organization is faced with a "disappearing quorum," the presence or absence of a quorum at a particular time can be established by counting the members present and entering the number on the minutes.

Practice Projects

1. From the following data, compute the quorum for each of the following organizations:

1. Quorum provision in bylaws: "One-sixth of the active members."

Total membership list:	64
Associate members:	6
Delinquent members:	3
Members debarred from voting by personal interest:	5

What is the number required for quorum?

2. Quorum provision in bylaws: none.

Total membership list:	212
Delinquent members and those who have moved away:	9
Members in good standing:	203

What is the number required for quorum?

3. Quorum provision in bylaws:

Quorum provision in bylaws:	10%
Total membership list:	96
Delinquent members:	7

What is the number required for quorum?

2. What quorum provisions would you recommend for the following organizations:

1. The One Hundred Club, which has a fixed number of members and meets monthly

2. The East Side Swimming Club, which has a membership of from 50 to 75 members

3. A committee on conservation, which has 20 members

4. A convention of the Fur Cutters' Association

5. A neighborhood club with 60 members whose usual attendance at its meetings varies from 20 to 30

6. The East Bay Council of Religion, which meets annually each August

CHAPTER 9

VOTE REQUIRED

MEANING OF MAJORITY VOTE

In organizations which are operating under democratic principles, almost every decision is made by a majority. The phrase "majority vote" raises the question, "A majority vote of what?"

There are several possible meanings for the term "majority vote,"

and the term must be qualified to define the particular meaning intended. In this text the term "majority vote" always refers to a majority of the legal votes cast, unless some other qualifying phrase is used.

It is important that the constitution, bylaws, or rules of an organization define the exact meaning of the term "majority vote" in each instance where the phrase is used. A majority vote might mean any of the following:

1. A majority of all the members
2. A majority of the positions or memberships in organizations having a fixed membership
3. A majority of the members present
4. A majority of a quorum
5. A majority of the total votes cast
6. A majority of the legal votes cast

The following example illustrates how a majority vote may be variously computed. Let us suppose that an organization has 300 members. The quorum is defined in the bylaws as "one-sixth of the active members." At a meeting there are sixty-five members present, and on a vote by ballot, thirty-one members vote and five votes are declared illegal. A majority vote in this situation would be variously computed as follows:

1. A majority of all members   151
2. A majority of the members present   33
3. A majority of a quorum   26
4. A majority of the total vote cast   16
5. A majority of the legal votes cast   11

In any organization whose rules do not define the type of majority required for various decisions, a majority of the legal votes cast binds the organization.

Majority of the Members

By "a majority of all the members" is meant a majority of all the members, both present and absent. Thus, if there are fifty members, a majority vote of twenty-six is necessary to take any legal action. If all fifty members are present, the vote of a majority of the members is required to take any action; but if only twenty-six members are present, a unanimous vote of those present is required.

This high requirement for a legal vote is ordinarily used only in organizations where the members are acting in a representative capacity and where every member is expected to be present and to vote.

Majority of the Memberships

To take an action in organizations having a fixed membership, "a majority of all the positions or memberships" is often required. For example, a board of education having a membership of five might require a vote of three memberships in order to decide a measure. This same vote would be required, even if there was a vacancy, because three is a majority of the positions or memberships on the board.

Majority of the Members Present

A few organizations require that any action to be taken by the body must have "a majority vote of the members present." The fact that some members do not vote does not reduce the number of affirmative votes

FAIRLY RUGGED INDIVIDUALIST

I always vote the way I think,
I bow to no authority.
And yet, I hardly need repeat,
I really find it very sweet
To be with the majority.

required. If there are ninety members present, an affirmative vote of forty-six is necessary, regardless of the number voting.

Majority of a Quorum

"A majority of a quorum," or a majority of the number who are authorized to do business for the organization, is frequently required for important decisions involving policy or large expenditures of money. If the quorum of an organization is thirty-two, seventeen votes would be required for the majority of a quorum. This number of affirmative votes is not changed by the fact that some members do not vote.

Examples of important questions which some organizations specify must be approved by at least a majority of a quorum are:

1. Amendment of constitution and bylaws
2. Dissolution of organization
3. Adoption of budget
4. Sale, mortgaging, or purchase of property of organization
5. Changes in organization policy
6. Change in custody of funds
7. Expulsion of members
8. Major financial expenditures

Majority of the Legal Votes Cast

When no other type of majority is specified, the common law provides that "a majority of the legal votes cast" is required to take any action. This requirement means that at times decisions are made by a very small proportion of the members.

The theory which allows the vote of a majority of those voting to decide a question, provided a quorum is present, is that every member present has the right and the opportunity to vote if he chooses. If he does not vote, he voluntarily waives that right and opportunity and consents that others should determine the will of the majority.

A majority may consist of only one vote. Sometimes when a motion is proposed in which the members have little interest, or when they are confused or do not wish to express their opinion, the chairman calls for the affirmative vote and the proposer of the motion votes "Aye." The chairman then calls for the negative vote and there is no response. The courts have held that a single affirmative vote, when no other votes are cast, constitutes a majority of the votes cast and is sufficient to carry a motion.

If several questions are being voted upon by ballot, the majority of the votes cast on each question must be computed separately, and a majority of the legal votes cast on that particular question is required.

A TIE VOTE

A tie vote means that an equal number of members have voted in the affirmative and in the negative on a question, or that two candidates for the same office have received an equal number of votes. A tie vote does not carry a measure or elect a candidate for which a majority vote is required.

In case of a tie, the chairman, if he is a member of the organization and has not already cast a vote, may vote to break the tie. If he has already voted, he cannot cast a second vote to break the tie unless this right is specifically given him by the bylaws. If the chairman is not a member of the organization, he cannot vote to break a tie unless he is specifically authorized to do so by the bylaws.

A PLURALITY VOTE

A plurality vote is a vote of at least one more than the number received by any opposing candidate or measure. It is possible to have a plurality vote only when there are three or more candidates or alternative measures. Thus, when there are more than two candidates, the candidate receiving the highest number of votes has a plurality.

A plurality vote does not elect a candidate or carry a measure unless there is a specific rule of the organization to that effect.

An example of a plurality vote is as follows:

Candidate	*Vote*
A	23
B	22
C	21
	——
	66

Candidate A received a plurality vote.

A TWO-THIRDS VOTE

A two-thirds vote means two-thirds of the legal votes cast, unless it is qualified in some other way. A two-thirds vote is seldom required except for an amendment to the bylaws or constitution, or on motions which restrict or shut off debate or suspend the rules.

ACTIONS WHICH NO VOTE CAN MAKE LEGAL

Actions on the following questions are never legal, regardless of the vote they receive:

1. Any motion which conflicts with the laws of the nation, state, or community, or with the provisions of the constitution or the bylaws of the organization.

2. Any motion forcing a member to reveal his opinion on a question which is to be, or has been, voted upon by ballot. For example, a motion to make a vote unanimous is illegal unless this motion is itself voted upon by ballot and is unanimously adopted.

3. Any motion which proposes to waive or suspend a rule protecting absentees. For example, a motion to disregard the required notice for a special meeting, or a motion to change a provision of the bylaws without due notice.

Practice Projects

1. An organization has 250 members and the quorum is defined as "one-fifth of the members." There are 52 members present, and on a vote by ballot 3 votes are declared illegal. Compute the majority in this instance for:

1. A majority of all the members
2. A majority of the members present
3. A majority of a quorum
4. A majority of the total vote cast
5. A majority of the legal vote cast

2. In a country club of 100 members, the quorum requirement is "a majority of the total membership." At a meeting 73 members are

present; the vote on a certain measure is 47 affirmative, 25 negative; one of the latter votes was declared illegal. Compute the majority in this instance for:

1. A majority of all the members
2. A majority of the members present
3. A majority of a quorum
4. A majority of the total vote cast
5. A majority of the legal vote cast

CHAPTER 10

METHODS OF VOTING

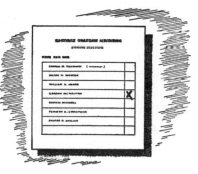

THE RIGHT TO VOTE

A member's right to vote is the most fundamental of all the rights of membership. It is also his greatest privilege.

Except in governmental bodies, no member can be required to vote. Penalties for refusal to vote may be provided in the bylaws of an organization, but voting which results from coercion is not in accordance with democratic principles and fails to accomplish a useful purpose.

Governmental bodies, however, have the right to compel the attendance of their members and to require them to vote. The members of these bodies are elected or appointed to perform certain duties, one of which is voting. If a member of a governmental body refuses to vote, he may be disciplined by the body and may even be expelled.

HOW VOTES ARE TAKEN

A vote is usually taken by one of the following methods:

Voice vote, rising or show of hands, roll call, ballot, mail, or unanimous consent. Each method is suited to a particular situation. The presiding officer or the members of the group have the right to decide which method should be used in voting on any question, unless the bylaws or rules require that a particular method be used.

In taking a vote, the presiding officer should give specific directions for voting by whatever method is to be followed. In taking a voice vote, for example, if he says, "Those in favor, signify by the usual sign," the members may be confused.

Voice Vote

The voice vote (viva voce) is the commonly used method of deciding most questions. It allows the vote to be determined rapidly but is not an accurate method of counting votes. It is useful for routine and commonly agreed-upon motions.

The presiding officer puts a question to vote by stating the motion and adding:

"Those in favor, say 'Aye.' . . . Those opposed, say 'No.' "

If there is no doubt in the mind of the chairman as to the result, he announces it by saying:

"The motion is carried," or "The motion is lost."

If the presiding officer is doubtful about the result of the vote, he should call for a second voice vote or for a rising vote.

If any member is in doubt as to the exact result of the vote, or if he does not agree with the chairman's announcement of the result, he may call for "a division of the assembly" in order to verify the vote. This request requires the chairman to take a vote by rising or show of hands. The call for division must be made before any other business intervenes and for this reason can interrupt a speaker.

Rising Vote

A vote by rising or by show of hands is desirable when a vote is being taken on an important question, or when accuracy is essential, or when there is an obvious difference of opinion. This method consumes a little more time than a voice vote, but it is more accurate and allows members to see who is voting and how.

In small assemblies, when a rising vote is close, the members should always be counted, either by the presiding officer or by the secretary. In a larger organization, if it is evident that there is no doubt as to the result of the vote, it is not necessary for the chairman to ask that a count be taken unless the body requests it.

When a count is taken, the chairman announces the result as follows:

"The vote is affirmative—62; negative—98. The motion is lost."

Motions which require a specific vote, such as a two-thirds vote or a majority of a quorum, should never be put to vote by a voice vote, since an accurate method of counting is required. In such instances, a rising vote is usually taken.

A vote by rising is necessary when a division of the assembly is called for to verify an indecisive voice vote. If it is more convenient, the chairman may ask members to vote by raising their hands. This vote is counted just as is a rising vote.

When visitors, or guests, or alternates who are not entitled to vote are present at a meeting or convention and are seated with the delegates, the chairman should call for rising votes only. This is done in order to be certain that only those who are entitled to vote are voting.

Voting by Roll Call

A vote by roll call ("yeas and nays") is accurate but consumes valuable time. It is ordinarily used only when members are voting in a representative capacity, so that those whom they represent will have an exact record of how their delegates voted, or when the bylaws require a vote by roll call.

When taking a vote by this method, the presiding officer states the motion to be voted upon and then says:

"Those in favor of the motion will answer 'Yes' as their names are called. Those opposed to the motion will answer 'No.' The secretary will please call the roll."

The names of all members eligible to vote are then called in alphabetical order, or by districts, or in some other agreed-upon sequence, and the vote of each member is recorded. If a member does not wish to vote, he may answer "Present," unless the rules of the organization forbid this response. When the vote by roll call is completed, the chairman announces the result:

" 'Yes'—80. 'No'—23. The motion is carried."

Voting by Ballot

Voting by ballot is the only method which enables a member to keep his opinions and his vote secret. This method is frequently required when electing officers, voting on amendments to the constitution or bylaws, or deciding other important matters.

A motion to vote by ballot or by any other method can be proposed at any time as an incidental motion and requires a majority vote.

When a vote by ballot is required by the constitution or bylaws, it is not possible to move to dispense with this requirement or to suspend the provision requiring the ballot vote.

NO SECRET

A vote by voice or a show of hands
Or the kind where the voter up and stands
Is saving of time and, it may be, pelf,
But it's frightfully hard to vote for yourself.

Such a motion is not in order, because it compels a member to reveal his opinion upon the proposition or candidate. For example, if a member proposes that the secretary cast a ballot for Mr. Quinlan, this motion should be ruled out of order. No member should be forced to reveal his opinion on a matter requiring a vote by ballot. A member could not oppose this motion without making public his opinion.

Mechanics of Balloting

The presiding officer appoints at least three tellers, one of whom he names as chairman, to assist him in taking the vote.

If the vote is on candidates for office, the list of tellers should include a friend or supporter of each candidate, at least for the most important or most hotly contested offices.

If the candidates or measures to be voted upon are known ahead of time, printed ballots are desirable. If these are not practicable, the secretary should prepare typed or multigraphed ballots. Such ballots result in far fewer errors than ballots written by each individual member. If it is not possible to have prepared ballots, uniform slips of paper should be distributed.

It is the duty of the tellers to see that each member who is entitled to vote receives one ballot. If a member makes an error which cannot be easily corrected, he may hand his ballot to the presiding officer, who destroys it and requests the teller to furnish another ballot.

After the tellers have distributed the ballots, the presiding officer should ask, "Is anyone without a ballot?" It is the duty of the tellers to see that all members have pencils or other facilities necessary for voting.

The presiding officer should give careful directions for voting and marking ballots.

He reads the title of the office and the names of all the candidates for that office and then asks the members to vote on the candidates. He then reads the title of the next office and the candidates for it. The same procedure is followed for propositions, which are voted on by number.

The presiding officer should instruct all members to fold their ballots. He should give explicit instructions to the tellers regarding how and where the ballots should be counted; but the tellers themselves have the sole authority to collect the ballots, to count them, to determine which ballots are legal, and to report the results to the presiding officer.

Counting Ballots

It is customary to observe the following rules in counting ballots:

1. When two or more ballots are folded together, they are counted as one illegal vote.

2. A vote for an ineligible person is counted as an illegal vote.

3. Blank ballots are ignored, except to determine the total number of votes cast.

4. Use of a nickname, or an error in spelling or in the initials of the candidate, does not invalidate a ballot when the intent of the voter is clear.

5. A ballot containing errors, where the intent of the voter is impossible to determine, is illegal.

6. If more ballots are cast than there are legal voters present, the vote must be retaken.

Any member has the right to be present while the ballots are being counted; but he cannot interfere in any way with the teller's work, since he is in the position of an observer only.

Teller's Report of Ballot Vote

The chairman of the tellers, when called upon by the presiding officer, reads the report of the tellers but does not state whether the propositions have carried or failed, or which candidates are elected. This report must contain the results with reference to all candidates or propositions. He then hands the report to the presiding officer, who announces the final result by stating which propositions have carried or which candidates have been elected.

The chairman of the tellers gives the ballots to the secretary in a sealed envelope. The secretary keeps them, unopened, for a reasonable time, in case a recount should be ordered by vote of the organization.

A teller's report on a vote by ballot is usually phrased in some such form as the following:

CLAREMONT COUNTRY CLUB

Teller's Report on Propositions I and II

Proposition I: To pay off the mortgage on the clubhouse:

Total vote cast	217
Illegal votes (five ballots not intelligible)	5

Total legal votes	212
Number necessary to pass (majority of quorum)	50
Votes for proposition	163
Votes against proposition	49

Proposition II: To establish a depreciation fund:

Total vote cast	209
Illegal votes (four ballots not intelligible)	4
Total legal votes	205
Number necessary to pass (majority of quorum)	50
Votes for proposition	81
Votes against proposition	124

Acting by Unanimous or General Consent

Organizations frequently decide routine and noncontroversial subjects without the formality of taking a vote. When there is unanimous or general agreement, considerable time may be saved by this procedure. However, acting by unanimous consent is never permissible in deciding controversial or important matters.

When a routine matter of business comes before an organization, the chairman frequently says, for example, "You have heard the reading of the minutes and corrected them. If there is no objection, the minutes will stand approved as corrected."

A member may also request that the assembly act by unanimous consent. He may say, "The credentials committee is not ready to report at this time, and I ask unanimous consent to have the program committee present its report instead."

The chairman then replies:

"If there is no objection, the program committee will report immediately."

The chairman should hesitate long enough to give members an opportunity to state an objection.

If any member wishes to object, he says, "I object."

If objection is raised, some member may propose a motion authorizing the procedure which has been objected to. This motion is considered and voted upon in the usual manner.

If the presiding officer has already announced that a particular action is being taken by unanimous consent, and any member objects before other business has intervened, the presiding officer must state the proposed action in the form of a motion and take a vote upon it.

Acting by unanimous consent is a valuable procedure on matters where there is no disagreement. It is inadvisable procedure, however, where there is a difference of opinion. Decision as to the advisability of proceeding by unanimous consent rests largely with the presiding officer. A competent chairman is alert to those matters which can be decided by unanimous consent, and likewise recognizes the controversial subjects which require that every rule of parliamentary procedure be carefully observed.

When a Member Cannot Vote

It is a general principle that no member can vote upon a motion in which he has a direct personal or financial interest. For example, a member cannot legally vote upon a motion awarding a contract to himself. If, however, a considerable number of members have a direct financial interest in such a question, the courts have held that all members may vote. An example of this would be a motion fixing the permanent amount to be allowed delegates to conventions. The establishment of the compensation of members is another example of a question on which all members may vote, even though they have a personal or financial interest.

However, if the salary of only one member were involved, that member would be ineligible to vote, and if his vote were necessary to validate his election or to fix his compensation, the vote would be void.

When charges have been preferred against a member or a small proportion of the members, those against whom charges are preferred cannot vote. However, if charges are preferred against a substantial proportion of the members, they are not debarred from voting. There are several cases on record where a few members named all the rest of the members in charges and thus attempted to gain control of the organization.

A member who has been nominated for office may legally vote for himself. This is quite customary in small boards, where one vote is a substantial proportion of the total.

Changing a Vote

A member has a right to change his vote, if he asserts that right promptly. In order to give finality to a vote, it is necessary that there be a fixed time limit beyond which a member cannot change it. The final announcement of a vote by the chairman terminates the right of any member to change his vote.

If the vote is a recorded one, no member may change his vote after the chairman's announcement, unless he can furnish definite proof that there has been an error in recording his vote. When a vote has been taken by ballot, the member's right to change his vote terminates as soon as he has dropped his ballot into the ballot box or delivered it to a teller.

Announcing the Result of a Vote

It is the duty of the presiding officer to announce the result of a vote accurately and according to the facts. If the presiding officer makes a mistake or makes an untrue or incorrect announcement of a vote, this fact does not change the true vote. The vote as cast by the majority is still the true vote, and in case of dispute the courts will examine the facts.

Voting by Mail

This form of voting is useful in organizations whose membership is scattered over a state or country or throughout the world, and whose members do not come together except at long intervals. Usually, these organizations vote by mail on questions such as amendments to the bylaws, election of officers, or important changes of policy.

Voting by mail is permissible only when there is provision for it in the bylaws of an organization. A motion to vote by mail on some particular question is not permissible unless the bylaws specifically authorize this type of vote.

Any method of voting by mail which is clear to the members and which safeguards the secrecy of their vote may be followed, unless a specific method is established in the bylaws. Usually it is the duty of the secretary to prepare printed ballots containing the numbered propositions and the names of the candidates. If members need information about the propositions or the candidates to be voted upon, an equal amount of material is furnished by the proponents and the opponents of the measures, or by the sponsor of each candidate.

The secretary mails a ballot to each member, together with full directions for marking it and any information which is to be included.

These ballots must be marked and returned to the secretary within a specified time. One way to ensure secrecy is to require each member to seal his ballot in the official envelope, with no mark of identification upon it, and to enclose it in another envelope which bears his signature. The secretary then checks the signature against the list of members entitled to vote, opens the outer envelope, and delivers the unidentified envelope, still sealed, to the tellers, who count the ballots and give a report to the president. Usually, a report of a vote by mail is sent to each voter.

Voting by Proxy

Voting by proxy means that a member casts a vote in the place of, and with the authorization of, one or more absent members. The member or members who are entitled to vote give to another member written permission to cast their vote. This member is then entitled to cast as many votes as he holds proxies.

The member voting must show a written assignment, signed by the member or members whose votes he is casting, giving him permission to vote for them by proxy.

Voting by proxy is not customary except in corporations where membership is based upon the possession of stock, and where a certain amount of stock entitles a member to a proportional number of votes. Voting by proxy in an ordinary organization, where all members have an equal right in voting, is highly inadvisable and is never permissible unless specifically authorized in the bylaws. The reason for this rule is that, in the usual type of organization, the right to vote is equal, and voting should be exercised only by members who are present and able to hear the discussion before voting.

Practice Projects

1. Take a vote by ballot on the following propositions:

No. 1: *Resolved,* That this organization select a controller at a salary of $450 per month.

No. 2: *Resolved,* That a payment of $10,000 be made on the Association's mortgage.

No. 3: *Resolved,* That the meadows in the rear of the club property be sold and the proceeds invested in government bonds.

The vote required to pass each proposition is a majority of the legal vote cast. A few students may prepare illegal ballots to give the tellers practice in counting votes. The report of the tellers should be presented in writing.

2. In which of the following motion situations would you, as presiding officer, take the vote by asking unanimous consent:

1. "I move that we replace the manager of our magazine."

2. "I move that the report of the auditors be filed."

3. "I move that a letter, protesting the rise in the county tax rate, be sent to the Board of Supervisors."

4. "I move that we postpone the reading of the minutes so that we can hear Senator Goodspeed immediately."

5. "I move that we endorse the candidacy of Mrs. Rosefield for the County Board of Education."

6. "I move that we recess for five minutes."

7. "I move that the Student Council withdraw its representative from the Area Board."

8. "I move that the two members who were found guilty of perjury by Superior Court today be dropped from membership in this organization."

3. An organization provides in its bylaws that any member who does not vote at the annual election of officers shall be fined. Discuss this provision.

4. What method of voting would you select as most suitable in the following situations:

1. A society has received an offer from a chain store to purchase its club property. There is sharp disagreement on whether or not to accept the offer.

2. The delegates at a convention are to vote on a motion to raise local payments to the national organization five dollars per year.

3. An association has a provision in its bylaws that "officers shall be elected by ballot at the annual meeting." A vacancy has occurred in the vice-presidency and a new vice-president must be chosen at a special meeting.

4. A board of education has before it a motion to thank the mayor for his assistance during "Public School Week."

5. At a convention where delegates are not seated apart from visitors, a motion to hold the next convention in Chicago is to be voted on.

6. In a meeting of the Carpet Manufacturing Association, the minutes have been read and someone moves that they be approved.

7. The Fireman's Benefit Association routinely refers all bills to its finance committee for approval. Someone moves to refer the monthly bill for rent to the finance committee.

PART TWO: MOTIONS

CHAPTER 11

THE MAIN MOTION

PURPOSE

The purpose of a main motion is to bring business before the assembly in a form in which it may be considered and voted upon.

FORM

PROPOSER: "I move that we appropriate three thousand dollars for the enlargement of our swimming pool."

or

"I move that we accept the offer of the National Executive Board to send a speaker for the state convention."

or

"I move that we approve the resolution of our Committee on Finance, providing an increase of three dollars in our dues."

or

"I move that we confirm the agreement with the First National Bank."

or

"I move the adoption of the following resolution:

"Resolved, That this organization express its gratitude and admiration for the fine and unselfish work carried on during the past two years by our National Chairman on Conservation, and that a copy of this resolution be sent to Mr. Levinthal, our National Chairman; to the Director of the United States Park Service; and to the newspapers of this city."

EXPLANATION

The main motion is the most commonly used of all the motions, and consideration of main motions is usually the chief business of organizations. A main motion presents a subject to an assembly for discussion and decision. Though it varies greatly in form and scope, it is always introduced by the words:

"I move . . . ."

The main motion deals with any subject which may properly be brought before the assembly. Some general main motions have particular names such as a motion to ratify, adopt, confirm, appoint, approve, or reject.

Any main motion proposing to do something which is illegal or which is completely unsuitable for the assembly to consider should be ruled "out of order" by the presiding officer and is not stated to the assembly.

Phrasing a Main Motion

If there is time, a motion should be carefully thought out before it is presented. A long or complicated motion should be written out and a copy of it given to the secretary at the time the motion is proposed.

Practice and skill are required to phrase motions effectively. It is important to cultivate this ability, because the good or bad phrasing of a motion influences its adoption or rejection and may either expedite business or tangle it.

In a recent meeting of a local Rotary Club, a member rose and inquired of the chairman why the club was not taking a more active part in the current Red Cross drive.

Immediately another member leaped to his feet, calling out "Mr. Chairman!" The president recognized him, and he blurted out a hastily improvised motion:

"I'm ashamed of our club! I move that all of us take Wednesday and Thursday off from our business, and go down to the Red Cross Headquarters and offer them our services, and that any member who doesn't comply be fined $250."

Another member seconded the motion, and as soon as it was stated by the chairman, the meeting was thrown into confusion.

"Wednesday and Thursday are my days in surgery," protested a physician. "Both days are filled with scheduled operations."

"I can't leave the plant those two days," another member objected. "Wednesday is the day we pour concrete, and I've got to be there. Neither can I afford to give to the Red Cross and then pay a $250 fine— that's outrageous!"

"Are both of you opposed to the Red Cross?" challenged the maker of the motion.

An outsider listening to the heated discussion which followed might have thought that the entire club was completely out of sympathy with the aims of the Red Cross, as shouts of "No!" defeated the motion.

A more experienced member then arose and offered the following motion:

"I move that our organization select a committee to cooperate with the Red Cross directors, and that the committee find out, first, which members can give time to the campaign and, second, arrange for whatever help our group can reasonably give."

This well-phrased motion carried unanimously.

Tests for Checking a Main Motion

There are simple tests which the proposer of a motion may use to check on how well his motion is phrased.

1. Is the motion *clear* and *definite?* If a member proposes a motion "that we help to make a happier Christmas for some of the less fortunate," the motion does not tell what form of help is to be given, who is to receive it, or what cost is involved.

On the other hand, a motion "to appropriate three hundred dollars to buy toys for the patients in the Children's Hospital," is clear and definite.

2. Is the motion capable of only *one reasonable interpretation?* If a motion is proposed "that flowers be sent to the family of every member when they die," it is not quite clear whether the members, the families, or the flowers are expected to die.

3. Is the motion *complete?* Does it cover all necessary points? For example, a motion "that we enlarge our membership" is so vague that it leaves undecided the number of members to be added and the method by which they are to be secured.

WHAT WAS THAT AGAIN?

Every little motion has
A meaning of its own.
Unless it's clearly stated, though,
The meaning won't be known.

4. Is the motion as *brief* as possible? The motion that "this organization contribute fifty of the outstandingly beautiful elm trees, which are so characteristic of our Eastern countryside, to the Park Department which has done so much to beautify our beloved and progressive city, and that we let the members of the Park Department know that each and every one of the members of the Bayview Horticultural Society is extremely grateful for what they have done for Bayview and is truly proud of them," is much more effective when phrased as:

"I move that the Bayview Horticultural Society contribute fifty elm trees to the Park Board in appreciation of its work."

5. Does the motion contain anything which is *irrelevant or confusing?* For example, a motion that "the Finance Committee be commended by all of us who have enjoyed its savings, particularly in view of the rising national tax budget and the high cost of living which is generally prevalent, and are grateful for its efforts," is phrased in a confusing way and part of the material is irrelevant.

6. Does the motion *carry out its intended purpose?* A club was discussing how the people of China might be made more familiar with the way democracy works in America. A member, trying to be helpful, offered the following motion:

"I move that we collect thousands of the popular books which we have already read and send them for distribution to the people of China."

It is obvious that, since the average Chinese does not read English, the motion would not carry out its intended purpose.

7. Is the motion suitably phrased to *meet the situation?* If an organization is discussing a new idea with which most of the members are unfamiliar, a simple motion phrased in general terms is the most suitable one. This type of motion seeks to win general agreement on the main idea or principle, and leaves details to be settled by later motions or by a committee. For example, if the United Automobile Workers, Local 810, is suddenly faced with a national emergency, a motion phrased in very general terms might meet the situation:

"I move that Local 810 offer full cooperation to the International Executive Board in this emergency."

If, on the other hand, there is a general agreement on the principle that the union should cooperate in an emergency with the International Executive Board, and numerous plans had been proposed for cooperating, a very specific motion would be preferable, such as:

"I move that Local 810 levy a special assessment of one dollar per member to be contributed to the emergency fund of the International Executive Board, and that a committee of five be appointed by the chairman to collect this fund."

Motions stated in general terms may be used to determine policy, and subsequent motions may provide details.

A careful analysis of the situation which a motion is designed to meet will often determine its most effective phraseology.

If a motion is poorly phrased, the presiding officer should request the maker of the motion to restate it in more suitable form. If a member has difficulty in phrasing his motion, the presiding officer should help him to state it as clearly as possible.

Reasoning out Rules

Reasoning out the rules governing a motion is a simple and logical process. In the case of a main motion, it is approximately as follows:

Since the assembly can consider only one general subject at a time, a main motion cannot interrupt a speaker.

It requires a second, except in committees or small groups or in legislative bodies, because it is logical that there should be proof that at least two people are in favor of the presentation and consideration of any main motion.

Since the object of the main motion is to present a proposal for discussion and decision, a main motion is, of course, debatable.

Likewise, since a main motion can be varied in form and may need to be changed, it can be amended to make it express the wishes of the group.

Since all decisions of assemblies, with a few exceptions, are made by the majority, a main motion requires a majority vote.

A main motion, if lost, cannot be renewed or proposed again at the same meeting or convention. When a vote on such a motion has been taken, it should continue in effect for the duration of the meeting if business is to proceed.

RULES GOVERNING A MAIN MOTION

1. Cannot interrupt a speaker, because it does not require immediate decision.

2. Requires a second, to ensure that more than one person is interested in its consideration.

3. Is debatable, because it presents a subject for consideration.

4. Can be amended, to make it express the wishes of the organization.

5. Requires a majority vote.

6. Has the lowest rank of precedence.

7. Applies to no other motion.

8. Can have applied to it all subsidiary motions, specific main motions, and the motions to withdraw and to object to consideration.

9. Cannot be renewed at the same meeting or at the same convention. In order to expedite business, it is important that main motions, when once acted upon, are disposed of for the remainder of the meeting or convention.

Some of the rules (such as those on application and renewal) governing each different motion have not been explained up to this point, but they are included to make the list of rules complete.

Practice Projects

1. Which motion in each of the following groups do you consider preferable? Give the reasons for your choice. What defects can you point out in the remaining motions?

1. "I move that a committee of three be appointed by the chairman to study the question of increased storage facilities for the water supply of the City of Davenport, and that they report their findings at the annual meeting."

2. "I move that we study the question of the water supply."

3. "I move that something be done about this scandalous situation and that some kind of committee be appointed right now to see about getting a better water storage place."

4. "I move that we demand that the City Council come to our next meeting and explain to us why we do not have an adequate water supply after talking about it for sixteen years. I also move that we insist that the City Council employ an expert to tell us what is wrong with our water storage system."

1. "I move that we have a joint Memorial Day program, and that we arrange to have some other organizations help, and that everybody think up some plans."

2. "I move that we follow the suggestion of Al Brown for Memorial Day."

3. "I move that we definitely do something to remember our buddies on Memorial Day."

4. "I move that our Post combine with the Riverdale Post of the American Legion and with the other veterans' organizations of the county to plan Memorial Day services."

1. "I move that we let our congressmen hear from us about the negligent way in which they are proceeding to appropriate our money, and that we give them to understand that we did not elect them to play fast and loose with our tax money which we turn over to them."

2. "I move that the American Bankers Association go on record as opposing any further increase in our national budget at this time, and that copies of this motion be sent to each member of Congress."

3. "I move that we write and tell every senator and representative what we think of their extravagant proposals for bankrupting the country through punitive taxation."

4. "I move that we take up the matter of reckless government spending with the members of Congress."

2. If you were presiding, which of the following motions would you:

1. State to the assembly verbatim?
2. Ask the proposer to rephrase?
3. Rule out of order?

Give the reasons for your decisions. How would you rephrase those motions which are legal but which are poorly phrased?

1. "Mr. Jackson, the treasurer, tells me that this organization is practically broke. I move that we give some serious thought to raising the dues."

2. "I move that this organization pay each of the delegates seventy-five dollars toward his expenses to the national convention."

3. "I move that we turn in a fire alarm to test the efficiency of our

City Fire Department, and that we time the interval between the turning in of the alarm and the arrival of the first fire engine."

4. "I move that we do not favor the refusal of the City Manager not to allow the Municipal Lake to be used for purposes which are not purely civic."

5. "I move that a committee be appointed for studying ways and means of enlisting new members for this organization."

6. "I move that we disregard the constitutional provision against voting at the same meeting on new members, and that we vote on the name of Mr. Johnson at once."

7. "I move that all dog owners be required to have muzzles on them whenever they appear on the city streets."

8. "I move that the Secretary of the Sailors' Union of the Pacific, Local 468, be authorized to open all letters addressed to brothers whose whereabouts we do not know. And if there is anything important in the letter, he should try to get them to the brothers."

9. "I move that we come to some decision on the matter of instructing or not instructing our delegates to the County Convention."

10. "I move that we appropriate six thousand dollars from our Charities Fund for the Home for Tubercular Children at Lake Arrowhead."

3. As a member of the following organizations, what motions would you propose, to meet the situations indicated? Examine each motion critically from the standpoint of brevity, clearness, definiteness, completeness, and suitability to the situation.

1. The Fairview Debating Club has been having poor attendance at its Tuesday-night meetings, because the prize fights occur on the same evening. The members wish to change their meeting time.

2. The Oakdale City Council plans to hold a civic parade as a welcome to the Vice-President of the United States who is returning for a brief visit to his home town. The money to pay for the expenses of the celebration is to come from the Mayor's contingent fund.

3. At a general meeting, the Associated Students of the University of Texas are disturbed by the charge that the editorials of the college daily newspaper continuously fail to represent the views of the majority of the students. The editor is an elective official and there is no provision for recalling him.

4. The Garbage Collectors' Union, Local 173, is in a turmoil because citizens are not properly segregating garbage. The members want to send a circular to each householder to enlist cooperation.

5. The members of the Ladies' Aid Society of the First Methodist Church wish to thank their pastor and express their appreciation for the cooperation and help which he and his wife have given the society during the past year.

6. The King's River Chapter of the Benevolent and Protective Order of Elks is planning to build a new clubhouse. Mr. Turnbow is the low bidder. The members wish to accept his bid and sign a contract.

Parliamentary procedure involves skill in group practice. No one can become a football player by sitting and reading a book on how to play football. Similarly, parliamentary drill should be carried on in a group, and fully one-third of the group's class time should be devoted to actual practice.

Each presiding officer should choose a secretary who will take notes and read motions and keep a record of motions proposed. The secretary should be ready to inform the chairman or any member of exactly what motion is pending at any time.

Rotate the chairmanship so that several students will have the experience of presiding for short periods—say five minutes. Propose various motions, both good and bad ones, discuss them, and vote upon them. Correct every small error in procedure.

CHAPTER 12

MOTIONS TO ENFORCE CORRECT PROCEDURE

REQUIRING CONFORMITY TO RULES

In order that a group may work together effectively and smoothly, it is necessary that the members conform to general procedural rules. To secure this conformity, members have available certain motions which help to ensure that correct procedure is followed.

Enforcement of correct procedure is primarily the duty of the presiding officer. However, he cannot be expected to detect every error or omission, so this duty is shared with the members.

If the chairman does not notice a mistake or an omission, or if he notices it and fails to correct it, there are four motions which members may use as tools to enforce observance of correct procedure. These are:

a. Point of order
b. Appeal
c. Inquiry
d. Division of the assembly

These motions arise incidentally out of the main motion which is pending before the assembly. They may be proposed at any time and must be decided as soon as they arise.

Point of Order

PURPOSE

The purpose of a point of order is to call attention to a violation of the rules, to an omission, or to a mistake in procedure.

FORM

PROPOSER (without waiting for recognition): "Mr. Chairman, I rise to a point of order."

CHAIRMAN (without waiting for a second): "State your point of order."

PROPOSER: "The motion just proposed is out of order because it conflicts with Bylaw 3."

CHAIRMAN: "Your point of order is *well taken*. The motion just proposed is out of order because it conflicts with Bylaw 3 on membership."

or

"Your point of order is *not well taken*. The chair believes that there is no conflict between this motion and Bylaw 3."

EXPLANATION

A point of order may deal with a mistake of the presiding officer or of any member, with a violation of the rules or of procedure, or with an error or omission.

Raising a point of order is equivalent to calling the attention of the assembly to the error and requesting that the presiding officer rule upon it; that is, state his opinion as to whether the point is correct or incorrect.

A point of order must be raised immediately after the mistake, error, or omission occurs. It cannot be raised later, after other business has intervened, unless it concerns a violation of the law or of the constitution or bylaws, or concerns an error in the minutes. It is never too late to correct a violation of the law, or of the constitution or bylaws, or to rectify an error in the minutes.

Since it is important that a mistake should be corrected as soon as possible, the member who rises to a point of order may interrupt a speaker or the taking of a vote. When a member is interrupted by a point of order, he should immediately sit down until the point of order has been decided.

Instead of seeking recognition in the usual way, the member who is raising the point of order says, "I rise to a point of order," so that the chairman will know why the member wishes to obtain the floor.

BIG MOMENT

A brilliant thought has come to me,
  I now recall the rule.
I'll show them up—I'll make them see
  That I am not a fool.

    My tied-up tongue is loose at last,
      My heart has ceased to pound,
      My momentary fright has passed,
        I calmly look around.

  I know precisely how to say
      The thing that in me burned,
But oh, alas, alackaday,
      The meeting has adjourned!

As soon as the member has stated his point of order, the presiding officer must rule upon it; that is, he must declare that it is "well taken" or "not well taken." He usually gives his reason for the ruling.

If a point of order raises a question which is unusually important, difficult, or complicated, the chairman may ask for time to get more information and may defer his decision until he has had an opportunity to study the matter. His decision, however, cannot be unreasonably delayed, since no action can be taken on the pending motion until the point of order is disposed of.

If the chairman is in doubt about the correctness of a point of order, or if he does not wish to take the responsibility for making the decision, he may refer the matter to the assembly and ask the members to decide. He may say:

"Mr. Andrews has raised the point of order that the motion which we are discussing is in conflict with Bylaw 3. The secretary will please read Bylaw 3."

After the secretary has read this bylaw, the chairman continues:

"The question is, 'Is this motion in conflict with this bylaw?' Those who believe it is, say 'Aye.' . . . Those who believe it is not, say 'No.' . . . The decision is in the negative. The chair therefore rules the point of order not well taken. Is there any further discussion on the motion before the assembly?"

In rare instances a chairman may not only refer a point of order to an assembly for decision, but may also call for discussion on it as well. However, unless the chairman asks for discussion, none is possible.

RULES GOVERNING POINT OF ORDER

1. Can interrupt a speaker, because a mistake should be corrected immediately.

2. Requires no second, because it is a request or demand and not a true motion.

3. Is not debatable, because the presiding officer decides it.

4. Cannot be amended, since it is a demand or request.

5. Requires no vote, since it is not a motion.

6. Takes precedence as an incidental motion and must be decided whenever it arises.

7. Applies to any mistake, error, or omission.

8. Can have no motions applied to it, except withdraw. The decision on the point of order may be appealed.

9. Cannot be renewed during the same meeting or convention.

Appeal

PURPOSE

The purpose of an appeal from a decision of the chairman is to enable any member to have the assembly decide by vote whether the chair's decision should be upheld or overruled. This motion is useful when someone believes that the presiding officer has made a decision which is wrong or unfair.

FORM

PROPOSER (immediately following the chairman's decision, and without waiting for recognition): "Mr. Chairman, I appeal from the decision of the chair."

CHAIRMAN (after hearing a second): "The decision of the chair has been appealed from. Do you wish to state the grounds for your appeal?"

The member may state the reason for his appeal briefly. The chairman may state the reasons for his decision either before or after giving an opportunity for discussion. He takes the vote on the appeal by saying:

"Those in favor of sustaining the decision of the chair say 'Aye.' . . . Those opposed, 'No.' . . . The decision of the chair is sustained (or overruled)."

EXPLANATION

An appeal usually arises from a chairman's decision on a point of order. The appeal enables the assembly to review the decision of its presiding officer. Any decision of the presiding officer is subject to appeal, but the announcement of a vote or an answer to a parliamentary inquiry is not a decision, and therefore cannot be appealed.

If, after the decision is given, other business intervenes, or there has been progress in debate, it is too late to appeal. The fact that a member has started to speak does not prevent another member, if he acts promptly, from interrupting the speaker and presenting his appeal.

An appeal is debatable. This is logical because it may relate to an important matter on which the assembly needs to hear the opinions of both sides before voting. Usually, debate should be limited to a statement by the member of the grounds for his appeal, and a statement by the chairman of the reasons for his decision.

If the chairman should become convinced during the discussion that his decision was wrong, he may change or reverse his decision, and the appeal is automatically dropped. The member making the appeal can, in like circumstances, withdraw his appeal.

If the assembly votes to sustain the chair's decision, his decision becomes the final decision of the assembly. If the vote does not sustain the chair's decision, his decision is overruled.

A majority vote, or a tie vote, sustains the decision of the chairman on an appeal. A tie vote sustains the chairman's decision because a majority vote is necessary to overrule his decision. The presiding officer, if he is a member of the organization, may vote to sustain his own ruling.

RULES GOVERNING APPEAL

1. Can interrupt a speaker, because it requires immediate decision, and because it has a time limit on its presentation.

2. Requires a second, since it is equivalent to a motion to overrule the decision of the presiding officer.

3. Is debatable, since it may need explanation in order to vote upon it.

4. Cannot be amended, since it is invariable in form.

5. Requires a majority or a tie vote to sustain the chairman's decision.

6. Takes precedence as an incidental motion, and therefore must be decided as soon as it is proposed.

7. Applies to no motions, but does apply to any decisions of the presiding officer.

8. Can have applied to it the motions to postpone temporarily, postpone definitely, vote immediately, limit debate, and withdraw.

9. Cannot be renewed, because it must be made promptly after the situation arises.

Parliamentary Inquiry

PURPOSE

The purpose of a parliamentary inquiry is to enable a member to obtain information from the presiding officer. This information must relate to a question of procedure which arises out of the motion before the assembly, or to a matter which is to be brought before the assembly immediately.

A request for information concerning the question before the assembly and a request to ask a speaker a question are slightly varied forms of a parliamentary inquiry.

FORM

1. *Parliamentary Inquiry*

PROPOSER (without waiting for recognition): "I rise to a parliamentary inquiry."

CHAIRMAN (without waiting for a second): "State your inquiry."

PROPOSER: "Is it possible to take a vote on this motion by ballot?"

CHAIRMAN: "Yes, if the assembly wishes."

2. *Request for Information*

PROPOSER (without waiting for recognition): "I rise to a parliamentary inquiry."

CHAIRMAN (without waiting for a second): "State your inquiry."

PROPOSER: "I should like to know whether this motion will increase our dues."

CHAIRMAN: "No, this appropriation would not cause an increase in dues."

3. *Request to Ask a Question*

PROPOSER (without waiting for recognition): "I should like to ask the speaker a question."

CHAIRMAN (if he feels that the request is suitable): "Is the speaker willing to answer a question?"

SPEAKER: "Yes," or "No," or "I prefer to answer the question later."

EXPLANATION

Every member has the right to know at all times exactly what question is being considered and what its effect will be. He also has the right to ask for information concerning a matter before the assembly, or to ask procedural questions about a matter that may come before the assembly immediately.

A parliamentary inquiry may interrupt a speaker if it requires an immediate answer. No member, however, has the right to interrupt a speaker if his inquiry can reasonably wait until the speaker has finished.

When a member rises to a parliamentary inquiry, he should immediately announce, "I rise to a parliamentary inquiry." The presiding officer will then know that the member rising has a right to the floor.

A parliamentary inquiry is always addressed to the presiding officer and is answered by him. If it concerns procedure, the presiding officer may consult the parliamentarian or some authority before answering the question.

When a member asks a question on procedure which is pertinent to the pending question, the presiding officer should answer the question if he can. It is not a duty of the chairman, however, to answer general questions on parliamentary law which are not related to the pending business.

If a member wishes to ask a question of a speaker, he rises and states his request to the presiding officer. The presiding officer, if he feels the request is reasonable, first asks the speaker whether or not he wishes to answer a question at this time. If the speaker is willing, the presiding officer tells the questioner to state his query. Both question and answer are directed to the presiding officer.

The presiding officer should never permit members to rise to parliamentary inquiries for the purpose of annoying a speaker, and he should refuse to recognize any member who rises for this purpose. If a member presents an inquiry which, in the opinion of the chairman, does not call for an immediate reply, he may tell the member that his inquiry will be answered later, and direct the speaker who was interrupted to continue with his discussion.

When a parliamentary inquiry is raised, it interrupts all business until the chairman either answers the query or states that he will answer it when the speaker has finished.

Questions which are really debate should be ruled out of order if they are presented as parliamentary inquiries; for example, if someone asks, "Is it not true that this type of proposal is unpatriotic?"

RULES GOVERNING PARLIAMENTARY INQUIRY

1. Can interrupt a speaker, because it may necessitate an immediate answer.
2. Requires no second, because it is a request and not a true motion.
3. Is not debatable, because it is a request which is decided by the chairman.
4. Cannot be amended, since it is not a true motion.
5. Requires no vote, because it is decided by the chairman.
6. Takes precedence, as an incidental motion, of the question out of which it arises.
7. Applies to no other motion.
8. Can have no motion applied to it except withdraw.
9. Cannot be renewed.

Division of the Assembly

PURPOSE

The purpose of a request for a division of the assembly is to verify a vote which is in doubt or to secure a more accurate count of a vote which has just been taken.

FORM

PROPOSER (immediately after the vote is taken or announced, and without waiting for recognition): "I call for division."

or

"Division!"

CHAIRMAN: "Division has been called for. Those in favor of the motion that (stating the motion just voted on), please rise. The secretary will please count. . . . Be seated. Those opposed, please rise. . . . Be seated. The affirmative vote is 29; the negative vote is 17. Therefore, the motion is carried."

EXPLANATION

Any member, without waiting for recognition, may call for a division of the assembly at any time after the question has been put to vote. He may do this even after the vote has been announced and another member has the floor, provided the division is called for quite promptly.

A call for a division is, in effect, a demand that a vote be verified. The vote may be verified by taking it in a more accurate manner. A voice vote, for example, may be verified by a rising vote or a show of hands. It is not necessary that an actual count of the members raising their hands, or rising, be taken if it is evident that either the affirmative or the negative has a distinct preponderance of votes.

The responsibility of announcing a vote rests upon the chairman. If he is in doubt, he may himself retake a voice vote or ask for a rising vote and, if necessary, for a count.

No member can use the privilege of demanding a division of the assembly to obstruct business by calling for a division on a vote where the results are evident and leave no room for doubt.

RULES GOVERNING DIVISION OF THE ASSEMBLY

1. Can interrupt a speaker, because it must be acted upon before other business intervenes.

2. Requires no second, because it is a request or demand and not a true motion.

3. Is not debatable, because it is decided by the chairman.

4. Cannot be amended, since it is not a true motion.

5. Requires no vote, because it is decided by the chairman.

6. Takes precedence, as an incidental motion, of the question out of which it arises.

7. Applies to no other motion.

8. Can have no motion applied to it.

9. Cannot be renewed, because the demand must be made immediately following the vote.

TOO CLOSE FOR COMFORT

When the vote is so close
    That some person stands
And calls, in loud voice,
    For a show of hands,

From the way it is asked,
    The way he insists,
What one rather expects
    Is a show of fists.

Practice Projects

1. Would you, as chairman, rule that the points of order in the following situations are well taken, or not well taken? Give reasons to support your answer.

Meeting: Long Horn Mesa Cattlemen's Association
Situation: A motion is pending to oppose an increase in the land which is under the jurisdiction of the National Park Service.

MR. ARTHUR: "It's time we cattlemen stopped taking a back seat to the sheepherders in this district. Those good-for-nothing wool-covered termites haven't left a blade of grass or a . . . ."

MR. BENSON: "Mr. Chairman, I rise to a point of order."

CHAIRMAN: "State your point of order."

MR. BENSON: "My friend here is talking off the point."

CHAIRMAN: "Your point of order is . . . ."

Meeting: New Jersey Nurses Association
Situation: A bylaw of the association provides that no appropriation in excess of two hundred dollars can be voted by the members unless notice of the proposed appropriation has been given at the previous meeting.

MISS CARSON: "I move that we donate fifty dollars a month for the next year to the Mental Hygiene Association."

MRS. LOWRY: "I second the motion."

MRS. MOFFITT: "I rise to a point of order."

CHAIRMAN: "State your point of order."

MRS. MOFFITT: "That motion means an expenditure of six hundred dollars. If I remember correctly, our bylaws say we can't appropriate more than two hundred without . . . ."

MISS CARSON (interrupting): "Why, I said only fifty dollars a month."

CHAIRMAN: "Your point of order is . . . ."

Meeting: Associated Plumbing Contractors of Webster County

Situation: The bylaws provide that recommendations for important political appointments are to be made only by the national executive board of the organization.

MR. BROWN: "I move that our county unit send a letter to the President of the United States, recommending that Mr. Finn McCumaill, our leading contractor and an outstanding patriot, be appointed to fill the present vacancy on the War Production Board."

NUMEROUS MEMBERS: "I second the motion."

MR. LAWRENCE: "I rise to a point of order."

CHAIRMAN: "State your point of order."

MR. LAWRENCE: "This kind of recommendation has to come from our national executive committee."

CHAIRMAN: "Your point of order is . . . ."

Meeting: Poultrymen's Association

Situation: The convention is discussing a motion that one thousand dollars be appropriated to the State University for research in increased egg production.

MR. KENWOOD: "I rise to a point of order."

CHAIRMAN: "State your point of order."

MR. KENWOOD: "I think that universities don't know as much about poultry as the average poultryman, and we haven't any right to turn over our money to them."

CHAIRMAN: "Your point of order is . . . ."

Meeting: Chamber of Commerce of Morningside Heights

Situation: A business meeting is in progress.

MR. HENES: "I move that we try to get the city council to put in new electroliers along Main Street."

CHAIRMAN: "That seems a sensible motion. Is there any discussion on the motion that . . . ."

MR. MARCO (interrupting): "I rise to a point of order."

CHAIRMAN: "State your point of order."

MR. MARCO: "Mr. Henes' motion was not seconded."

CHAIRMAN: "Your point of order is . . . ."

Meeting: Windy Harbor Yachtmen's Association

Situation: A motion is pending to hold a regatta on the Fourth of July.

COMMODORE EMILE: "It seems to me that we will face stiff competition on the Fourth of July because the Chamber of Commerce is holding a barbecue, and the American Legion has a dance planned for . . . ."

MR. WAYNE (interrupting): "I rise to a point of order."

CHAIRMAN: "State your point of order."

MR. WAYNE: "The Commodore is not speaking on the subject."

CHAIRMAN: "Your point of order is . . . ."

While practicing points of order, it is advisable to raise a point of order on every small error.

2. The chairman's rulings on the following points of order are incorrect. Present an appeal from the chair's decision and state the grounds for your appeal.

Meeting: The Midvale Knitting Society

Situation: The society is discussing a motion to import French yarn for the members.

MRS. CHERIE: "I think it would offend our local merchants if we bought our yarn in France. After all, they have to live and they do business with our husbands. The same principle was involved when the town meeting voted to have that statue of General Peabody carved in Italy and . . . ."

MRS. STEPHENSON: "I rise to a point of order. Mrs. Cherie is not speaking on the subject."

CHAIRMAN: "Your point of order is well taken."

Meeting: The South City Sanitary District

Situation: The members are discussing a motion to enlarge the facilities for disposal of garbage. Members are conversing with each other, walking about, and paying little attention to the speaker.

MR. NERVIG: "Mr. Chairman, I rise to a point of order."

CHAIRMAN: "State your point of order."

MR. NERVIG: "My point of order is that the members of this assembly are out of order."

CHAIRMAN (indignantly): "The chair rules your point of order not well taken."

Meeting: The Ponderosa Pine Association

Situation: The Association's bylaws provide that all assessments require notice at a previous meeting.

MR. LOOMIS: "We need funds badly. I move that we make an assessment immediately of five dollars per member."

MR. EVANS: "Mr. Chairman, I rise to a point of order."

CHAIRMAN: "State your point of order."

MR. EVANS: "My point of order is that our bylaws say that no assessment can be levied unless notice is given at a previous meeting, and we've had no notice."

CHAIRMAN: "The chairman rules your point of order not well taken. We need the money immediately, so we ought to go ahead with the assessment anyway."

Meeting: Union of Aviation Mechanics, Local 368.

Situation: The charter of the union forbids it to take independent action in any political matter.

BROTHER WILLIAMS: "I move that our local endorse the work of our congressman from this district to lower the cost of living."

MR. ECKHOFF: "I rise to a point of order."

CHAIRMAN: "State your point of order."

MR. ECKHOFF: "We are forbidden in our charter to take any independent political action, therefore Brother Williams' motion is out of order."

CHAIRMAN: "The chairman rules your point of order not well taken. This is not a political action."

3. If a motion that Typesetters' Local 428 sponsor a course for the training of apprentices is pending, which of the following might be correct inquiries?

1. "How much would this plan cost the Local?"

2. "Why should the Local spend money to help other people when we need it ourselves?"

3. "Is a motion to amend in order?"

4. "When is the annual banquet to be held?"

5. "What does Bylaw 16 say about expenditures?"

6. "I'd like to ask the maker of the motion how the apprentices are to be selected."

7. "Is it possible to take a ballot vote on this motion?"

8. "How many other locals have apprentice courses?"

9. "How long would the course run?"

10. "Can I pay my dues now?"

CHAPTER 13

MOTIONS TO CHANGE MOTIONS

ALTERATIONS ARE OFTEN NECESSARY

Proposals are sometimes presented in a form which is not acceptable to the entire group. Phrasing a motion is difficult, and many motions require correction. As discussion develops, it frequently becomes evident that the motion as originally presented is inadequate and that it is unacceptable unless it can be changed.

Often the members favor a part of the motion, and either disagree with another part of it or are convinced that it can be improved by dividing or changing it.

To meet these situations, the motion to amend and the request to divide a question have developed. Amendments may be proposed to the original motion to put it in a form which is acceptable to the members; or the proposal may be divided into separate motions which can be considered individually.

The legitimate use of both motions is to improve the original proposition; to aid and to perfect the motion to which they are applied; to befriend the original motion and to make it more worthy of support and adoption.

Occasionally both motions are purposely misused by the opponents of the original motion to make it unsuitable for adoption and thus to defeat it. The presiding officer can rule out amendments which are, in his opinion, proposed solely to delay action on the original motion.

The perfection of a proposal by amendment or division is an important deliberative process and requires even more skill and experience than adequate phrasing of an original motion.

Motion to Amend

PURPOSE

The purpose of the motion to amend is to change or modify a motion or resolution which is being considered by the assembly so that it will more accurately and fully express the will of the group. It applies to any motion which is variable in form; that is, any motion which could have been phrased in some other way.

FORM

Assume that the following main motion is under consideration:

"I move that this organization send representatives to the Board of Education and to the State Superintendent of Public Instruction to present the need for more school playgrounds in this county."

The following are the usual types of amendments which may be applied to the pending motion:

1. *Amendment by Addition* (*Insertion*)

PROPOSER: "I move to amend the motion by inserting the word 'five' before the word 'representatives.' "

CHAIRMAN: "It has been moved and seconded to amend the motion by inserting the word 'five' before the word 'representatives.' "

When restatement is necessary to a clear understanding, the chairman should continue:

"So that, if amended, the motion would read, 'that this organization send five representatives to the Board of Education and to the State Superintendent of Public Instruction to present the need for more school playgrounds.' Is there any discussion on the amendment? . . . Those in favor of the amendment, say 'Aye.' . . . Those opposed, 'No.' . . . The amendment is carried (or lost). Is there any discussion on the motion (or on the motion as amended)?"

2. *Amendment by Elimination* (*Striking Out*)

PROPOSER: "I move to amend the motion by striking out the words 'and to the State Superintendent of Public Instruction.' "

CHAIRMAN: "It has been moved and seconded to amend the motion by striking out the words 'and to the State Superintendent of Public Instruction,' so that the motion, if amended, would read, 'that this organization send representatives to the Board of Education to present the need for more school playgrounds, etc.' "

TINKERS' DAMN

There are always those about us
  Who await a motion's birth
And then fluster us and flout us
  And propose, with wicked mirth,

One amendment on another,
  Each a little bit more wild,
Till the motion's poor old mother
  Doesn't recognize her child.

3. *Amendment by Substitution* (*Striking Out and Inserting*)

a. Substituting words:

PROPOSER: "I move to amend the motion by striking out the word 'representatives' and inserting the word 'our president and secretary.' "

CHAIRMAN: "It has been moved and seconded to amend the motion by striking out the word 'representatives' and inserting the words 'our president and secretary' so that the motion, if amended, would read 'that this organization send our president and secretary to the Board of Education to present the need for more school playgrounds.' "

b. Substituting a new motion or paragraph:

PROPOSER: "I move to amend the motion by substituting for it the following motion: 'I move that representatives of this organization hold a conference with the State Director of Recreation to determine how we can best cooperate in securing more school playgrounds.' "

CHAIRMAN: "It has been moved and seconded to amend the motion 'that this organization send representatives to the Board of Education and the State Superintendent of Public Instruction to present the need for more school playgrounds in this county' by substituting for it a new motion 'that representatives of this organization hold a conference with the State Director of Recreation to determine how we can best cooperate in securing more school playgrounds.' Is there any discussion on the amendment?"

EXPLANATION

Number of Pending Amendments Limited

Amendments are of two ranks. Amendments applied to the original motion are amendments of the first rank, and amendments applied to the proposed amendment are amendments of the second rank, or amendments to the amendment. *Only one amendment of each rank may be pending at any one time.* When one amendment to a motion is under consideration, no other amendment to that motion is in order, but an amendment to the amendment is in order. An amendment to an amendment cannot itself be amended.

Whenever an amendment is adopted or defeated, another amendment of the same rank is in order. Any number of amendments may be offered in succession, provided that only one amendment of each rank is pending at one time. As soon as a pending amendment of the second rank has been disposed of, another of the same rank may be proposed. As soon as the pending amendments of both ranks have been disposed of, another amendment of each rank is in order.

For example, if the motion "that this organization hold a banquet next Friday night" is before the assembly, some member may move to amend it by adding the words "at the Palmer House." While discussion is in progress on this amendment, another member may move to amend the amendment by adding the words "in the Empire Room." This would be in order because it is an amendment to the amendment.

If, however, someone moved to strike out "Friday" and insert the word "Wednesday," this would be another amendment of the first rank and would be out of order until the original amendment to the motion had been voted upon.

An amendment to a constitution or to bylaws, or to any motion which has previously been adopted, is itself a main motion, not an amendment, and is, therefore, subject to amendments of both ranks.

Amendments Must Be Germane

The most important fact to remember about amendments is that an amendment must be germane. Germane means "relevant to" or "having direct bearing upon" the motion which the amendment seeks to change.

For example, if a motion is pending "that this organization hire an executive secretary," the motion could be amended by adding the words, "at a salary of $500 per month," or by adding "who shall work under the direction of the president," or by striking out the word "executive," and inserting the word "program." All these amendments relate directly to the subject of the main motion, which is the hiring of a secretary.

On the other hand, if a member proposed to amend this same motion by adding the words "and that we raise our dues," or "that this organization dispense with one business meeting each month," or "that our initiation fee be raised," each of these amendments would be ruled out of order by the presiding officer because it was not germane to the subject of the original motion. No subject which is different from the motion under consideration can be admitted under the guise of an amendment.

An amendment to change one type of motion into another type of motion is never in order. For example, a motion to postpone another motion temporarily cannot be amended to make it a motion to postpone indefinitely.

Amendments May Be Opposed to Spirit of Motion

An amendment may be opposed to the spirit or intent of the main motion. It may even nullify the main motion. For example, if a motion is pending to endorse the report of the labor commissioner, an amendment might be proposed to strike out the word "endorse" and insert the word "deplore." Such an amendment would be hostile to the intent of the original motion. However, the amendment would be in order because it is germane to the subject matter of the motion, which is to express an official opinion on the report.

No amendment is in order which merely changes a question from affirmative to negative. For example, a motion "that we raise the dues one dollar per month" cannot be amended to read "that we do not raise the dues one dollar per month."

Debate on Amendments

Debate on an amendment is limited to a discussion of the amendment and does not open the original motion to debate. It may be necessary, however, in discussing the amendment, to refer to the main question, in order to make the effect of the amendment clear. The same rule applies in the case of an amendment to an amendment. In discussing an amendment to an amendment, it may be necessary to explain it by reference to the amendment and to the main motion itself. It is not in order, however, to discuss the merits of the main question during discussion of an amendment.

While an amendment is being discussed, a member may think of a still better amendment. It is permissible for him to state that if the pending amendment is voted down, he will propose a new one, and to state or describe it briefly.

When a motion is not debatable, proposed amendments are likewise not debatable.

Withdrawing and Modifying Amendments

A member has the right to modify his own motion, without going through the process of amendment. He must do this, however, before the motion has been stated to the assembly by the presiding officer. If a member wishes to modify his motion after it has been stated to the assembly by the presiding officer, he can do it only by unanimous consent or by formal vote of a majority.

The proposer of an amendment has the right to withdraw it before it has been stated by the presiding officer. After it has been stated, but not yet voted upon, he may still withdraw it if he obtains the consent of the assembly.

If the maker of a motion wishes to accept a proposed amendment, he may rise and, without waiting for recognition, state:

"Mr. Chairman, I accept the amendment."

The chair then asks if there is any objection, and if there is none, the proposed amendment becomes a part of the pending question. If there is an objection, the amendment must be voted upon in the regular way.

When several amendments would be necessary to make a motion acceptable to an assembly, it is better to propose an amendment in the form of a new substitute motion. The substitute may revise the motion completely, so long as it is germane to the subject of the original motion.

This proposed substitute amendment is itself subject to an amendment.

Voting on Amendments

When a motion, an amendment, and an amendment to an amendment are pending, the vote is taken first on the amendment to the amendment, next on the amendment, and last on the motion.

If a substitute motion is offered as an amendment, the vote is taken on whether to substitute it for the original motion. If the substitution is approved, the substitute amendment becomes the main motion and is subject to amendments of both ranks.

One nineteenth-century writer borrowed the complicated machinery of the House of Representatives and allowed the friends of the substitute amendment and the friends of the original motion to perfect each motion before taking a vote on the substitution. This complicated procedure is confusing and unsuited to ordinary bodies.

An amendment to a pending motion requires only a majority vote, even though the motion itself may require a two-thirds vote. An amendment to any amendment requires only a majority vote.

An amendment to a constitution or to bylaws requires whatever vote is provided for in those documents. If there is no special provision, only a majority vote is required by parliamentary law.

When an amendment is adopted or rejected, the same amendment, or substantially the same amendment, or question, or idea, even though expressed in different words, cannot be proposed again at the same meeting or convention. The vote on the amendment, however, may be reconsidered. This rule gives finality to an amendment which has once been decided, and prevents further tampering with the amended motion.

Filling Blanks

Motions are frequently presented with blanks left to be filled in by vote of the assembly. For example:

"I move that a committee consisting of Mr. ————, Mr. ————, and Mr. ———— be selected to decide on the plans for landscaping the grounds."

or

"I move that we build an annex to our clubhouse, the cost of which shall be limited to $————."

or

"I move that we sell all of our property facing on Cedar Street for a price of $————, including commission of $————."

The words or figures to be inserted in these blanks are not treated as amendments—they are alternative propositions.

The chairman asks for names or amounts or numbers to fill the blanks, and these are suggested by members. No second is required. There is no restriction on the number of alternative names, amounts, or numbers which may be suggested, unless a limitation is established by a special rule or by a motion.

When all suggested names, amounts, or numbers have been submitted, they are voted upon. To ensure fairness, a ballot vote should be taken, so that all names or amounts or numbers can be voted upon simultaneously. If the assembly does not wish to take a ballot vote, a rising vote should be taken, beginning with the smallest or the largest number, whichever is the least likely to win the approval of the assembly.

The entire list of suggestions should be voted upon both affirmatively and negatively, and the suggestion receiving the highest number of votes (provided that the number of votes received is a majority of the members voting on the suggestion) is declared accepted. If no suggestion receives the necessary vote, or if there is a tie vote, the two suggestions which have received the highest affirmative votes are voted on again. After the blanks have been filled, the motion is open for discussion and is then voted upon.

RULES GOVERNING MOTION TO AMEND

1. Cannot interrupt a speaker because it does not require immediate decision.

2. Requires a second.

3. Is debatable, unless applied to an undebatable motion.

4. Can be amended.

5. Requires a majority vote, even though the motion to which it applies requires a two-thirds vote or more.

6. Takes precedence over the main motion and the motion to postpone indefinitely.

7. Applies to any motion which may be varied in form.

8. Can have applied to it all subsidiary motions, reconsider, and withdraw.

9. Cannot be renewed at the same meeting or convention, but may be reconsidered.

Request for Division of a Question

PURPOSE

The purpose of a request to divide a question is to enable a member to insist on a division of a motion composed of two or more independent parts or ideas into separate motions which may be considered and voted on individually.

FORM

Assume that the following motion is pending:

"I move that we have an annual get-together banquet, and that the initiation fee of this organization be raised to seventy-five dollars."

PROPOSER (without waiting for recognition): "I request that the motion just proposed be divided into two parts:

First, a motion to have an annual get-together banquet and

Second, a motion to raise the initiation fee of this organization to seventy-five dollars."

CHAIRMAN (without waiting for a second, if in his opinion the question contains more than one distinct proposal): "It is requested that the motion be divided into two parts. This will be done. The motion now before the assembly is 'that we have an annual get-together banquet.' Is there any discussion?"

EXPLANATION

A member has the right to request the division of a question whenever the motion contains two or more distinct propositions, each of which is capable of standing alone, and each of which may be considered and voted upon independently of the other. A member may also request the division of a question when a group of amendments covers different points, or when a committee report contains a number of recommendations.

When a member requests a division of a question, the presiding officer must rule upon whether the motion or resolution can be divided. If the motion is divisible, he agrees to the division and states the first independent portion of the motion and calls for discussion on it. If, in his opinion, the question cannot be divided, he explains this fact.

A request to divide a motion must not require the secretary to do more than separate the proposition into the proposed parts. If considerable rewriting is involved, a motion to divide the proposition is necessary. This motion must list the separate motions into which it is proposed that the proposition be divided. If a motion requires extensive rewriting, it is often wise to refer it to a committee with instructions to clarify or divide it.

Instead of requesting that a question be divided, a member may propose a motion that the question be divided. This is an incidental main motion and is governed by the rules of a main motion. Some other member may propose a motion outlining a different division. These motions are not amendments, but are alternative propositions which must be discussed and voted upon in the order in which they were proposed.

QUESTIONS WHICH ARE NOT DIVISIBLE

The following principles guide the presiding officer in deciding whether or not a question is capable of division:

1. If a motion contains only one subject, no matter how complicated it may be, it cannot be divided by a request, but it may be divided by a motion.

2. A question which contains several distinct propositions, any of which would not be suitable for adoption if all the others failed, cannot be divided.

For example, a motion that the club buy a multigraph machine and share it with the state office of the organization for part-time work, could not be divided, because obviously a multigraph machine which was not purchased could not be shared with anyone.

RULES GOVERNING REQUEST FOR DIVISION OF A QUESTION

1. Cannot interrupt a speaker, since it does not require immediate decision.

2. Requires no second, because it is a request or demand and not a true motion.

3. Is not debatable, because it is not a motion.

4. Cannot be amended, because it is a request.

5. Requires no vote, because it is decided by the chairman.

6. Takes precedence as an incidental motion.

7. Applies to main motions, amendments, and committee recommendations.

8. May have no motion applied to it except withdraw.

9. Cannot be renewed at the same meeting or convention.

The motion to divide a motion is governed by the same rules as a main motion.

Practice Projects

1. Assume that the following motion is pending before the assembly:

"I move that we reorganize our office staff by dropping one of our secretaries and hiring an assistant editor for the monthly magazine."

Give the proper response of the presiding officer to each of the following proposals:

1. "I move to amend the motion by striking out the word 'one' and inserting the word 'two.' "

2. "I move to amend the motion by adding the words 'at a salary to be determined by the executive board' after the word 'magazine.' "

3. "I move to amend the motion by substituting for it the motion 'that this organization combine with the Association of Nevada Poultry Producers.' "

4. "I move to amend the motion by striking out the word 'assistant' before the word 'editor.' "

5. "I move to amend the motion by striking out the words 'for the monthly magazine' and inserting in their place the words 'for all of our publications.' "

6. "I move to amend the amendment by adding the words 'except our weekly news letter' after the word 'publications.' "

7. "I request that the motion be divided into a motion to reorganize our office staff and into a motion that we hire an assistant editor for the monthly magazine."

8. "I move to amend the motion by inserting the words 'refuse to' before the word 'reorganize.' "

9. "I move to amend the motion by striking out the word 'assistant' and inserting the word 'managing.' "

10. "I move to amend the motion by striking out the word 'an' after the word 'hiring,' and inserting in its place the word 'two.' "

11. "I move to amend the motion by substituting for it the following motion: 'that we refer the whole matter of office reorganization to the standing committee on publications.' "

12. "I move to amend the amendment by adding the words 'with full power to act as they see fit.' "

2. Suggest a suitable amendment, and an amendment to that amendment, for each of the following motions:

1. "I move that this organization start a circulating library which shall be open to all active members."

2. "I move that the Northampton Automobile Club authorize the purchase of the three antique automobiles that are being offered for sale by the Brown Motor Company."

3. "I move that this organization create a standing committee on ways and means, and that the monthly dues of active members be increased to ten dollars, and that juvenile members pay an initiation fee of fifty dollars."

4. "I move that the Pinecrest Apartment House Association employ an attorney on a retaining fee, who shall give advice without charge to members of the association."

5. "I move that the Indiana Boxers and Wrestlers Welfare Association put on a benefit in Indianapolis on the night of February 17."

3. Which of the following motions are properly divisible by a request for division?

1. "I move that our club lounge be completely refurnished, and that a party be given for all members and their families to raise funds for the refurnishing of the lounge."

2. "I move that we erect a new clubhouse, and that we hire Mrs. Taylor to do all the decorating."

3. "I move that our organization plan to incorporate under the state laws, and that we build a clubhouse."

4. "I move that a bonus equal to ten per cent of their salaries be given to all employees at Christmas time, that the Monday following Christmas Day be declared a holiday at this plant, and that we launch a publicity campaign to encourage more employees to take their vacations during the winter months."

5. "I move that we purchase our supplies for the orphanage in January and in June of each year, and that a building be erected on the orphanage grounds so that the younger children may be segregated from the older ones."

4. Suggest amendments which will improve the following motions:

1. "I move that this organization let the state association know that we certainly don't like the way they send out notices without giving us time to plan ahead for the executive committee meetings."

2. "I move that we petition the County Board of Supervisors to pass an ordinance that no one shall be permitted to carry a loaded gun on the highways of this county except for the purpose of shooting an obnoxious animal or a policeman in the discharge of his duty."

3. "I move that we no longer refuse to permit nonmembers of the organization to attend our regular meetings, as is now forbidden, provided they are accompanied by members who are in good standing as it states in the bylaws."

4. "I move that the members of the Bayview Hospital Association provide a plaque honoring our first president, and that our new superintendent be authorized to employ an additional pediatrician at a salary not to exceed $5,000 per year."

5. "In view of the recent railway accident involving a school bus, I move that our organization request the governor's committee on safety to pass the following resolution:

'*Resolved,* That when two trains approach each other on a common crossing, they shall both stop and neither shall proceed further until the other has passed beyond the full length of the other train!' "

CHAPTER 14

MOTIONS TO CONTROL DEBATE

RIGHT TO CONTROL DEBATE

The object of deliberative bodies is to reach the considered decision of the assembly after a free interchange of thought and discussion. Freedom of discussion is necessary for reaching decisions in a group. It is also the cherished right of individual members.

However, every organization has an inherent right to control its discussion. It may limit the time which is to be devoted to the debate on a question, it may change or extend that limitation, or it may shut off or close debate altogether.

One method of regulating the duration of discussion on a question is to fix a time at which all discussion must cease. Another method is to limit the number of speakers or the length of their remarks. Any of these limitations cuts down debate but gives all members equal opportunity to discuss.

Discussion of a question may also be regulated by extending the time to be devoted to the question or the time apportioned to speakers.

There are times when limiting debate is not sufficient. In some instances discussion must be avoided entirely or cut off, subsidiary motions must be cut off, and the pending question brought to an immediate vote. Sometimes, if business is to be completed before adjournment, discussion must be prevented or terminated. Frequently discussion has been so prolonged that it is no longer profitable, and business must be expedited by shutting off debate.

There are also occasions when the group must protect itself against filibustering.

Motion to Limit or Extend Limits of Debate

PURPOSE

The purpose of the motion to limit debate is to restrict the length of time to be devoted to the discussion of a question.

142

The purpose of the motion to extend the limits of debate is to modify or remove restrictions already imposed, in order that the time allotted for discussion on a question or to a speaker may be increased.

FORM

PROPOSER: "I move to limit the time of each speaker on this motion to five minutes."

or

"I move to limit debate on this question to four speeches in its favor and four speeches against."

or

"I move to limit debate on the question to one-half hour."

or

"I move that the time of the speaker be extended twelve minutes."

EXPLANATION

There is wide variation in the forms of the motion to limit debate. Limitations may be applied to the total length of time to be devoted to the question, to the number of speeches, to the number of speakers who may discuss the question, to the length of time each speaker's discussion may take, or to any combination of these restrictions.

When one form of limiting debate is proposed and is pending, another form of limitation may be proposed as an amendment. For example, if a motion is pending "to limit the number of speakers to four," an amendment might be proposed to add the words, "and to limit the length of each speech to ten minutes."

If several motions are pending before the assembly, and the proposer of a motion to limit debate does not specify to which motion his proposal is intended to apply, the immediately pending question *only* is affected.

The motion to extend the limits of debate is governed by the same rules as the motion to limit debate. The most common form of this motion is to extend the time allotted to a particular speaker.

Both the motion to extend the limits of debate and the motion to

IT'S A PLEASURE
TO BE HERE THIS EVENING

The speaker worked for days and days
Rehearsing every sparkling phrase.
He wrote down words and underlined them,
So that his fleeting eye could find them.
He practiced long before the mirror;
His wife was frequently his hearer.
Rewording, cutting out, extending,
And checking time from start to ending,
He polished till as if spontaneous
His "few remarks . . . extemporaneous."

restrict the limits of debate remain in force only during the current meeting or convention at which they are passed. If the motion to which they are applied is postponed by the assembly to another meeting, and is brought up again at that meeting, the motion limiting debate has no effect.

Both motions require a two-thirds vote, on the basis that the motion to limit debate infringes on the principle of full and free discussion, and the motion to extend debate sets aside an already established limit. However, when there is general agreement, both motions are frequently decided by unanimous consent.

RULES GOVERNING MOTION TO LIMIT OR EXTEND LIMITS OF DEBATE

1. Cannot interrupt a speaker, because it does not require immediate decision.
2. Requires a second.
3. Is not debatable.
4. Can be amended only as to time allowed for debate, length of speeches, number of speakers, or other similar limitations or extensions.
5. Requires a two-thirds vote, for the reason that a motion to limit debate infringes on the principle of full and free discussion, and a motion to extend debate sets aside an already established limit on debate.
6. Takes precedence of the motions to postpone definitely, refer to a committee, amend, and postpone indefinitely.
7. Applies to all debatable questions.
8. Can have applied to it only motions to amend and withdraw.
9. Can be renewed at the same meeting, after change in the parliamentary situation.

Motion to Vote Immediately (Previous Question)

PURPOSE

The purpose of the motion to vote immediately (previous question) is to stop all discussion on the question before the assembly, to prevent the proposal of further subsidiary motions (except to postpone temporarily), and to bring the question to an immediate vote.

LIMITED APPEAL

A debate,
As it goes on, loses weight.
Its strength
Is in inverse ratio to its length.
So jam it up,
Dam it up,
Compress it,
And though you might not guess it,
It will get shinier
As it gets tinier. . . .
A bit of limit
Will never dim it.

FORM

PROPOSER: "I move that we vote immediately on the motion to . . . ."

or

"I move to vote immediately on all pending questions before the assembly (or on the amendments, etc.) . . . ."

or if preferred, the old form may be used:

"I move the previous question."

CHAIRMAN: "It has been moved and seconded to vote immediately on the motion before the assembly. Those in favor of voting immediately, please rise. . . . Be seated. Opposed, please rise. . . . Be seated. There being a two-thirds vote in the affirmative, the motion to vote immediately is carried. We will now vote on the main question."

EXPLANATION

The motion to vote immediately, or "to move the previous question," as the old form of the motion was phrased, has a long and interesting history. It was first used, in 1604, in the House of Commons. Sir Robert Howard, who evidently had no liking for either the motion or its author, observed, "This 'previous question' is like the image of the inventor— a perpetual disturbance."

The "previous question" was originally used to suppress motions "of a delicate nature as to high personages." The name "previous question" has always caused confusion, and the use of the motion has so changed in America that the old English form is entirely misleading.

The motion is sometimes called the motion to "close debate," but this name is neither accurate nor descriptive, because the effect of the motion, if carried, is threefold:

1. It prevents or cuts off debate.

2. It prevents the proposal of further subsidiary motions except the motion to postpone temporarily.

3. It forces the assembly to vote immediately on the question or questions to which it is applied.

The term "vote immediately" is therefore accurate and clear. It is widely used and approved.

If there are several motions pending before the assembly, and the motion to vote immediately is made without any qualifications, it applies only to the *immediately* pending question. If, however, a qualification is stated in the motion, as, for example, "I move that we vote immediately on everything that is pending," the effect of the motion, if carried, is to force an immediate vote as stated in the qualification—in this case on all pending questions—and its effect continues until the main question before the assembly is voted upon.

For example, this is the procedure if a main motion, an amendment, and a motion to postpone to the next meeting are pending, and a motion to vote immediately "on all pending questions" is carried. A vote is first taken on the motion to postpone to the next meeting; then, if it is lost, a vote is taken on the amendment; and finally, a vote is taken on the main motion.

The effect of a motion to vote immediately terminates with the meeting at which the motion was adopted. If, after the motion to vote immediately on a main motion has carried, the assembly should vote to postpone the matter temporarily, and the question should be brought up for decision later in the same meeting, there could be no debate on the main motion. If, however, the main motion was not brought up until the next meeting, the effect of the motion to vote immediately would have terminated, and discussion would be called for upon the question.

Like the motions to regulate debate, the motion to vote immediately requires a two-thirds vote, because it infringes on the principle that every motion is entitled to full and free discussion.

RULES GOVERNING MOTION TO VOTE IMMEDIATELY (PREVIOUS QUESTION)

1. Cannot interrupt a speaker, because it does not require an immediate decision.
2. Requires a second.
3. Is not debatable, since its object, which is to shut off debate, would be defeated if it were debatable.

4. Cannot be amended, but its proposer may qualify or limit its application.

5. Requires a two-thirds vote for the reason that it sets aside the fundamental principle that decisions on questions should be arrived at after full and free debate.

6. Takes precedence over all subsidiary motions except postpone temporarily.

7. Applies to any debatable motion.

8. Can have no motion applied to it except withdraw.

9. Can be renewed at the same meeting, after change in the parliamentary situation.

Practice Projects

1. In the following situations, which motion to control debate would you use, and how would you state it?

1. At a meeting of the University Dramatic Club, when new business is called for, a member moves "that the Dramatic Club merge with the Footlighters' Club to form one strong organization." There are two opposing factions, and a prolonged discussion is in prospect.

2. At a convention of the Association of Clay Brick Manufacturers, just a half hour before time to adjourn, a member proposes that "this organization undertake a campaign to send representatives abroad to find new markets." He declines a request to withdraw his motion and insists that it be considered. Only one other member favors the motion. The two supporting members have explained their beliefs.

3. At a meeting of Theta Sigma Phi, a motion is proposed to request the National Executive Committee to raise the standards for the admission of new members. The members present are almost evenly divided on the question and the hour is 10 P.M. There is thirty minutes' time before adjournment.

4. At a meeting of the Education Majors' Club, a motion to recommend that more elective courses be permitted is being discussed. Discussion on this motion has already taken an hour and a quarter at a previous meeting, and this is an adjourned meeting called to continue the discussion. The debate has made it clear that all members except a small group favor the motion. The time is 11:30 P.M.

5. The City Council of Taft has discussed, for two hours, the question of rezoning a district, and there seems to be little prospect of anyone's changing his mind. Every member has spoken several times, but one councilman has spoken for twenty minutes.

2. What is the traditional difference in attitude on motions to control debate in the Senate and in the House of Representatives?

3. What can the presiding officer do to help ensure that discussion is not prolonged unduly?

CHAPTER 15

MOTIONS TO DEFER ACTION

REASONS FOR POSTPONEMENT

Some motions seem to be proposed at an inopportune time. For this reason two motions are employed for postponing action on a motion until a more advantageous time.

There are many reasons why an assembly may wish to defer action on a matter. For instance, a motion may be presented late in a meeting when many members have left. Naturally, the supporters of the motion would prefer to wait until a more suitable time, when the motion can receive more favorable consideration. Or perhaps the motion has been proposed when other more pressing business is waiting, and there is little time left for discussion.

Another reason for postponement may be that the motion is so important that its consideration should be set for a time when every member can plan to be present. Or perhaps some emergency has arisen that makes it important for the assembly to decide some other matter at once. Or perhaps the assembly considers the motion an unfortunate proposal and wishes to dispose of it without offending its maker.

Frequently, when discussion has been animated, or there is a sharp divergence of opinion on the motion, members realize that a cooling-off period would be beneficial. Members who differ in their opinions are more likely to reach an agreement if they have had time to think over the problem. Differences in points of view, which seem very important in the heat of discussion, often assume their true proportions and prove to be minor variances after time has elapsed.

All these and numerous other reasons justify the two motions whose aim is to defer action. These are:

a. The motion to postpone temporarily (lay on the table)
b. The motion to postpone definitely

They have the same general purpose but differ in specific aims and details.

151

PROGRESS REPORT

At meetings of clubs I've attended,
  I've found there was room for improvement.
More effort, I fear, was expended
  Making motions than making much movement.

Motion to Postpone Temporarily

PURPOSE

The purpose of the motion to postpone temporarily (lay on the table) is to set aside the consideration of a motion until some later, but as yet undetermined, time. It allows a matter to be set aside without prejudice. It also provides that the matter may be taken up again by the motion to resume consideration (take from the table) at any time the assembly wishes. The motion to resume consideration has preference over any other new main motion.

FORM

PROPOSER: "I move that the motion that this board sign a contract with the Eastway Supply Company be postponed temporarily."

or if preferred, the old form of the motion may be used:

"I move that the motion be laid on the table."

EXPLANATION

When a motion is pending before an assembly, it frequently happens that the members may wish, either before discussion has taken place or during discussion, to put the whole question aside.

The motion to postpone temporarily removes the question from the consideration of the assembly and puts it aside until the assembly votes to resume its consideration. There are no time limits within which the question must be taken up again. As soon as other business has been disposed of, the assembly may resume consideration of a question which has been postponed temporarily. On the other hand, the question may never be taken up again.

When a motion is postponed temporarily, it is postponed to an undetermined time. If a motion sets a specific time for postponement, it is not a motion to postpone temporarily but a motion to postpone definitely.

The old forms of the motion were to "lay on the table" or to "take from the table." This term grew out of the custom of laying a bill on the clerk's table, where it stayed until the assembly decided to pick it up and hear it again. Both the terms "postpone temporarily" and "lay on the table" are commonly used.

The motion to postpone temporarily applies only to a motion which is before the assembly. If a main motion is postponed temporarily, all pending amendments and all adhering motions—that is, all motions which have been applied to the main motion—are postponed with the main motion, since they are inseparable from it. Likewise, if an amendment is postponed temporarily, the main motion is postponed with it.

The effect of a motion to postpone temporarily is to remove the main motion from the consideration of the assembly, with all its amendments and adhering motions, until such time as the matter is reopened by a motion to resume consideration.

HOW CONSIDERATION OF A QUESTION IS RESUMED

When a motion has been postponed temporarily, it can be brought before the assembly again whenever no business is pending. This is done by a motion to resume consideration.

When a motion to resume consideration is proposed, it takes precedence over any new main motion which a member seeks to propose at the same time. It is a specific main motion, and may be proposed at any time when a main motion is in order. The usual form is:

"I move that we resume consideration of the motion to enlarge our golf course, which was postponed temporarily (laid on the table) at the last meeting."

or

"I move to take from the table the motion to enlarge our golf course."

If the motion to resume consideration carries, consideration of the motion is taken up again at the point where it was interrupted. Any pending motions which were attached to the motion are still pending.

RULES GOVERNING MOTION TO POSTPONE TEMPORARILY (LAY ON THE TABLE)

1. Cannot interrupt a speaker, because it does not require immediate decision.

2. Requires a second.

3. Is not debatable, because one of its objects is to postpone debate.

4. Cannot be amended, because it is invariable in form.

5. Requires a majority vote.

6. Takes precedence over all other subsidiary motions.

7. Applies to main motions, amendments, and appeals.

8. Can have no other motions applied to it except withdraw.

9. Can be renewed at the same meeting, after a change in the parliamentary situation.

Motion to Postpone Definitely

PURPOSE

The purpose of the motion to postpone definitely, or to a certain time, is to postpone consideration of a motion and to fix a definite time when it shall be considered, or further considered. Whereas the motion to postpone temporarily defers the motion until an *undetermined* time, the motion to postpone to a definite time postpones it to a *determined* time and makes the question which has been postponed an "order of the day" for that day or time.

FORM

PROPOSER: "I move to postpone consideration of the motion until the next meeting" or "until Monday at eight o'clock" or "until the report of the delegates has been received this afternoon."

or

"I move that the question be postponed and made a special order for next Friday at three o'clock."

CHAIRMAN: "It has been moved and seconded that (stating the motion) be postponed until the next meeting. Is there any discussion on the postponement of this question?"

EXPLANATION

The motion to postpone definitely is useful in many instances. It may be that some other matter should be decided before the pending motion

SUSPENDED MOTION

Oh, how I'd like, if I were able,
To rise and lay upon the table
The chap whose motion has (the swine)
Just done precisely that to mine.

can be voted upon. The supporters of the pending motion may seek a more favorable time for its consideration, or more support for it. More information may be needed before it can be decided judiciously. Postpone definitely is often proposed by the supporters of a measure.

When a motion or subject is postponed to a definite day or hour, it becomes a general order for that day or hour. This means that time on a definite day or at a certain hour is reserved for the consideration of the question that has been postponed. When that day or hour arrives, the general order does not interrupt discussion of any pending motion, but as soon as any pending motion is disposed of, the chairman must immediately present to the assembly the question which was postponed definitely.

A matter which is postponed to a definite time may be made a "special order" for that time. When such time arrives, the presiding officer must interrupt any pending business and place the special order before the assembly for consideration. A motion which is postponed and made a special order requires a two-thirds vote, because it interrupts pending business or suspends the regular order of business.

LIMITATIONS ON DEFINITE POSTPONEMENT

The motion to postpone definitely cannot be used in such a way that its effect would be essentially the same as that of the motion to postpone indefinitely. The following limitations are therefore placed upon the motion to postpone definitely:

1. It is not permissible to postpone a question beyond the next regular meeting or the end of a convention, or to any time when it would be too late to act upon the question. This would be equivalent to a motion to postpone indefinitely, because the effect would be to kill the question.

2. The motion to postpone definitely cannot be amended to convert it into a motion to postpone indefinitely.

3. A question cannot be postponed to a special meeting, or to an adjourned meeting, unless the time for that meeting has already been fixed or is fixed in the motion to postpone, because this would be equivalent to postponing indefinitely.

CHANGING TIME OF CONSIDERATION

The motion to postpone definitely may be amended by changing the time to which the motion is postponed.

Once a motion has been postponed to a definite time, the members of an assembly have the right to be certain that the question will come up at that time and will not be taken up before that time. The only way a motion that has been postponed to a definite time can be taken up before the time set for its consideration is by a motion to suspend the rules. Such a change must be safeguarded by strict observance of requirements for notice to all members.

When the bylaws or rules set a definite time for considering a matter, it cannot be postponed until that time arrives except by a motion to suspend the bylaw or rule. For example, if an election is set for a particular meeting, and weather conditions make it impossible for most of the members to attend, those who do attend can postpone the election. But it cannot be postponed beforehand, except by suspension of the bylaw if suspension of a bylaw is provided for and by observing all requirements of notice to each member.

If for any reason the matter which was postponed to a definite time is not taken up at the time set, it becomes unfinished business and goes over until the following meeting.

RULES GOVERNING MOTION TO POSTPONE
DEFINITELY

1. Cannot interrupt a speaker, because the motion does not require immediate decision.

2. Requires a second.

3. Open to restricted debate on the propriety of postponing the particular question to a particular time. It does not open the main question to debate.

4. Can be amended only as to the time of postponement, since it is otherwise invariable in form.

5. Requires a majority vote.

6. Takes precedence of the motions to refer to a committee and to postpone indefinitely.

7. Applies to main motions only.

8. Can have applied to it only the motion regulating debate, amendments as to time, and withdraw.

9. Can be renewed at the same meeting, after a change in the parliamentary situation.

Practice Projects

1. In your opinion, which motion to defer action would be more suitable in the following situations:

1. The Executive Committee of the State Highway Patrol is considering a motion to hold a safety conference in Atlantic City. You favor the motion and are disturbed because several of the members who feel as you do have left for an early dinner and will not return until the evening meeting.

2. At a meeting of the Audubon Society, a motion is proposed to discontinue support of the national magazine. You are opposed to the motion and fear that it will carry. It will take some weeks to educate the members on the need for continuing support of the magazine.

2. Discuss the essential differences between the motion to postpone temporarily and the motion to postpone definitely.

3. Outline five hypothetical situations in which you feel that the motion to postpone temporarily would be suitable.

4. Outline five situations indicating the use of the motion to postpone definitely.

CHAPTER 16

MOTION TO REFER TO A COMMITTEE

PURPOSE

The purpose of a motion to refer to a committee is to transfer a motion or question from the assembly to a smaller group of members working under the authority and direction of the assembly.

FORM

PROPOSER: "I move to refer the motion to a special committee of five members, to be appointed by the president," or "consisting of Mrs. L., Mr. M., and Mr. B."; or "to a committee to be elected by the assembly," or "to the Finance Committee."

CHAIRMAN (after hearing a second): "It has been moved and seconded to refer the motion to a committee consisting of five members to be appointed by the president. . . . Is there any discussion on referring this question to a committee?"

EXPLANATION

There are numerous reasons why a member may wish to have a question considered by a committee.

The most common reasons for referring a matter to a committee are:

1. To have an unsatisfactory motion rephrased, amended, or divided
2. To expedite business by having a matter considered by a small group and thus save the time of the assembly
3. To secure more adequate investigation of a matter and recommendation on it
4. To ensure privacy in considering a delicate matter
5. To permit more informal consideration

6. To have a piece of work carried out

7. To hold hearings on the subject

8. To save a motion from defeat or from indefinite postponement

9. To delay a proposal, or perhaps to kill it, by reference to a hostile committee

10. To help develop a consensus of opinion

The motion to refer to a committee varies considerably in its form. The proposer of the motion may specify details in his motion, such as the type of committee (standing or special), and may give instructions to the committee. If it is a special committee, the proposer may include provisions covering the number and manner of selection of members and the selection of a chairman, the type of report desired, the date of the report, and other instructions.

If none of these details are included in the motion to refer a matter to a committee, the chairman may settle these questions by referring them to the assembly. He may ask such questions as: "How large a committee should this be?" "How shall the members be chosen?" "What instructions should be given to the committee?" "When should the committee report?" These questions may be decided either before or after the motion to refer to a committee is voted upon.

Instructions defining the powers and duties of the committee may be included in the original motion to refer, or as an amendment to the motion, or they may be stated in a separate motion after the first motion has been voted upon.

The question of whether reference to a committee should be made is the chief point which is debatable. The merits of the motion or resolution which it is proposed to refer are not at issue and, strictly speaking, are not debatable. But some latitude must be permitted in discussing the merits of the matter to be referred, together with the propriety of reference.

Referring a motion to a committee is not the final action on the motion referred. Additional instructions may be given to the committee at any time while it is considering the question, or the whole question may be withdrawn from the committee and returned for consideration by the assembly.

When there is no motion pending, and a motion is made which creates a committee and refers a matter to it, this is a main motion and is

NOTE TO CHAIRMEN

Want to dodge the irksome task?
   Want to scram, and leave the city?
Here's my honest, frank advice:
   Refer it to a subcommittee.

governed by the same rules as a main motion. For example, someone may move "that a committee be appointed to study the question of improvements to our clubhouse," or "that a committee be appointed to audit the treasurer's books." These motions are main motions.

No motion can be referred to a committee with instructions to report at some impossible time, such as an hour after adjournment of a meeting, or after the close of a convention. Such instructions would make the motion to refer to a committee, in effect, a motion to postpone indefinitely.

RULES GOVERNING MOTION TO REFER TO A COMMITTEE

1. Cannot interrupt a speaker, because it does not require immediate decision.

2. Requires a second.

3. Is open to debate, only on the advantage of referring the question to a committee. A motion giving instructions to a committee is open to limited discussion on the instructions.

4. Can be amended with reference to such matters as

   a. Type or number of committee
   b. Method of selection
   c. Who is to be chairman
   d. Instructions to the committee

5. Requires a majority vote.

6. Takes precedence of the motion to amend and to postpone indefinitely.

7. Can be applied only to main motions and amendments.

8. Can have applied to it only the motion to amend, the motions regulating debate, and withdraw.

9. Can be renewed at the same meeting, after a change in the parliamentary situation.

Practice Projects

1. Outline a meeting situation which illustrates each of the ten most common reasons for referring a matter to a committee.

2. Have you ever seen an assembly try to decide a matter in a meeting, when it could more profitably have been referred to a committee? Describe the situation.

3. Prepare instructions to a committee in the form of:

1. A part of the motion to refer to a committee
2. An amendment to the motion to refer to a committee
3. A separate motion proposed after the motion to refer to a committee has carried

CHAPTER 17

MOTIONS TO SUPPRESS MOTIONS

RIGHT TO SUPPRESS A MOTION

Every member of an organization has the right to present propositions to the assembly for discussion and decision. The assembly, however, has the right to decline to consider, or to vote to suppress, propositions which, for any reason, it may consider undesirable. The proposer of a motion also has the right, for a limited time, to remove his motion from the consideration of the assembly by withdrawing it.

Sometimes a motion is presented which is regarded by a majority of the members as useless, inexpedient, tactless, or unsuitable. The assembly has the right to refuse to consider such a motion.

The three motions which have the effect of suppressing a proposition are:

1. Object to consideration
2. Withdraw a motion
3. Postpone indefinitely

All three motions aim, not at suppressing debate on the motion, but at suppressing the proposition itself.

A motion can always be killed by a direct negative vote. The above-listed motions usually kill a motion without running the risk of allowing the motion itself to come to a direct vote.

Object to Consideration

PURPOSE

The purpose of the motion to object to consideration is to avoid entirely, and prevent discussion on, a question which the assembly feels is embarrassing, contentious, unsuitable, or unprofitable, or one which it simply does not wish to consider.

165

FORM

PROPOSER (without waiting for recognition): "Mr. Chairman, I object to the consideration of this question."

CHAIRMAN (without waiting for a second): "Objection has been raised to the consideration of this question. Those in favor of considering the question, please rise. . . . Be seated. Those opposed, please rise. . . . Be seated. There being a two-thirds vote in the negative, the objection is sustained and the question will not be considered."

or

"Since the objection has failed to receive a two-thirds vote, the objection is not sustained, and the question will now be considered."

EXPLANATION

Main motions are occasionally proposed which are completely unsuitable for consideration. Other motions are proposed which are tactless, foolish, or unnecessary. Objection to consideration heads off the discussion of such motions before discussion has begun.

Objection to consideration of a motion must be raised immediately following the statement by the chairman of that motion. After progress in debate, or after some other motion has been applied to the motion, it is no longer possible to object to its consideration.

The effect of proposing objection to consideration is to shut off immediately all debate on the main motion until the objection is decided. If the objection carries, the motion objected to cannot be brought up again at the same meeting or convention except by unanimous consent or by a motion to suspend the rules.

Objection to consideration applies only to main motions or to communications such as letters or telegrams. It cannot be applied to committee reports or to amendments to the constitution or bylaws. Communications from a superior body, such as letters from a national officer to a local unit, cannot have objection to consideration raised against them.

The following are examples of the logical use of objection to consideration:

If the national president is visiting a local unit, and some member moves that an investigation of the treasurer's books be made, the motion would, of course, be embarrassing. Some member might properly object to its consideration at that particular time.

In a literary society, if a member proposed a motion to endorse a particular member as a candidate for senator, consideration of this motion might very properly be objected to on the ground that the society takes no part in politics.

At a meeting of a city Board of Education, if a motion is proposed to undertake an investigation of the conduct of the State Board of Education, this motion might properly be objected to on the grounds that the local board has no authority to make such an investigation, or no reason to believe that such an investigation is necessary.

Whenever objection to consideration is appropriately made, the chairman must immediately put the question of consideration to vote without calling for discussion. A two-thirds vote against consideration is required to sustain the objection, because ordinarily any member of an organization has the right to propose a motion and to have it considered. The vote on an objection to consideration should be taken by raising of hands or by rising, so that it may be accurately determined whether there is a two-thirds vote in the negative.

If the chairman feels that any motion is made purely for the purpose of delaying a vote, heckling, embarrassing, or creating confusion, or that it is obviously frivolous or unsuitable for consideration by the assembly, he may rule it out of order on his own authority without waiting for an objection. Or if objection to its consideration is raised, he may rule it out of order without taking a vote on the objection. Of course, members may appeal from his decision.

RULES GOVERNING OBJECTION TO CONSIDERATION

1. Can interrupt a speaker, because the objection must be raised before progress in debate is made.

2. Requires no second, because it is an objection and not a true motion.

3. Is not debatable, since its purpose is to avoid all debate on the question.

4. Cannot be amended, because it is invariable in form.

5. Requires a two-thirds negative vote to prevent the consideration of the motion, because it sets aside the fundamental right of members to have consideration given to motions which they introduce.

6. Takes precedence as an incidental motion.

7. Applies to main motions only.

8. Can have no other motion applied to it except withdraw.

9. Cannot be renewed, because the objection can be raised only immediately following the presentation of the main motion.

Withdraw a Motion

PURPOSE

The purpose of the request to withdraw a motion is to enable a member to remove from the consideration of the assembly a motion which he has proposed.

FORM

PROPOSER (of the original motion, after receiving recognition): "I ask leave to withdraw my motion."

or

"I wish to withdraw my motion."

CHAIRMAN (without waiting for a second): "Mr. Lawrence asks leave to withdraw his motion. Is there any objection?" (Waiting a moment, to permit possible objection), "There being no objection, the motion is withdrawn."

If any member objects, the presiding officer may take a vote on the question of allowing the motion to be withdrawn; or the proposer or any other member, after obtaining recognition, may propose the following motion:

"I move that permission be granted to withdraw the motion."

EXPLANATION

The request to withdraw a motion can be made only by the proposer of the motion. Before a motion has been stated by the chairman, its proposer is allowed to modify it or withdraw it at his pleasure, under the theory that the motion is still under his control. If he desires to withdraw it, he simply says:

"I withdraw my motion."

Once the motion has been stated to the assembly, however, it becomes the property of that body, and a member may withdraw his motion only if no objection is raised, or if he is given permission to withdraw it by a majority vote.

Sometimes a member is requested to withdraw a motion. Until the motion has been stated to the assembly, the presiding officer or any member may request the mover to withhold making, or to withdraw, his motion. This request is usually made because some urgent business needs prior consideration or because the motion seems unsuitable for consideration by the assembly. Requesting a member to withdraw his motion is a more tactful way of avoiding consideration of a motion than objecting to its consideration.

If the mover declines to withdraw his motion, the chairman proceeds as though no such request had been made.

A motion can be withdrawn, with permission, up until the moment the final vote on it is taken. It may be withdrawn even though other motions affecting it may be pending, or debate has been closed.

Withdraw is the only motion which can be applied to every other motion.

The effect of withdrawing a motion is to remove it immediately from the consideration of the assembly, as though it had never been proposed. No mention need be made, in the minutes, of a motion which was withdrawn.

RULES GOVERNING REQUEST TO WITHDRAW A MOTION

1. Cannot interrupt a speaker, because it does not require immediate decision.
2. Requires no second, because it is a request.
3. Is not debatable.
4. Cannot be amended, because it is invariable in form.
5. Requires no vote, because it is a request. It is granted by unanimous consent or defeated by an objection.
6. Takes precedence as an incidental motion.

REST IN PEACE

Indefinite postponement is
A clever little dodge.
It's often used to do the biz
In club as well as lodge.

There's just a trace of hope in it,
It's surely not the end.
It seems to live and breathe a bit,
And yet, my trusting friend,

The motion thus postponed that's still
As something sick in bed,
Instead of being merely ill
Is just as good as dead.

7. Applies to every motion.

8. May have no motion applied to it.

9. May be renewed at the same meeting, after change in the parliamentary situation.

The motion granting leave to withdraw a motion is governed by the same rules as the request to withdraw, except that, being a motion, it requires a second and a majority vote.

Motion to Postpone Indefinitely

PURPOSE

The purpose of the motion to postpone indefinitely is to suppress the question pending before the assembly, without allowing it to come to a vote.

FORM

PROPOSER: "I move that the motion before the assembly be postponed indefinitely."

CHAIRMAN (after hearing a second): "It has been moved and seconded that the motion before the assembly be postponed indefinitely. Is there any discussion?"

EXPLANATION

The term "postpone indefinitely" is misleading. The motion to postpone indefinitely, if carried, does not postpone but kills, or suppresses, the main question.

The motion to postpone indefinitely applies to main motions only. If the motion to postpone indefinitely carries, its effect is equivalent to a negative vote on the main motion.

The motion to postpone indefinitely is debatable and opens the main question, to which it is applied, to debate. The main motion is open to debate on the principle that any motion which seeks to dispose finally of the main question opens it to debate.

This motion is sometimes used for parliamentary maneuvering. Members who have exhausted their right to speak on the main motion propose the motion to postpone indefinitely and thereby gain a second chance to debate the main motion.

Opponents of the main motion sometimes move to postpone it indefinitely in order to watch the vote and learn who is in favor and who is opposed to the main motion, without the risk of adopting it.

RULES GOVERNING MOTION TO POSTPONE INDEFINITELY

1. Cannot interrupt a speaker, because it does not require immediate decision.

2. Requires a second.

3. Is debatable, because it is equivalent to a negative vote on a main motion and finally disposes of it. It opens the main question to debate for the same reason.

4. Cannot be amended, because it is invariable in form.

5. Requires a majority vote.

6. Takes precedence of nothing but the main motion.

7. Applies to main motions only.

8. Can have applied to it only the motion to withdraw, vote immediately, or limit debate.

9. Cannot be renewed during the same meeting or convention.

Practice Projects

Which of the three motions to suppress a motion would you propose in the following situations? Give the reasons for your choice.

1. A member of the Parent-Teacher Association has just introduced a motion "that we write a letter to France objecting to their exporting their perfume to this country."

2. You have just introduced a motion that the club read the list of members who are delinquent in their dues, when a delegation from the Civic Association arrives to observe your club during its business meeting.

3. You have just proposed a motion "that a picnic be planned for Labor Day." Before it is seconded, the secretary announces that all the members will be required to march in the parade during most of Labor Day.

4. The St. Mary's Home Finding Society is discussing a motion to move its headquarters from Kansas City to Topeka. It is not clear how a majority of the members feel on the subject and you would like to know.

Review Project

The following is a verbatim report of a portion of a meeting of a club that we shall call the West Brae Neighborhood Association. Comment on the effectiveness of the presiding officer and the discussion, and the methods used by various members to win others to their viewpoints.

CHAIRMAN: "Is there any new business?"

MR. ALDEN: "I move that the West Brae Neighborhood Association heartily endorse the proposed plan of the Board of Directors of the Brookline Private School to purchase the old Garvey mansion and to remodel it as a school for children between the ages of three and eight."

CHORUS OF MEMBERS: "Second the motion!"

MR. MASON: "Mr. Chairman, I object to the consideration of this motion."

CHAIRMAN: "You're out of order, Mr. Mason. You cannot object yet because the motion has not been stated by the chairman. It has been moved and seconded that . . . ."

MISS YOUNG: "Mr. Chairman, I rise to a point of order."

CHAIRMAN: "State your point of order."

MISS YOUNG: "This motion is definitely out of order. This organization was formed to consider neighborhood affairs which vitally affect all of us. Many of us have no children and so . . . ."

CHAIRMAN (interrupting): "Pardon me, Miss Young, but your point of order is not well taken. The chair rules that the endorsement or rejection of a plan for using the Garvey mansion as a private school *is* a matter of concern to this neighborhood group. The secretary will please read the motion."

The secretary reads the motion.

MRS. LAWRENCE: "Mr. Chairman, I move to amend the motion by adding the words 'and that we send this endorsement to the City Planning Commission.' "

MR. JOHNSON: "Second the amendment."

MISS SESSIONS: "I rise to a parliamentary inquiry."

CHAIRMAN: "State your inquiry."

MISS SESSIONS: "I should like to know why it is that the members of this organization who have children are constantly imposing their children on those of us who are not so fortunate, or unfortunate, as to have children. Some of us are not even married, and to bring into this neighborhood more little hellions than we already have, trampling all over our . . . ."

MR. MOORE: "Mr. Chairman, I rise to a point of order."

CHAIRMAN: "State your point of order."

MR. MOORE: "My point of order is that Miss Sessions is not raising an inquiry. She is discussing the question, and not too impersonally at that."

MR. RISPATO: "Second the motion!"

CHAIRMAN: "Your point of order is well taken, Mr. Moore. Miss Sessions, you will have to wait until discussion is called for on the amendment."

MRS. JOHNSON (interrupting): "I appeal from the decision of the chair. Miss Sessions is one of our most generous contributors and I think she has a right to express her convictions. My pansy beds . . . ."

CHAIRMAN: "Mrs. Johnson, you'll be given a chance to discuss this motion in a moment. The decision of the chair has been appealed from. The chair rules that Miss Sessions was out of order because she rose to a parliamentary inquiry and started discussing the amendment before discussion was called for, instead of stating an inquiry. Mrs. Johnson, do you wish to state the grounds for your appeal?"

MRS. JOHNSON: "Indeed I do! This club is divided right down the middle between those who have children and those who haven't. I think if Miss Sessions objects to having more children in our neighborhood, we should heed her words. 'The wise man listened with an open mind,' said Plato. Or was it Aristotle?"

CHAIRMAN: "The decision of the chair has been appealed from. All those in favor of sustaining the decision of the chair that Miss Sessions was out of order, say 'Aye.' . . . All those opposed, 'No.' . . . The decision of the chair is sustained."

MR. GARFIELD: "I call for a division."

CHAIRMAN: "Those in favor of sustaining the decision of the chair will please rise. The secretary will please count. . . . Be seated. Those opposed, please rise. . . . Be seated. The vote is 21 in the affirmative, 20 in the negative. The appeal is lost. Is there any further discussion on the amendment to add the words, 'and that we send this endorsement to the City Planning Commission'?"

MRS. JOHNSON: "I want to talk about my hobby. My pansy beds . . . ."

CHAIRMAN: "Mrs. Johnson, you are out of order unless you confine your discussion to the amendment."

MR. MASON: "I object to the consideration of this whole motion about the school."

CHAIRMAN: "Your motion is out of order, Mr. Mason. The time has passed when it was possible for anyone to object to the consideration of this motion."

MR. JACKSON: "Mr. Chairman."

CHAIRMAN: "Mr. Jackson."

MR. JACKSON: "I feel that this amendment is a good one because there is no point in our taking action if we don't let the Planning Commission know about it. Naturally, as the proud father of five 'little hellions,' I'm anxious to see good educational privileges provided for in our own neighborhood. And we all know well enough that our public schools are overcrowded to the point where our children are in danger."

CHAIRMAN: "Is there any further discussion on the amendment to the motion?" (Pause.) "All those in favor of the amendment that the words 'and that we send this endorsement to the City Planning Commission' be added to the motion, so that the motion, if amended, will read 'that the West Brae Neighborhood Association heartily endorse the proposed plan of the Board of Directors of the Brookline Private School to purchase the old Garvey mansion, and to remodel it as a school for children between the ages of three and eight, and that we send this endorsement to the City Planning Commission,' say 'Aye.' . . . Opposed, 'No.' . . . The chair is in doubt. Those in favor, please rise. The secretary will please count. . . . Be seated. Those opposed, please rise. . . . Be seated. The vote is 26, affirmative—16, negative. The amendment is carried. Is there any discussion on the motion as amended?"

MR. CORNISH: "I move that we postpone this question until next Friday night at eight o'clock."

MR. ROSE: "I rise to a point of order. On Friday at eight o'clock we will be here listening to a speech by Mayor Bronson. Besides, next Friday is not a business meeting."

CHAIRMAN: "Your point of order is well taken. The chair rules that the motion to postpone until next Friday at eight o'clock is out of order, because next Friday's meeting is not a business meeting. Is there any further discussion of the motion as amended?"

MRS. HENES: "Mr. Chairman."

CHAIRMAN: "Mrs. Henes."

MRS. HENES: "I move that we postpone this question indefinitely."

ANOTHER MEMBER: "Second the motion."

CHAIRMAN: "It has been moved and seconded that we postpone this question indefinitely. Is there any discussion?"

MR. YALE: "Mr. Chairman."

CHAIRMAN: "Mr. Yale."

MR. YALE: "I think it is extremely unwise to postpone this question at all. The Garvey mansion has been reduced to a very low price, and someone else will snap it up. If the Board of Directors does not pay a deposit on it soon . . . ."

MR. MASON: "I object to the consideration of the motion."

CHAIRMAN: "Your objection is out of order. It is only main motions which you can object to considering. This is a motion to postpone indefinitely."

MISS THOMAS: "I object strenuously to having this matter postponed. It is an urgent problem to find suitable school facilities, particularly for the children of this neighborhood. As a teacher, I know how overcrowded the public schools are."

CHAIRMAN: "If there is no further discussion on the motion to postpone indefinitely, we will vote. All those in favor of the motion to postpone the matter indefinitely, say 'Aye.' . . . Those opposed, 'No.' . . . The motion is carried."

MRS. JOHNSON: "My pansy beds . . . ."

CHAPTER 18

MOTIONS TO TERMINATE MEETINGS

ASSEMBLIES CAN TERMINATE MEETINGS AT WILL

The motions to terminate meetings have the highest rank of precedence. Necessity determines the precedence of any motion, and the urgency of motions to terminate meetings has given them the right to secure immediate attention over all other motions.

The theory of this urgency, which allows motions to adjourn and to recess to be brought up at any time and to take precedence over any other motion, is that a deliberative body should not be kept in session against its will. If it were so restrained against its will, there could not be free deliberation or discussion. If the members of the assembly wish to terminate the meeting, they should be allowed to do so at once.

Motion to Recess

PURPOSE

The purpose of the motion to recess is to permit an interlude in a meeting.

FORM

PROPOSER: "I move that we take a recess of ten minutes."

or

"I move that we recess until tomorrow night."

CHAIRMAN: "It has been moved and seconded that this assembly take a recess of ten minutes. Those in favor, say 'Aye.' . . . Those opposed, 'No.' . . . The motion is carried. The meeting is recessed for ten minutes."

POPULAR ACCLAIM

Which motions have the most success?
    For which do persons yearn?
One is the motion to recess,
    The other, to adjourn.

EXPLANATION

There are many reasons why it is necessary or convenient to recess during a meeting. The members may be tired and want to relax for a few minutes, a committee report may be delayed, or an election committee may be counting ballots. Many other similar instances may make it desirable to have a pause in a meeting.

The motion to recess differs from the motion to adjourn in that an adjournment terminates a meeting, while a recess is an interval during a meeting. A motion to recess and a motion to adjourn to an adjourned meeting, however, are really the same motion. Each has the effect of providing a temporary interval during which the meeting is interrupted.

The motion to recess may be amended only as to the time or the duration of the recess. It takes effect immediately unless the motion specifies otherwise. A recess cannot extend beyond the time set for the next regular meeting. When the meeting reconvenes after the recess, or after the motion to adjourn to an adjourned meeting, business is resumed at the same point where it was interrupted.

Like all privileged motions, the motion to recess loses its privileged character and becomes a main motion if made when nothing else is before the assembly, or when the recess is set for a future time.

RULES GOVERNING MOTION TO RECESS

1. Cannot interrupt a speaker, because it does not require immediate decision.
2. Requires a second.
3. Is not debatable, since it is a simple procedural motion, and particularly because its high precedence is incompatible with debate.
4. Can be amended only as to time or duration of the recess, since it is otherwise invariable in form.
5. Requires a majority vote.
6. Takes precedence of all motions except the motion to adjourn.
7. Applies to no other motion.
8. Can have applied to it only the motion to amend or withdraw.
9. Can be renewed at the same meeting, after change in the parliamentary situation.

Motion to Adjourn

PURPOSE

The purpose of the motion to adjourn is to terminate formally a meeting or convention.

FORM

1. Unqualified Form

PROPOSER: "I move we adjourn."

CHAIRMAN: "It has been moved and seconded that we adjourn. Those in favor, say 'Aye.' . . . Those opposed, 'No.' . . . The motion is carried. The meeting is adjourned."

2. Qualified Form

a. Future adjournment
"I move we adjourn in fifteen minutes."

or

"I move we adjourn at ten o'clock."

b. Adjournment to adjourned meeting
"I move that this meeting adjourn to an adjourned meeting to be held on Friday night at eight o'clock."

c. Final adjournment of convention
"I move that this convention now adjourn."

EXPLANATION

There are two forms of the motion to adjourn. The *unqualified form,* which is the usual motion "I move we adjourn," is a highly privileged motion, which calls for an immediate adjournment, if carried, and has no reference to any future meeting.

A *qualified* motion to adjourn, "I move we adjourn in ten minutes," or "I move we adjourn at five o'clock," is a main motion and subject to all the rules of a main motion. It has the lowest rank of precedence and, as a main motion, is debatable and may be amended or have any other motion applied to it.

The motion to adjourn to an adjourned meeting is a qualified motion to adjourn. No exact form of stating the motion is required, but the motion must make clear that the meeting is to continue at a later date, and the time and place of the adjourned meeting must be stated. This motion is equivalent to a motion for a recess.

When Adjournment Would Dissolve

The rule that an unqualified motion to adjourn is a privileged motion has one important exception: If an unqualified motion to adjourn is made, which would have the effect of dissolving the organization, the motion to adjourn is a main motion and is governed by all the rules of a main motion.

If an unqualified motion to adjourn is proposed when there is no provision in the constitution, bylaws, rules of order, or program, for another meeting, this motion is, in fact, a motion to dissolve.

If adoption of the motion would dissolve the organization, the presiding officer should call the attention of the assembly to the fact that the motion to adjourn is a motion to dissolve. It is important that full discussion and opportunity to amend the motion should be given. Therefore, when there is no provision for a future meeting, a simple, unqualified motion to adjourn is, in fact, a motion to dissolve and is a main motion, subject to all of the rules of a main motion.

A final adjournment which has the effect of dissolving the assembly or closing the convention is termed "adjournment sine die," or adjournment without day.

Avoiding Too Hasty Adjournment

When a motion to adjourn is made, it is the duty of the presiding officer to see that no important business is neglected, before putting the motion to vote. Even though the unqualified motion to adjourn has been moved, the presiding officer may call the attention of the assembly to important matters which it may have overlooked. If there are questions which should be settled before adjournment, he may ask that the proposer of the motion to adjourn withdraw it until the business has been completed.

A lack of provision for the next meeting, the necessity of fixing a time

for the next meeting, important announcements or business should all
be called to the attention of the assembly by the presiding officer, before
voting on adjournment.

The motion to adjourn is the only motion which can be voted upon
when less than a quorum is present.

Voting on Adjournment

The presiding officer should be careful to find out which type of
adjournment the proposer of a motion to adjourn intends, and to rephrase the motion if necessary to make it clear.

For example, a member may say, "I move that we adjourn until next
Wednesday at eight o'clock." If the next regular meeting is scheduled
for that date and hour, the member is merely calling attention to the
time of the next regular meeting, and is not moving to adjourn to an
adjourned meeting. In this instance, the chairman should state the
motion, "It has been moved and seconded that we adjourn."

In announcing the result, the chairman may add, "We now stand adjourned until our next regular meeting on Wednesday at eight o'clock."

In putting any qualified motion to adjourn to vote, the chairman
should state whether it fixes the hour for future adjournment, whether
it is an adjournment to an adjourned meeting, or whether the adjournment is sine die or, in fact, a dissolution.

It is good practice for the presiding officer, in declaring any meeting
adjourned, to state the time and place for reconvening.

When a specific time for adjournment has been fixed in the bylaws
or by the adoption of a program or rule at some previous meeting, it is
the duty of the chairman, when that hour arrives, to interrupt the speaker
or any business which is pending, and call attention to the fact that it
is time to adjourn. A member must then move either to adjourn or to
suspend the rule requiring adjournment.

Effect on Unfinished Business

The effect of adjournment upon unfinished business is as follows:

1. When a meeting is adjourned, the business which is interrupted
by adjournment comes up first under unfinished business at the next
meeting. It is taken up at the point at which it was interrupted.

2. When a series of meetings or a convention is adjourned, the business which was interrupted is dropped and can be introduced only as new business at a future meeting.

3. When a meeting adjourns to an adjourned meeting, business is resumed at the same point at which it was interrupted.

RULES GOVERNING MOTION TO ADJOURN (UNQUALIFIED)

1. Cannot interrupt a speaker, because it does not require immediate attention.
2. Requires a second.
3. Is not debatable, since it is a simple, procedural motion, and particularly because its high precedence is incompatible with debate.
4. Cannot be amended, because it is invariable in form.
5. Requires a majority vote.
6. Has the highest precedence of any motion.
7. Applies to no other motion.
8. Can have no other motion applied to it except withdraw.
9. Can be renewed at the same meeting, after a change in the parliamentary situation.

Practice Projects

1. Discuss the reasons why a group should not be kept in session when a majority wish to adjourn.
2. Can you recall any meetings which adjourned so hurriedly that important business was overlooked? Describe the situation.
3. In what type of situation can those members favoring a motion profit by proposing a recess?
4. Discuss some of the methods which might be used during a recess to gain support for a measure.
5. Why is a qualified motion to adjourn always a main motion and not a privileged motion?
6. How might an organization inadvertently dissolve itself?
7. Who has the major responsibility to see that this does not happen?

CHAPTER 19

MOTIONS TO MEET EMERGENCIES

NEED FOR EMERGENCY PROCEDURES

Even in the best planned meetings, unforeseen situations often arise. It becomes necessary to take some action which is not in order at that time or is not permitted by the rules of the organization.

Two procedures are designed to meet these emergencies: one, a motion to suspend the rules which interfere with some action the assembly desires to take; and the other, a request for a privilege to be granted to the assembly or to one of its members.

Both procedures are temporary expedients to meet a sudden need of the assembly or of a member to do something which, according to the rules, is impossible. Both are limited to the accomplishment of a specific purpose, and their effect terminates when that purpose is accomplished.

These procedures are not violations of the rules. They are regular means set up to meet emergencies in a legal and proper manner.

Motion to Suspend Rules

PURPOSE

The purpose of the motion to suspend rules is to allow an assembly to take some emergency action or to do something which is forbidden by the rules of parliamentary procedure, by a program already adopted, or by a rule of the organization.

FORM

PROPOSER: "I move to suspend the rules of our order of business so that we may listen to Mayor Brown immediately."

CHAIRMAN: "It has been moved and seconded to suspend the rules of our order of business so that we may listen to Mayor Brown immediately. Those in favor, please rise. . . . Be seated. Those opposed, please rise. . . . Be seated. The vote is affirmative, 29—negative, 0. The rules are suspended."

EXPLANATION

The motion to suspend rules is an incidental motion which seeks to meet emergencies. It frequently happens that an assembly has adopted rules or a program which make it impossible to cope with a situation which arises suddenly.

For example, an organization may have a rule that all large expenditures shall first be approved by the Board of Governors. A motion may be proposed to send $2,500 to the Red Cross for relief of flood sufferers in a nearby town. During discussion of this motion, someone may point out that according to the rules this motion would first have to be approved by the Board. Someone could move as an incidental motion "that the rules which interfere with the sending of $2,500 immediately to the flood sufferers be suspended."

At a meeting of an organization, open to members only, if a motion on sewage disposal is being discussed, a member might move to suspend the rules forbidding the attendance of guests, so that the commissioner and the assistant director of sanitation could explain the sewage problems.

The motion to suspend rules is generally concerned with rules relating to priority of business, or business procedure, or procedural rules.

Rules may be suspended only for a specific purpose and for a limited time. If rules were suspended for an indefinite period, this would be equivalent to amending the rules. For this reason the object of the suspension must be specified, and only the act or acts named in the motion can be performed under the suspension. Just as soon as the specified acts are performed, for which the rules were suspended, the suspended rule automatically becomes effective again.

The provisions of a constitution or of bylaws cannot be suspended unless there is specific provision in the constitution or bylaws for their suspension.

No rules which are designed to protect absentees, such as rules re-

HANGING ON

A rule's not broken
  When suspended,
In fact it isn't
  Even bended.

quiring notice of meetings or fixing a quorum, can be suspended at any time. It is, of course, impossible to suspend any provision of a statute or charter.

The motion to suspend rules may be made when no question is pending, or while a question is pending if it pertains to that question.

If no motion is pending, the motion to suspend the rules is a main motion and follows all the rules of a main motion except that it requires a two-thirds vote.

RULES GOVERNING MOTION TO SUSPEND RULES

1. Cannot interrupt a speaker, because it does not require immediate decision.

2. Requires a second.

3. Is not debatable.

4. Cannot be amended, because it is invariable in form.

5. Requires a two-thirds vote, because it sets aside rules of the assembly or rules of procedure.

6. Takes precedence as an incidental motion.

7. Applies to no other motions.

8. Can have no motion except withdraw applied to it.

9. May be renewed at the same meeting, after change in the parliamentary situation.

Question of Privilege

PURPOSE

The purpose of a question of privilege, or of a motion of privilege, is to secure immediate action on some matter which concerns the comfort, convenience, rights, or privileges of the organization or of one or more of its members.

FORM

1. *Question of Privilege of the Assembly*

PROPOSER (without waiting for recognition): "Mr. Chairman, I rise to a question of privilege."

CHAIRMAN (without waiting for a second): "State your question."

PROPOSER: "I suggest that the building superintendent be asked to turn on the heat in this wing of the building. Some of us are cold."

CHAIRMAN: "Will the sergeant at arms please find the superintendent and ask him to turn on the heat."

2. *Question of Personal Privilege*

PROPOSER (without waiting for recognition): "Mr. Chairman, I rise to a question of personal privilege."

CHAIRMAN (without waiting for a second): "State your question."

PROPOSER: "The secretary has just read a statement concerning me in the minutes which is in error. I did not second Mr. B.'s motion at the last meeting. I was, and still am, opposed to that motion."

3. *Motions Involving Question of Privilege*

PROPOSER: "As a question of privilege, I move that this meeting be moved immediately to a quieter part of the building. Most of us here in the back can't hear with the band practicing next door."

CHAIRMAN (without waiting for a second): "As a question of privilege, it has been moved . . . ."

EXPLANATION

Questions of privilege which relate primarily to a *particular* member are termed questions of *personal* privilege. Questions of personal privilege are concerned with the rights and privileges which belong to the *individual* member.

Questions which relate to the privilege of the *entire assembly* are known as questions of privilege of the *assembly* and, in case of conflict, have precedence over questions of personal privilege. Questions of privilege of the assembly frequently are concerned with such problems as heating, lighting, ventilation, seating of members, accuracy of reports, conduct of officers, members, or employees, control of noise or disturbance, ability to hear speakers, or the functioning of the public-address system.

Questions of privilege, when proposed as requests, are usually decided by the presiding officer. The emergency nature of a question of privilege allows the member proposing it to interrupt a speaker. While a question of privilege is being decided, the person interrupted should be seated. As soon as the speaker has stated his question of privilege, the presiding officer must rule on it immediately by stating that it is granted or denied. Any member may appeal from this decision.

If the question of privilege interrupts a speaker, the presiding officer may rule that it is a legitimate question of privilege but that it is not of sufficient immediate importance to interrupt further. He states this and tells the member that the privilege will be granted as soon as the speaker has concluded.

If the presiding officer decides that the question of privilege is a legitimate privilege and is sufficiently urgent, he grants the request immediately. As soon as the question of privilege has been disposed of, the speaker who was interrupted resumes his discussion.

Questions of privilege which are stated as motions are usually concerned with privileges which are not within the power of the presiding officer to decide and which therefore require a vote of the assembly.

To be a true motion of privilege, the matter must be of immediate urgency, but it need not relate to the motion which is pending before the assembly. When a matter is presented as a motion of privilege it is, after being stated by the chairman, subject to all the rules applicable to a main motion. Its status as a motion of privilege extends only to the fact that, because of its urgency, it can interrupt when another main motion is pending before the assembly, and can gain precedence for its consideration and decision.

RULES GOVERNING A QUESTION OF PRIVILEGE (NOT A MOTION)

1. Can interrupt a speaker, because it requires immediate decision.
2. Requires no second, because it is a request and not a true motion.
3. Is not debatable, because it is decided by the presiding officer.
4. Cannot be amended.
5. Requires no vote, because it is decided by the presiding officer.
6. Takes precedence of all motions except the motions to recess and to adjourn.
7. Applies to no other motion.

8. Can have no other motions applied to it except withdraw.

9. Cannot be renewed at the same meeting.

When a question of privilege is presented as a motion, it is privileged as to its precedence only, and after being stated by the chairman, is subject to all the rules of a main motion.

Practice Projects

1. From your own observation, can you recall any instance when it was necessary to suspend the rules? Have you ever seen an action taken illegally when a motion to suspend the rules would have given legal sanction to the action? Discuss.

2. Should a rule be suspended indefinitely?

3. If there is need for indefinite or frequent suspension of a rule, what other action should be taken?

4. Outline several situations in which a question or motion of privilege would solve a problem and expedite the meeting.

CHAPTER 20

MOTIONS AFFECTING
PREVIOUS ACTIONS

GETTING THINGS UNDONE

The usual purpose of a meeting is to get things done. Perhaps because "getting things done" is the chief task of a deliberative assembly, little attention has been given to the less frequent but sometimes important problem of getting things undone. But there are times when actions have to be undone—when decisions on matters have to be reevaluated, re-decided, reversed, or repealed.

Meetings are quite often confronted with the problem, "But we've already voted on it. What can we do about it now?"

The possible answers can best be considered together, and their relationship to each other explained. To understand the problem of how to undo previous actions, it is necessary to consider some new motions and some which are already familiar.

Procedures which may be applied to previous actions are the following:

a. Reconsider
b. Renew
c. Rescind or repeal
d. Amend by a new motion

Two of these procedures, renew and reconsider, apply to actions which have been lost; and three of them, rescind, amend, and reconsider, apply to actions which have been passed. The one overlapping procedure, which applies to votes that have been *either* carried or lost, is the motion to reconsider.

Reconsider must be brought up at the same meeting or convention during which the motion to be reconsidered was voted upon. Many

191

motions, if lost, cannot be renewed at the same meeting or convention. The remaining procedures have no time limit and may be proposed at any time after the meeting at which the action was originally taken.

The following list shows which procedures apply to actions that have been lost, and which apply to actions that have carried:

Motions Affecting Actions Already Taken

Actions Lost	*Actions Carried*
May have applied to them:	May have applied to them:
a. Reconsider	*a.* Reconsider
b. Renew	*b.* Rescind or repeal
	c. Amend by new motion

Motion to Reconsider

PURPOSE

The purpose of the motion to reconsider is to enable an assembly to set aside a vote previously taken on a motion or resolution and to consider the matter again as though no vote had been taken.

FORM

PROPOSER (without waiting for recognition): "I move to reconsider the vote by which the motion to add a wing to the hospital was passed earlier in this meeting."

CHAIRMAN (*a.* If no other business is pending and after a second): "It has been moved and seconded to reconsider the vote by which the motion to add a wing to our hospital was passed this evening. Is there any discussion? . . . Those in favor of reconsidering the vote by which the motion to add a wing to our hospital was passed, say 'Aye.' . . . Those opposed, 'No.' . . . The motion to reconsider is carried. Therefore, the question of adding a wing to our hospital is again open for discussion. Will the secretary please read the motion."

(*b.* If other business is pending): "The secretary will please note the motion to reconsider. It will be taken up as soon as the business now before the assembly has been disposed of."

EXPLANATION

What Votes May Be Reconsidered

The general rule is that when a proposition has been adopted, it must stand.

It is necessary to give finality to votes on propositions so that the will of the majority may be carried out; otherwise a minority could obstruct the execution of the majority's will for a long period of time. However, to guard against any possibility of too hasty action, or of a change of mind by the majority of the members, a vote is subject, for the current meeting, to reconsideration.

The final vote on any main motion, or amendment to a main motion, may be reconsidered during the same meeting or convention at which the vote to be reconsidered was taken. After the meeting at which the vote on it was taken, no motion can be reconsidered.

What Votes May Not Be Reconsidered

A vote cannot be reconsidered in the following instances:

a. When something which cannot be undone has been done as a result of the vote. For example, when an officer has been elected and has qualified for his position, when a contract has been awarded and signed, or when a sum of money has been authorized in payment and has been paid.

b. When a motion or rule which requires previous notice has been passed. For example, if the constitution or bylaws have been amended, the vote on these amendments could not be reconsidered without notice, because this would amount to amending without notice.

c. The vote on procedural motions cannot be reconsidered. When such a motion has carried, it is much simpler to accomplish the purpose of reconsideration by another procedural motion. For example, if a motion has been referred to a committee, it is easier to withdraw it from the committee than to reconsider the vote. On the other hand, when such a motion has lost, it is easier to renew the lost motion after progress in debate than to reconsider the vote.

TO THE REAR

The move to reconsider,
  Made by woman, child, or man,
Undoes everything we did or
  Hoped to do since we began.

It's a strictly rearward movement
  Which will, after fuss and stir,
Lead us onward to improvement
  Or right back to where we were.

Who May Move to Reconsider

Any member may move to reconsider. One of the early parliamentary writers insisted that only those members who voted "on the prevailing side" could propose the motion to reconsider. This well-intentioned requirement resulted in ridiculous subterfuges by members in order to qualify themselves to propose the motion to reconsider.

Some member of the minority would vote on the prevailing side, or if this move was overlooked, some member of the minority would hastily rise and change his vote. In voice votes, and in votes by ballot, it is impossible anyway to tell how anyone voted.

The courts have held that Jefferson and Cushing were right in following the historical principle that anyone can move to reconsider, unless the assembly has a special rule forbidding it.

The motion "to reconsider and have entered on the minutes" for action at the next meeting was a device by which two members could tie up, until the next meeting, even though that might be months away, any motion which had been passed by the majority, no matter how urgent. It has never had general acceptance as a rule of parliamentary law and exists only when specifically provided for in the bylaws or rules.

Time Limit on Motion to Reconsider

The time during which a motion to reconsider may be proposed is strictly limited. A motion which has been decided by vote of the assembly should not be subjected for long to attack by one or two members, and the will of the majority as expressed in the vote should be carried out with reasonable promptness.

Therefore, the motion to reconsider can be made only on the day that the vote to be reconsidered is taken or, in a convention, on the next business day. In an ordinary meeting, a motion to reconsider can only be proposed at the same meeting at which the vote to be reconsidered is taken. This rule lends stability to actions of an assembly and allows it to proceed with work which has been authorized by majority vote.

Proposal of Motion to Reconsider

The motion to reconsider, even though it is a specific main motion, can be proposed at any time during a meeting, even after a vote to adjourn has been taken, but before the adjournment has been announced.

It may be proposed even though other business is under consideration, and, if necessary, it may interrupt a speaker. When the motion to reconsider is proposed while some other business is pending, the secretary records its proposal, but it is not considered until the pending business has been disposed of.

Consideration of the Motion to Reconsider

A motion to reconsider, if proposed when no other business is pending, is considered immediately, unless its consideration is postponed to a definite time.

A motion to reconsider, if proposed when other business is pending, is considered as soon as the pending business is disposed of, unless its consideration is postponed to a definite time.

Debate on Motion to Reconsider

The motion to reconsider is debatable and opens the main question to be reconsidered to debate. Even though a member has exhausted his right to debate a question, he may discuss it again under the motion to reconsider.

Reconsidering Amendments

When it is desired to reconsider the vote on an amendment after a vote has been taken on the adoption of the main motion, it is necessary also to reconsider the vote on the main question. When it is necessary to reconsider two or three successive votes, one motion can be made to cover them all.

Effect of the Motion to Reconsider

The effect of proposing the motion to reconsider a vote is to suspend all action on the motion resulting from the vote, which it is sought to reconsider, until the motion to reconsider is acted upon. If, however, the motion to reconsider is made and not considered, its effect terminates with the meeting, or, in the case of a convention, with the next calendar day, unless the motion to reconsider is postponed to a later definite time.

When a vote is reconsidered, it is canceled as completely as though it had never been taken, and the original motion is again before the assembly and open for discussion as though it had not been voted upon.

RULES GOVERNING MOTION TO RECONSIDER

1. Can interrupt a speaker, because there is a definite time limit for the proposal of the motion.

2. Requires a second.

3. Is debatable and opens the motion, which it seeks to reconsider, to debate.

4. Cannot be amended, since it is invariable in form.

5. Requires a majority vote, even though the motion to be reconsidered, required a two-thirds vote.

6. The proposal of the motion has the highest rank of precedence, but the consideration of the motion ranks as a main motion.

7. Applies to votes on main motions and amendments.

8. Can have applied to it withdraw, vote immediately, limit debate and postpone indefinitely.

9. Cannot be renewed, as only one reconsideration is permitted.

Renewal of Motions

Renewal is a procedure, not a motion. Whether a motion can be renewed is one of the facts to learn about each motion. It is closely linked to reconsideration. There are only two ways to bring up, for consideration a second time, a motion which has been lost. One is by the motion to reconsider. The other is by renewing it.

The purpose of renewing a motion is to bring up the defeated motion again. Renewal is not concerned with how the motion was lost—whether it was postponed indefinitely or voted down. Most procedural motions can be renewed after "progress in debate," and that phrase is interpreted to mean "after a speech which might change the attitude of the assembly or an action which might change the situation."

Main motions and amendments can be reconsidered and therefore cannot be renewed at the same meeting. In order to progress with business, the disposition of main motions must be final, except that they may be reconsidered for a limited time.

No main motion which is lost may be renewed at the same meeting at which it was voted on, because during that time it may be reconsidered.

Procedural motions are renewable because they are usually not debatable, and the duration of their effect is quite brief. They must be available to meet changing situations.

It is the duty of the presiding officer to prevent the privilege of renewing a procedural motion from being used to obstruct business, and when it is evident that it is being misused, he should protect the assembly by ruling it out of order.

Motion to Rescind

PURPOSE

The purpose of the motion to rescind is to nullify or void a motion previously passed.

FORM

PROPOSER: "I move to rescind (or repeal, or annul, or cancel, or void) the motion, passed on November 9 of last year, by which this organization went on record as favoring a new bond issue."

CHAIRMAN: "It has been moved and seconded to rescind the motion, passed on November 9, by which this organization went on record as favoring a new bond issue. The secretary will please read the motion referred to. . . . Is there any discussion? . . . Those in favor of the motion to rescind this motion, please rise. . . . Be seated. Opposed, please rise. . . . Be seated. The motion to rescind is carried. The motion favoring a new bond issue is rescinded."

EXPLANATION

The motion to rescind is a specific main motion and applies only to motions which have been passed. The motion to rescind a motion can be proposed at any time and has no time limit. It applies only to main motions. Naturally, motions cannot be rescinded which have resulted in actions which the assembly cannot undo.

The motion to rescind requires a majority vote, even though the motion which is being rescinded required a higher vote.

The effect of a motion to rescind, if adopted, is to nullify the action which has been rescinded. The term "rescind" is synonymous with the terms "nullify," "void," "annul," or "cancel," and these words are frequently used in place of the word "rescind." All motions to rescind, whether proposed as motions to nullify, or void, and any other motions to the same effect, are governed by the same rules.

A motion which has been rescinded is left in the minutes of the organization, but a notation of its rescission is written in the margin beside it. The motion to rescind is not retroactive; that is, it does not overthrow action taken as a result of the main motion, but it prevents future action under the motion rescinded.

An interesting vote to rescind occurred on April 30, 1863 (*Hinds' Precedents,* Vol. LV, p. 27). The House of Representatives had previously adopted a resolution censuring Simon Cameron for alleged irregularities in proceedings as Secretary of War, in the matter of purchasing military supplies at the outbreak of the rebellion. The record of rescission reads: "And whereas, on the twenty-sixth day of the ensuing month, the then President of the United States, Abraham Lincoln, in a special message to Congress, assumed for the Executive Department of the Government, the full responsibility for the proceedings complained of—

"Therefore—

"Resolved, that this House, as an act of personal justice to Mr. Cameron, and as a correction of its records, hereby directs that said resolution be rescinded and that rescission be entered on the margin of the *Journal* where said resolution is recorded."

RULES GOVERNING MOTION TO RESCIND

1. Cannot interrupt a speaker, because it does not require immediate decision.
2. Requires a second.
3. Is debatable and opens to debate the question it proposes to rescind.
4. Cannot be amended, since it is invariable in form.
5. Requires a majority vote.
6. Takes precedence as a main motion.
7. Applies to main motions previously adopted.
8. Can have applied to it all subsidiary motions and withdraw.
9. Cannot be renewed at the same meeting.

Motion to Expunge

The motion to expunge is seldom used in ordinary organizations. It is a motion which really attempts an impossibility, because it seeks to blot out of the record an action which was taken and recorded. No action can really be blotted out, because it must remain to show what was expunged. The motion is governed by the same rules and has much the same effect as the motion to rescind, but in addition it usually indicates what amounts to an apology for the original action and expresses strong disapproval of it. The motion to expunge is frequently combined with the motion to rescind.

The most famous instance of the use of the motion to expunge occurred in the Senate of the United States during the term of office of President Jackson. When he took office, there were numerous banks chartered by the individual states. Also Congress had chartered the United States Bank. Jackson was hostile to this bank, because of his resentment toward the moneyed interests, which it represented.

To show his disapproval of the United States Bank, Jackson withdrew the Federal government's deposits. Immediately, bankers and businessmen protested to Congress, blaming business distress on the President's action in removing these Federal deposits. As a result the Senate of the United States passed this resolution:

> *"Resolved,* that the President, in the late executive proceedings in relation to the public revenue, has taken upon himself authority and power not conferred by the constitution and laws but in derogation of both."

Senator Benton, who was a close friend of President Jackson, immediately began a campaign to expunge the resolution. It was defeated, but at each new session of Congress he renewed the motion to expunge. Each time the motion was brought up, it gained a few more votes. Those votes were gained by pressure brought on individual senators by the legislatures of their states. In the last session of Congress during President Jackson's term of office, the motion to expunge the condemnatory resolution came to vote again.

The audience hissed and booed, and Benton ordered the sergeant at arms to clear the galleries. Finally he countermanded that order and brought the ringleader of the disturbance to the bar of the Senate. Quiet was restored, and the motion to expunge passed by a vote of 24 to 19.

In the original journal, a red line was drawn around the resolution, and across the record was written, "Expunged by order of the Senate this 15th day of January, in the year of our Lord 1837."

Since that episode, the motion to expunge has been used only a few times in Congress, and in ordinary deliberative assemblies it is rarely used.

All the purposes of a motion to expunge may be accomplished by the motion to rescind, and the denial of the passage of the original action which is made by the expungement is really a legal absurdity. The motion seeks to a certain degree to be retroactive, while the motion to rescind is effective only from the date of rescission.

Amendments to Actions Already Taken

An amendment to an action which has already passed must be made as a new main motion. The amending motion should state specifically what changes are to be made in the former motion. It should also clearly identify the action which it is proposed to amend; if possible, give the date or approximate date; and refer to the page in the minute book where the record of the action may be found.

Amendments to actions which have already been passed require a majority vote, unless they propose to amend the constitution, bylaws, or some other rule which contains a provision requiring a larger vote for amendments.

A good definition of the meaning of amendments to actions already passed is to be found in the court's opinion in the case of Faloner v. Robinson (Supreme Court of Alabama, June term, 1871. 46 Ala. 340, 348). "A motion which has already been passed is amended when it is in whole, or in part, permitted to remain, and something is added to or taken from it, or it is in some way changed or altered to make it more complete or perfect, or to fit it the better to accomplish the object or purpose for which it was made."

Repeal

The motion to repeal is identical with the motion to rescind.

"Repeal by implication" is not a motion but is the application of a principle to resolve a conflict between two actions. Occasionally an action already taken is found to be in conflict with a later action. This situation of conflict between the two actions gives rise to the principle known as "repeal by implication."

When there is a conflict between two motions, or actions, which cannot be reconciled, it is a well-established principle that the latter of the two actions, or motions, prevails. The need for the application of this principle usually arises because of the failure of the proposer of the second motion properly to identify a previous action which he proposes to change or because the amendment is not clear. Frequently, the proposer of a motion is not even aware of motions already adopted with which his motion conflicts.

When the proposer of a motion plans to supersede all or portions of an old motion by a new motion, he should state in his motion that it is intended to repeal the earlier action. If one motion overlaps another motion, the provisions of both remain in force unless there is a direct conflict between them. If there is a conflict, the latter repeals the earlier by implication only in so far as it is impossible to reconcile the two motions, or actions.

Practice Projects

1. Which of the following motions to reconsider or rescind would you rule out of order and why?

1. "I move to reconsider the vote by which we passed a motion at our monthly meeting last spring, that dues be raised for associate members."

2. "I move to reconsider the vote by which we just amended Bylaw 3."

3. "I move to reconsider the vote on the motion to refer the matter of a new driveway to a committee."

4. "I move that we reconsider the vote by which we sent a telegram at the beginning of this meeting to the National President, protesting the raise in assessment fees."

5. "I move that we reconsider the vote by which the motion providing for a new filing system was lost at our last convention."

6. "I move to reconsider the vote by which the treasurer was authorized earlier in this meeting to buy new chairs for the auditorium."

7. "I move to reconsider the vote by which the motion to set up a retirement fund was lost at our convention meeting yesterday."

8. "I move to rescind the motion, which we passed on June 9, authorizing the payment of thirty dollars a month to John Martin, the gardener."

9. "I move to rescind the motion which authorized the signing of a contract, in July of last year, for the maintenance by Schaeffer Brothers of our golf course for five years."

10. "I move to rescind the motion, passed last December, which authorized the treasurer to make a contribution of seven hundred and fifty dollars to the National Welfare Fund."

11. "I move that we rescind the motion electing Mr. King to membership in our organization, since he has not attended meetings since last December."

12. "I move to rescind the motion, passed at our November meeting two years ago, in which we expressed our disapproval of the military appropriation bill."

13. "I move to rescind the motion, which was passed at the beginning of the meeting, permitting trees to be thinned out on our property in Northern Pennsylvania."

14. "I move to rescind the motion to take a recess."

15. "I move to rescind the motion, passed on April 2, by which members were given the privilege of bringing their wives to dinner without charge on Ladies' Night."

2. What motion or procedure would you apply to each of the following situations involving actions already taken, and how would you phrase them?

1. A motion was passed five years ago by the Edenvale Chapter of the Benevolent and Protective Order of Elks to offer a prize of $100 for the best essay on "Americanism" written by a student of Eldridge High School. There are now two high schools in Edenvale, and the Elks wish to open competition in the essay contest to students of both.

2. The Atlanta Taxi Drivers' Association, at their regular meeting on March 5, passed a vote condemning the slowness of the chief of police in apprehending three murderers. Toward the close of the same meeting, the members learned that the three criminals had been apprehended. Naturally, the club members no longer desired the motion.

3. The Centerville Peace Officers' Association voted down a motion to ask for an immediate increase in the percentage to be set aside for

the Widows' and Orphans' Fund, at their April meeting. At the following September meeting, sentiment was much more favorable toward the increase, and the proposers of the motion wished to have it considered again.

4. At a meeting of the Bee Keepers' Association of Amador County, it was discovered that $306 was missing from the association's funds, which had been ordered placed in the bank. The treasurer was out of town, and the organization passed a resolution of censure against him for carelessness in handling the money and demanded that restitution of all missing funds be made to the association. At the next meeting, it was brought to the attention of the members that the apparent absence of $306 was due to an error by one of the bank clerks, and that the treasurer had not been responsible for any loss of funds. The association not only wished to apologize, but to take appropriate action expressing their regret.

5. The Lehigh Office Furniture Distributors, at their May meeting, voted to engage showrooms jointly with the Office Equipment Dealers' Association for the annual showing of their products. Later on in the same meeting, they learned that the Office Equipment Dealers did not plan to have any exhibit this year.

6. The Art Association of Auburn passed a motion at their annual art exhibit, twelve years ago, which stated that every member exhibiting a painting must pay a fee of two and one-half dollars. So few paintings were displayed at the last few annual exhibitions that the members wish to open the exhibition to anyone, without fee.

7. Four and one-half years ago, the United Automobile Workers' Local 682 passed a motion that no advertising could be solicited for the annual yearbook and report. At the September meeting this year, they passed another motion that advertising could be solicited from automobile agencies, distributors, and supply houses. They had forgotten about the first motion. What rules now govern the union with regard to advertising solicitations?

8. The Garden Club of Mount Holyoke passed a motion, many years ago, that seeds should be purchased and distributed free to all members of the club for their own use. The cost of seeds has increased, and the members no longer favor this motion.

CHAPTER 21

SUMMARY OF RULES
GOVERNING MOTIONS

RULES COMMON TO ALL MOTIONS

Now that you have studied all the important motions, it may be helpful to get an over-all view of the rules which govern them and thus to understand the general principles which determine these rules. This chapter is not intended to add new facts, but to summarize and generalize on facts already stated.

The first fact to learn about any motion is its purpose. If you understand the purpose of a motion, you will find that the rules governing it provide the logical means to enable the motion to accomplish that purpose. Certain of the rules are almost self-evident.

Nine basic rules govern motions. Some motions have additional rules, but the nine basic rules are common to all motions. The best way to learn these rules is not to memorize them, but to study the purpose of a motion, to understand the reasons for the rules, and to become familiar with the rules through practice.

The answers to the nine following questions form the basic rules which govern each motion. These are the questions which you should ask and answer about each motion:

1. What is its precedence?
2. Can it interrupt a speaker?
3. Does it require a second?
4. Is it debatable?
5. Can it be amended?

6. What vote does it require?
7. To what motions does it apply?
8. What motions can be applied to it?
9. Can it be renewed?

The answers to these questions vary with each motion, but they may be summarized under some rather general rules. Such a summary will give you a background which will help you to reason out the rules gov-

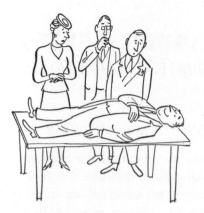

MOTIONLESS

When finally a vexing motion
Is laid upon the table,
We sometimes feel that we would also
Lie there if we were able.

erning individual motions. Do not memorize this summary, but read it carefully as background material.

The answers to the first question, "What is the precedence of the motion?" have already been analyzed in a previous chapter. The others will be discussed here.

Can the Motion Interrupt a Speaker?

When a speaker has been recognized, he is ordinarily entitled to the floor as long as he does not violate the rules of debate, and it is the duty of the presiding officer to protect him in this right.

There are, however, two types of motions which, because of their urgency, are permitted to interrupt a speaker.

The first type includes motions which have a time limit after which they cannot be proposed or considered. These motions must, of necessity, be permitted to interrupt. The motions which may interrupt a speaker because they are subject to a time limit are:

a. Reconsider
b. Object to consideration
c. Appeal
d. Division of assembly

The second type of motion which may interrupt a speaker is that relating to the immediate rights or needs of the assembly or of one of the members. These motions are:

a. Question of privilege
b. Point of order
c. Parliamentary inquiry

Does the Motion Require a Second?

Motions normally require seconds except in small organizations or committees, or in legislative bodies. This requirement of a second is justified on the principle that the assembly should have evidence that at least two members favor the introduction and discussion of a motion before it is considered by the body. However, recently some organizations have passed a special rule stating that seconds to motions are not required.

A number of procedures are listed as motions but are not true motions. They are actually requests, demands, privileges, or inquiries. None of these require seconds, because they are not true motions. A few of them can, in some instances, be proposed as motions. If they are stated as motions, they require seconds.

The following requests and demands do not require seconds:

a. Question of privilege
b. Point of order
c. Parliamentary inquiry
d. Request to withdraw a motion
e. Object to consideration
f. Division of a question
g. Division of an assembly

Is the Motion Debatable?

The business of an organization consists largely of the consideration and discussion of main motions which bring subjects before the assembly for decision. Main motions and their amendments are fully debatable.

Postpone indefinitely is debatable because it proposes what is equivalent to a negative vote on the main motion. Reconsider and rescind are themselves specific main motions. An appeal presents a substantive question, as does a main motion—"Is the decision of the chairman right or wrong?" All other motions are procedural motions and are therefore not fully debatable.

The following motions only are fully debatable:

a. Main motions
b. Amendments (unless applied to an undebatable action)
c. Postpone indefinitely
d. Appeal
e. Reconsider
f. Rescind

There are two motions which permit limited or restricted debate. They do not open the merits of the main question to discussion. The motions which allow limited discussion are:

a. Postpone definitely
b. Refer to a committee

All other motions are procedural motions and therefore can be decided without debate.

Can the Motion Be Amended?

A simple test may be used to determine whether a motion can be amended.

Is the motion variable in form? If its wording can be varied, it can be amended. If its form is fixed and invariable, it cannot be amended. If it could have been stated in more than one way when proposed originally, it is subject to amendment in order to state it in the form preferred by the members.

Few motions are variable in form. The only two motions which can be freely amended are:

a. Main motions
b. Amendments

Three motions can be varied only as to time and therefore can be amended only as to time. These motions are:

a. Postpone definitely
b. Limit debate
c. Recess

The motion to refer to a committee may be amended as to the name of the committee or the number of members, to give instructions to the committee, and in similar ways.

What Vote Does the Motion Require?

The theory of democratic government implies control by a majority, and almost all motions require a majority vote.

Common practice in ordinary organizations has led to the requirement of a two-thirds vote for a few motions which temporarily set aside a fundamental principle. The only motions which do not conform to the principle of a majority vote and which, by common practice, require a two-thirds vote are:

a. Vote immediately
b. Limit debate
c. Suspend rules
d. Object to consideration

To What Motions Can the Motion Apply?

A motion is said to apply to another motion when it is used to alter, affect, or dispose of the original motion.

For example, if a main motion, "that the Wildlife Conservation League accept the offer of the county to donate a strip of land to be used as a bird refuge" is pending, and a member moves to amend the motion by adding the words "and express our gratitude," the amendment is said to apply to the main motion.

Likewise, while this same motion is pending, if a member moves to postpone further consideration until the next meeting, this motion to postpone definitely is said to "apply" to the main motion.

The privileged motions cannot apply to any other motion, because they relate rather to the organization and its members and not to particular items of business. Very few incidental motions can apply to other motions, because they relate generally to the order or manner of considering business. The only incidental motions which can apply to other motions are:

a. Withdraw, which can apply to any motion

b. Object to consideration, which can apply to main motions

c. Division of a question, which can apply to main motions and amendments

The subsidiary motions all apply to main motions. The motions to control debate, which are vote immediately (previous question) and limit debate, naturally apply to all debatable motions.

The motion to amend can apply to any motion which is variable in form.

Specific main motions apply only to main motions, except that the motion to reconsider can apply to amendments.

What Motions Can Be Applied to the Motion?

When a motion is being considered, it is necessary to know what motions can be applied to it. In practice, this question involves very few difficulties, because the answer to the question is usually self-evident. These are a few guiding rules:

1. Every motion can have the motion to withdraw applied to it.

2. The privileged motions and the incidental motions can have no other motions (except withdraw) applied to them, except that the motion to recess may be amended; and an appeal may have applied to it the motions regulating debate and the motions to postpone definitely or temporarily.

3. All debatable motions can have the motions regulating debate (to vote immediately or to limit debate) applied to them.

4. All motions which can be stated in more than one way (which are variable in form) can have the motion to amend applied to them.

5. Main motions can have all the subsidiary motions applied to them and, in addition, the motions to object to consideration, reconsider, and withdraw. Amendments can have the same motions applied to them as main motions with the exception of the motion to object to consideration.

Can the Motion Be Renewed?

Renew means to propose again the same, or substantially the same, proposition at the same meeting or convention.

Main motions which have been lost, postponed indefinitely, or set aside by an objection to their consideration cannot be renewed at the same meeting or convention. However, they may be introduced as new motions at a future meeting or convention. The same rule naturally applies to amendments and to the motion to postpone indefinitely, which is really a negative form of the main motion.

The motions to reconsider and to rescind are themselves forms of a second consideration of a motion and consequently cannot be renewed.

Most procedural motions can be renewed after a change in the parliamentary situation which, in effect, makes the renewed motion a new question. Change in the parliamentary situation means that motions have been proposed or disposed of, debate has proceeded, or other events have occurred to create a new situation so that the assembly might reasonably take a different position.

Requests, demands, inquiries, or privileges cannot be renewed.

Objection to consideration, appeal, point of order, and call for a division logically cannot be renewed because they must be presented immediately after a specific situation arises. Otherwise the time limit for their consideration debars them.

In summary, most motions which bring a subject before the assembly cannot be renewed except as new motions at the next meeting or convention. Most procedural motions can be renewed after a change in the parliamentary situation, which makes the motion to be renewed, in effect, a new question.

Practice Projects

1. As you look over the different motions, do you notice any other generalizations which might be made about them?

2. Do any specific rules seem illogical or unreasonable to you? If so, explain your ideas and suggest solutions.

3. Why is it important to know the purpose of a motion?

PART THREE : ORGANIZATIONS
Their Structure and Functions

CHAPTER 22

CREATING A NEW
ORGANIZATION

TEMPORARY AND PERMANENT ORGANIZATIONS

Organizations may be divided into two groups according to the probable length of their existence.

A *temporary* organization is formed for a specific purpose or to accomplish a specific act, and is dissolved automatically as soon as its purpose has been accomplished. An example of a temporary organization is a mass meeting, or a meeting to endorse a candidate or to advocate a measure.

A permanent organization is formed with the intent of functioning for a longer time or indefinitely.

PLANNING FOR A NEW ORGANIZATION

There are many problems and decisions involved in the formation of a permanent organization which can best be determined by a small group or by a committee and which should be decided before a general meeting is called. Some of the preliminary questions to be decided are:

1. What is the purpose of the proposed organization?
2. How is this purpose to be accomplished?

FOUNDERS KEEPERS

No organizer of clubs am I,
  At thought of the same, I wince.
I was founder of one, back in Junior High,
  That's been foundering ever since.

3. What is to be the relationship of the new organization to other organizations?

4. How is the organization to be financed?

5. What are the policies of the organization?

6. Is the organization to be incorporated?

7. Is there to be more than one kind of membership?

8. Who are to be the temporary officers?

9. How are members to be selected?

PLANS FOR THE FIRST MEETING

When the founders have agreed upon answers to these and other preliminary questions, they are ready to make plans for the first meeting. Some of the questions to be decided about the meeting are:

1. What kind of initial meeting should be held?

2. Where and when is it to be held?

3. How are the people to be called together?

4. Who will call the meeting to order?

5. Who will be the chairman?

6. Who will nominate the chairman?

7. Who will explain the purpose of the meeting?

8. Who will prepare the resolutions or bylaws to be voted upon?

When answers to such questions as these have been agreed upon, a small group should prepare the resolution establishing the permanent organization and draft a set of bylaws.

THE FIRST MEETING OF AN ORGANIZATION

When the group has assembled in response to the initial call or invitation to a meeting, some member should rise and call the meeting to order:

"The meeting will please come to order. I nominate Mr. Keith as temporary chairman."

The member who has called the meeting to order may ask for nominations for chairman instead of proposing a chairman himself. Usually only one person is nominated for temporary chairman, but if several names are proposed, a vote is then taken on each name, in the order of

RECOGNITION

What happens when I wave my hand
And resolutely cry
And seek to gain the chairman's ear
Or anyhow his eye?

What happens when, from where I sit
Up in the second row,
I rise and stand upon my chair?
I think, my friend, you know.

Some person sitting far to rear,
Half hid behind a door,
Lifts up his little finger and,
By gad, he has the floor!

its presentation, until one nominee receives a majority vote of all the members voting. This candidate is declared elected and takes the chair as temporary chairman.

The temporary chairman then opens nominations for a temporary secretary, who is elected in the same manner.

When the temporary secretary has been elected, the chairman calls upon one or more members to explain the purpose of the meeting. When these purposes have been discussed or are generally understood, and opportunity has been given to ask questions, someone should present a resolution or motion that the assembly form itself into an organization.

RESOLUTION FORMING A TEMPORARY ORGANIZATION

A temporary organization usually operates under a resolution and does not require a constitution or bylaws, unless it becomes a permanent organization. The resolution should therefore contain a statement of the purpose and the general plan of work of the temporary organization.

The following is an example of such a resolution:

"Resolved, That this assembly form itself into a temporary organization for the purpose of electing Mr. Lamb as Congressman from the Thirty-eighth District, and be it further

"Resolved, That a chairman, secretary, and finance committee be elected who shall serve for the duration of this campaign, and be it further

"Resolved, That a copy of this resolution, signed by all persons present who desire to support the candidacy of Mr. Lamb, be sent to all newspapers in this congressional district, to the State Central Committee, and to Mr. Lamb."

RESOLUTION FORMING A PERMANENT ORGANIZATION

The resolution or motion which authorizes the formation of a permanent organization can and usually should be brief:

"I move that this assembly form a permanent organization to be known as the Westport County Civic League."

If this motion receives a majority vote, some member moves to select a committee to draft a constitution and bylaws. If these have already been prepared, the committee which drafted them is asked to report.

The constitution and bylaws are first read as a whole and then article by article. It is during this second reading that they may be amended and discussed.

When the constitution and bylaws have been adopted, the first business in order is the election of permanent officers. This election completes the formation of a permanent organization.

Practice Projects

1. Choose a group of students to meet and bring to class a plan and resolution for a temporary organization. They may then conduct an organizing meeting with the rest of the group attending as members.

2. Select a type of permanent association which would be suitable for the class to form, and go through all the procedure to create the organization. It is suggested that the permanent association be a type of organization that might actually serve a useful purpose. A current-events club, an adult study group, or a debating society can be formed to exist for as long as the members desire. It can also be used as the basis for practice in drawing up a constitution and bylaws and in revising them.

CHAPTER 23

CONSTITUTION, BYLAWS, AND STANDING RULES

RULES GOVERNING ORGANIZATIONS

An organization is always governed by law, and usually by a charter or a constitution, by bylaws, and by standing rules, or by several of these. If the organization is an incorporated group, the primary rules under which it operates are the corporation laws of the state in which it is incorporated. Next in rank are the rules in its charter, constitution, bylaws, and standing rules.

Organizations which are not incorporated operate under general laws which are applicable and under their constitution, bylaws, and standing rules. Many organizations combine their constitution and their bylaws into one document. This frequently is a desirable plan, because all of the provisions referring to one subject—for example, membership—appear in one place under subheadings. This set of rules is called the "constitution and bylaws," or the "bylaws."

Rules of procedure peculiar to the organization are sometimes included in a group of rules known as "standing" or "special rules."

In all situations not covered by law, the charter, the constitution, the bylaws, or the rules, the parliamentary authority adopted by the organization governs.

DRAFTING A CONSTITUTION

Usually the constitution and bylaws of an organization are prepared by a committee. It is important that the committee members talk over and understand thoroughly the purposes and plans for the proposed organization before they begin the actual drafting of provisions. Agreement and understanding of basic aims and methods simplify the actual writing of rules.

IRON CONSTITUTION

The constitution's what you go on,
What you really can't be low on,
What you plan by, work by, share by,
What, in short, you always swear by.
Having long revered, obeyed it,
Sometimes you forget you made it.

Even experienced members of the committee may find it difficult to establish theoretical provisions for the operation and government of an organization and to foresee how these provisions will actually work.

Some help in meeting this difficulty can be gained by a study of the constitutions and bylaws which have worked well for other similar organizations. However, it is inadvisable to "borrow" a complete constitution or bylaws from one organization and expect it to work effectively for another group with different conditions, problems, and needs.

Simple, basic structures work better than elaborate and complicated ones. Exact language is preferable to vague or technical phrases. The careful definition of the scope of work and the powers and duties of all officers, boards, and committees takes time, but it results in a better-functioning organization.

PROVISIONS OF A CONSTITUTION

A constitution is a compilation of the fundamental rules defining the structure and government of an organization. It should be brief and clear. It is customary to include a minimum of at least eight articles, and each article may be divided into sections and subsections. The basic articles usually include:

Article 1. Name of the organization
Article 2. Purposes, powers, and scope of the organization
Article 3. Qualifications of members
Article 4. Officers of the organization
Article 5. Provision for a board of directors, or governing board, or executive committee
Article 6. The time and place for regular meetings, and a procedure for calling special meetings
Article 7. Number constituting a quorum
Article 8. Method of amending the constitution, and the vote required

Many constitutions are preceded by a preamble, which states the purposes of the organization and introduces the articles.

PROVISIONS OF BYLAWS

The bylaws contain all provisions and details which are necessary to amplify and carry out the provisions of the constitution. If an organiza-

tion does not have a constitution, the provisions usually
included in it are placed in
the bylaws instead.

All bylaws relating to the
same subject should be
grouped together under one
article or section, which in
turn may be divided into sub-
headings. For example, under the article or bylaw entitled "Committees" should be grouped all provisions which relate to committees, including their names, their powers, and their duties.

Bylaws usually include provisions covering the following subjects:

1. Membership, including kinds of membership, requirements for
membership, limitations as to number of members, how members are
selected and admitted, the rights and duties of each class of membership,
and how membership is terminated.

2. Committees, including lists of all standing committees, method
of their selection, the scope of their work, definite statements of the
powers and duties of each, their quorum, time of meeting, and ex-officio
members, if desired. The governing board or executive committee should
have its duties and its powers carefully and explicitly defined. No committee has implicit powers or duties. Provisions should be included for
regular and special committee meetings and for reports.

3. Financial provisions, including dues, fines, tax on memberships,
initiation fees, assessments, bank accounts, bills, vouchers, audits, and
details for their administration.

4. The term of office, powers, and duties of each officer. No officer
has inherent powers or duties. Each duty an officer is expected to fulfill
and a careful definition of his powers and limitations should be included.
There should also be some provision for filling vacancies and for removing officers who do not perform their duties.

5. Provision for regular meetings and provision for special meetings,
including requirements for notice and agenda and attendance at meetings. Since the law requires strict observance of all provisions concerning notice of meetings, both regular and special, these requirements
should be set forth in detail.

6. Election, including dates and methods of nomination and election, and methods of voting. The method of selection, duties, and procedure of the nominating committee, and the vote required for election.

7. Order of business for meetings.

8. Parliamentary code adopted as the authority for the organization's procedure.

9. Vote and notice required for important decisions.

10. Procedure for suspending or amending bylaws.

11. Provisions for limiting debate, if desired.

12. Standing or special rules.

13. Quorum.

14. Conventions.

ADOPTION OF CONSTITUTION OR BYLAWS

When the chairman of the committee on constitution and bylaws presents his report, he concludes it by moving that the constitution and bylaws, or the constitution, or the bylaws, be adopted. The presiding officer may state the motion in this form:

"It has been moved and seconded that the constitution be adopted."

The secretary then reads the constitution as a whole, or if it has already been read by the chairman of the committee, the secretary may read the first section or subsection. As each section is read, the presiding officer calls for a discussion on it and asks for amendments to it. If amendments to a section are proposed, these are discussed and voted upon individually, but no vote is taken on the final approval of the section as a whole. After all sections have been read, discussed and amended, the presiding officer asks:

"Is there any discussion on the constitution as a whole or is there any further amendment to it?"

When any proposed amendment has been disposed of and if no one rises to discuss the constitution further, the chairman takes a vote on the original motion to adopt the constitution. A majority vote is sufficient to adopt a constitution or bylaws.

Following this vote, if there are separate bylaws, these are read, considered, and amended individually. The bylaws are then voted upon as a whole.

WHEN THE CONSTITUTION AND BYLAWS
GO INTO EFFECT

If no provision is contained in the constitution or bylaws as to when they should go into effect, they take effect immediately after the vote adopting them. If it is desired that a particular section of the constitution or bylaws should not go into effect until a later date, this reservation should be included in the motion to adopt. An example of the adoption of bylaws with a reservation is as follows:

"I move that the bylaws be adopted as last read, except that Bylaw 11, which establishes the dues of the organization, shall not go into effect until the November meeting."

REQUIREMENTS FOR AMENDING CONSTITUTION
AND BYLAWS

Both constitution and bylaws should contain provisions within themselves for their amendment. This provision usually includes two requirements. The first is a requirement for the notice that must be given when an amendment to the constitution or bylaws is proposed. The second is a requirement fixing the vote an amendment must receive for adoption.

The requirements on notice may vary widely. Some organizations provide only that notice be given at a previous meeting. Others require that the amendment be read and submitted in writing to the secretary and read at two preceding meetings. Still other organizations provide that the proposed amendment be sent to each member in printed form.

The essence of all these provisions for notice is that every member of the organization must know what the proposed amendment is and when it is to be voted upon.

CONSIDERING AMENDMENTS TO CONSTITUTION
OR BYLAWS

When a proposed amendment to the constitution or bylaws comes before the assembly for consideration, the discussion must be confined strictly to the consideration of the amendment as stated in the notice. No amendment may be proposed to any part of the constitution not mentioned in the notice. Unless the provision for amendment states specifically that no amendment may be made to the proposed amendment, such amendments as are germane to the subject are in order. For example, the notice may have read as follows:

Notice of Proposed Amendment to Bylaws

To amend Bylaw 4 on Membership by adding the following as Section 5: "Associate membership in this organization shall be open to all those teachers, recommended by the membership committee, who have taught for at least one year in the city school system and are now retired."

An amendment to strike out the phrase "recommended by the membership committee" would be germane to the amendment. And members, in reading their notice proposing the establishment of a class of members to be known as associate memberships, could anticipate reasonable changes in the amendment.

VOTE REQUIRED FOR AMENDMENTS

The second requirement which must be included in any provision for amending the constitution or bylaws is a statement of the vote which the proposed amendment must receive. Usually the constitution or bylaws provide that, notice having been given and a quorum being present, two-thirds of the legal votes cast is required. Some organizations require only a majority vote on the theory that, due notice having been given, the constitution or bylaws may be amended by the same vote by which they were adopted.

In some small organizations, a two-thirds vote of the total membership is required, but this high percentage would make it impossible for many large organizations to amend their constitutions or bylaws. If an organization has both a constitution and bylaws, usually the vote required for amending the constitution is somewhat higher, and the requirements of notice somewhat greater, than the notice and vote required for amending the bylaws.

REVISION OF CONSTITUTION AND BYLAWS

When it is necessary to amend several portions of a constitution or bylaws, it is usually advisable to select a committee on revision. This committee should invite suggestions from members. It should consider the constitution and the bylaws as a whole, so that proposed amendments will not conflict with provisions of other sections.

The committee usually holds hearings, so that other members will have a chance to appear and present proposed amendments. The committee should submit a report of suggested amendments which it favors, giving the reasons for each proposed change. If found desirable, it is possible to substitute an entirely new constitution or bylaws as a revision.

When the report of the committee is read at a meeting of the organization, it is equivalent to giving notice of a proposed amendment. The report of the committee cannot be acted upon until the time required for notice has elapsed.

When the time for considering the proposed amendments arrives, the committee report is read, and each section is discussed and opened to amendment.

STANDING RULES

An organization has the right, by majority vote and without notice, to establish standing rules. Standing rules cover points of procedure which differ from the adopted parliamentary authority or which are peculiar to the organization. They also cover other rules which are not of sufficient importance to be included in the bylaws. A standing rule may be amended or abolished at any meeting by a majority vote and without notice.

The following are examples of subjects frequently included in standing rules:

1. Limitations on length of speeches
2. Fines or penalties
3. Regulations concerning attendance of guests at meetings
4. Entertainment of guest speakers
5. Regulations concerning programs

ADOPTING A PARLIAMENTARY AUTHORITY

The courts hold that any deliberative body conducts its meetings subject to the rules of parliamentary law. This means that every organization, for its own protection as well as guidance, should adopt some code or book of rules on parliamentary law. This adopted authority furnishes the rules which guide an organization on all matters not covered by its charter, constitution, bylaws, or standing rules.

The name of the book adopted by the organization as its parliamentary authority should be stated in its bylaws. This bylaw is usually phrased in some such form as the following:

"In all matters not covered by its constitution or bylaws, this organization shall be governed by the *Sturgis Standard Code of Parliamentary Procedure.*"

or

"*The Sturgis Standard Code of Parliamentary Procedure* shall serve as the parliamentary authority of this organization for all rules and procedures not covered by its constitution, bylaws, or other rules."

A parliamentary authority should be chosen with great care. The fundamental principles of parliamentary law do not change, but the rules of procedure are always in process of development. As new court decisions are given, rules must conform to them. Ignorance of the correct rules of procedure, or the adoption of an obsolete manual, often results in legal entanglements or lawsuits.

The parliamentary authority chosen by an organization must be complete, so that all details are covered. Short summaries of rules are helpful but are not appropriate for adoption by organizations, because there are many situations which they do not cover. The law does not excuse any organization from legal requirements because of errors or omissions or ambiguities in the authority it has adopted.

In case of difficulty, organizations may always refer their questions to the author of their parliamentary guide for further interpretation or explanation. Most authors are glad to be helpful in this way.

Practice Projects

1. Select a committee to draft a set of bylaws for the organization chosen as a permanent group. When this committee reports, consider, amend, and adopt the bylaws.

2. Secure a constitution and bylaws from some existing organization, and select a committee from the class to revise these. Let the class consider, amend, and vote upon the suggested revisions.

CHAPTER 24

OFFICERS

THE PRESIDENT AS PRESIDING OFFICER

The president is the leader of the meeting. He sets its tone and its pace. In large measure he determines its achievements. His success as a presiding officer depends upon his ability, not merely to maintain order, but also to guide the meeting so that it moves rapidly and progressively

toward its goal. The presiding officer of any assembly is not in the position of a teacher, a speaker, a director, or a boss. He is the servant of the assembly and, while presiding, should be as impersonal and as impartial as a judge or an umpire.

Nothing will weaken the influence of a presiding officer more quickly than a feeling on the part of the members that he is partial in his conduct or in his decisions. If he obviously favors his friends, or advocates or opposes measures during meetings, or is biased in his rulings, he will fail to hold the respect of the assembly. He must not only be impartial but impersonal. To preserve his attitude of impersonality, he may refer to himself as "the chair" or "the chairman." He may say, "The chairman requests" or "The chair rules."

An efficient chairman maintains order at all times. He is alert to the first signs of disturbance and acts promptly to restore order and attention. A firm refusal to recognize any member or to entertain any business until order is restored will generally quiet an assembly. A good presiding officer uses his gavel sparingly. A chairman who has to resort to frequent gavel pounding is inefficient.

231

MEET OUR OFFICERS

The president, or chairman,
Should be a fair man,
And wise
Enough to recognize
People way back by the door
He has never seen before.

　　　　The vice-president, if ambitious
　　　　And slightly vicious,
　　　　Should use stealth
　　　　And never inquire openly about the
　　　　　　president's health.

The secretary
Should be very
Good at spelling, or at least writing,
Regardless of how dim the lighting.

　　　　As for the treasurer,
　　　　He should not be too much of a pleasurer
　　　　And playboy,
　　　　Else someone will say, "Say, boy,"
　　　　(This can be heart-rending)
　　　　"Isn't that our money you're spending?"

It is the responsibility of the presiding offcer to see that the meeting moves along and makes progress. This does not mean that he coerces the assembly into carrying out his will. It means, rather, that he must be alert to times when the assembly seems to move too slowly in carrying out its own will. Discussion that is too prolonged or not to the point, or confusion in applying parliamentary rules, slows up a meeting and causes members to lose interest. It is the chairman's responsibility to see that facts and procedures are clear, that discussion is to the point, that votes are taken promptly, and that the meeting marches along.

He must do this tactfully and not in a dictatorial manner. Presiding is an art that is hard to teach. The sensitive and tactful chairman is quick to observe the times when debate should be held to the minimum, and to sense when comprehensive discussion is necessary before a vote is taken. He knows how to encourage a postponement when tension mounts and time is needed to cool off, and how to dispose quickly of embarrassing or unsuitable motions. He understands how to encourage the shy member who speaks only when he feels strongly on a subject, and how to discourage the member who is overly fond of hearing his own voice.

The chairman creates the atmosphere, the spirit, and the attitudes of a meeting. He should be able to make members feel at ease, to encourage them to take part in discussion, to stimulate interest in the subject which is being discussed. By his own conduct he emphasizes courtesy, order, and mutual consideration.

A good presiding officer knows parliamentary procedure and knows how to use it. He realizes that procedure should serve the organization and not hamper it.

A member of the British Parliament once gave this recipe for an ideal chairman: "Two cups of common sense, well mixed with three pounds of tact and fairness, stirred, and plentifully sprinkled with a knowledge of parliamentary law. Bake with a few years of experience."

DUTIES OF THE PRESIDENT

Usually the most important duty of a president is to preside at all business meetings. When business is being considered, the presiding officer cannot delegate his duty to preside to a program chairman, or to the chairman of a convention, or to some other member.

In many organizations the presiding officer has duties in addition to the usual ones attached to his office. These additional duties should be specifically stated in the bylaws.

The usual duties of a presiding officer are as follows:

He calls the meeting to order at the appointed time.

He announces, in its proper order, the business which should come before the assembly.

He assigns the floor to members who desire to present motions or speak.

He states all motions which have been properly proposed and seconded and restates all motions which are not clear.

He restricts discussion to the question before the assembly.

He makes certain that members understand the pending business and explains the effect of a motion if it is not evident.

He answers parliamentary inquiries and questions and decides points of order and questions of privilege as soon as they arise.

He states the exact question to be voted upon and puts it to vote.

He votes in case of a tie or when he is authorized to do so by the bylaws.

He announces votes and the results of votes.

He signs all orders necessary to carry out the will of the assembly.

He acts as the representative of the organization to outside persons and to other organizations.

He. appoints committees as directed by the bylaws or by motion of the assembly.

He performs all other duties which may be assigned to him by the bylaws or rules of the organization.

THE VICE-PRESIDENT

The vice-president's chief duty is to be ready to assume temporarily the office and duties of the president in case of the absence or incapacity of that officer.

He must also be prepared, in the event of the resignation or permanent incapacity of the president, to assume the office of president. The second vice-president and other lesser vice-presidents, if there are any, then assume the office which is next above them.

When the vice-president is acting in place of the president, he has all the powers, duties, privileges, and responsibilities of that office. Unless there is provision in the bylaws that officers shall advance from one step to another at each election, there is no rule that a member who is a vice-president one year shall be elected president the following year.

The vice-president takes the president's place if it is necessary for the president to leave the chair, or when the motion is one in which the president has a personal interest.

In practice, the vice-president is usually assigned additional responsibilities by the bylaws or standing rules of the organization. He frequently heads some activity or important committee, or serves on the governing board.

THE SECRETARY

The secretary is the chief recording officer of the organization. He also acts as assistant to the chairman by taking notes and being ready to explain at any time exactly what business is pending. When the secretary is a member of the organization, he does not forfeit any rights of membership by reason of holding that office. He may introduce motions, discuss them, and vote on all measures.

In the absence of the president and vice-presidents, the secretary should be prepared to preside.

The chief duties of a secretary usually are as follows:

To keep a careful and authentic record of the proceedings of the organization

To be able to furnish the exact wording of a motion which is pending before the assembly

To authenticate all records by his signature

To read papers that may be called for by the assembly

To furnish information from the minutes, which may be requested by officers or members

To prepare a roll of members and to call it when necessary

To preserve all records, reports, and documents of the organization which are not assigned to others

To provide the chairman, at the beginning of each meeting, with a detailed memorandum of matters to come up under each section of the order of business

To provide the chairman of each committee with instructions for the committee, copies of correspondence, papers, or reports which may be of help to it, summary of policies of the organization which may be involved in the committees' work, and a statement of the powers and duties of the committee

To have available at each meeting a copy of the constitution, bylaws, standing rules, and parliamentary authority of the organization; a list of the organization's members and a list of all committees and their members

THE CORRESPONDING SECRETARY

In many organizations the duties of the secretary are divided between a corresponding secretary and a recording secretary. The duties of a corresponding secretary are to write official letters for the organization and to keep a file of all correspondence. The corresponding secretary does not initiate correspondence but prepares letters upon direction of the president, the executive board, or the organization itself.

THE EXECUTIVE SECRETARY

Many state and national organizations, and large local groups, employ an executive secretary. He is a paid official and is usually not a member of the organization. He is the chief administrator and serves as the working head of the group.

The executive secretary works under the direction of the president and of the governing board and is usually chosen by them. He is particularly necessary and helpful in organizations where the officers change annually or biennially. He is able to maintain stability in the organization by preserving a continuity of policy.

He is a great help to officers, to committees, and to the membership at large, and is an important asset to any group which has a large amount of work to do.

THE TREASURER

The treasurer is the official custodian of the funds of an organization. He is also the disbursing officer.

As custodian, he is responsible for collecting money due the organization and for its safekeeping. He must keep an accurate record of all funds collected and be able to furnish a statement at any time showing the financial condition of the organization.

As disbursing officer, he is responsible for checking all bills and vouchers which are presented for payment, and for issuing checks to cover them. He must also keep an accurate record of all disbursements.

A treasurer should be chosen for his financial integrity and his book-keeping ability. He should give a brief report or summary at each meeting, and a complete report annually. His books should be audited by a committee or by auditors selected by the organization.

THE SERGEANT AT ARMS

The sergeant at arms is an assistant to the presiding officer and works under his direction. In general, he is responsible for the comfort and the convenience of the assembly. He acts as chief usher, and it is his duty to see that only persons who belong in the assembly room are admitted. It is also his duty to see that they are properly seated.

He is responsible for the behavior of the members and, if the presiding officer so directs, he may expel members from the room.

In most organizations, the sergeant at arms has the duty of arranging the chairs, tables, and equipment before the assembly convenes. In larger organizations, he usually has a paid staff of assistants.

THE PARLIAMENTARIAN

The parliamentarian should be qualified by experience and knowledge to give professional and accurate advice on questions of parliamentary procedure. He is usually appointed by the president, sometimes with the approval of the executive committee or board of directors.

The parliamentarian serves in an advisory capacity to the presiding officer. His duty is to give advice upon request or when needed. He should not try to manage the presiding officer. He gives all opinions directly to the chairman. He may be a member of the organization, but he should not hold any other office, board position, or chairmanship, because he should be an impartial and objective adviser. When possible, it is desirable to secure for parliamentarian someone who is not a member of the organization.

A skilled parliamentarian can be helpful in many ways. He can keep the organization out of difficulties and expedite its work. He can be helpful in advising committees, in assisting with the preparation of reports, in planning for conventions, in planning elections, in revising bylaws, and in setting up agendas. In state and national organizations, the parliamentarian is usually a paid professional adviser. He is selected by the president and works under his direction in a relationship similar to that of a lawyer. His advice can be accepted or disregarded.

At a convention, the employment of an experienced and competent parliamentarian gives the president, the board, and the organization assurance that the proceedings of the convention will be well-planned, smooth, and legally correct.

An unqualified parliamentarian will usually be an interference rather than a help to an organization.

HONORARY OFFICERS

Some organizations provide, in their bylaws, for honorary members and officers. Created as a tribute to the members upon whom they are conferred, these titles carry with them the right to attend meetings and sometimes to speak, but not to preside, to propose motions, or to vote.

Honorary status is perpetual unless it is rescinded.

Practice Projects

1. Visit several organizations and give a report on the presiding officer. Evaluate his attitudes, knowledge of procedure, impartiality, ability to keep the meeting moving, and his general efficiency.

2. Discuss the concrete ways in which a good secretary can be helpful to an organization.

3. Discuss the qualifications and duties of a parliamentarian, with particular reference to the difference between the relationship of the parliamentarian and of the officers to the organization.

4. Why is it desirable, in some instances, to have honorary members or officers?

5. Comment on the conduct of the presiding officer in each of the following situations, and upon the probable effect of his conduct upon the members:

1. At a convention, the presiding officer called the meeting to order. When the delegates did not respond he pounded his gavel furiously, then shouted, "Sit down! Sit down and come to order! You're acting like a bunch of cattle. Stop your talking. Sit down!"

2. At a town meeting, the moderator was being heckled by a small group of troublemakers. He firmly announced, "Your chairman will not recognize any speakers or entertain any motions until this meeting becomes quiet and orderly. If a few citizens persist in their unmannerly tactics, your chairman must ask the sergeant at arms to escort them from the meeting."

3. At a meeting of a service club, the presiding officer said, "I am tired of long-winded speeches. If you fellows want to say something, say it in one or two sentences, or else don't speak. Also, stop asking questions whenever you don't understand something. If you keep quiet and listen, you'll probably find out the answer after a while. Hereafter I want you to use your heads and let me steer this meeting."

4. At a civic meeting, the voters were discussing the regrading of a road. One member said, "I don't think we know enough about the subject to decide right now. I move we put it all over until next meeting."

A member rose to a point of order, and said, "There is no such motion. Mr. Evans is out of order." The chairman replied, "Mr. Evans, you wish to postpone this motion until the November meeting, do you not? Is there a second to Mr. Evans' motion to postpone this motion?"

5. At a meeting of the Aeronautical Association, a motion to send letters to senators and congressmen, urging that the Air Force of the United States be expanded, was pending. The presiding officer said, "I urge every member to vote for this motion. You people who are against it are thinking more about the few dollars you will have to pay in increased taxation than about the good of this country. I hope every member will support this motion."

6. At the close of a meeting of the Laundry Owners' Association, several members approached the president and said, "Just out of curiosity we would like to know how you feel personally about raising the dues. During that two hours of argument, we couldn't even get a clue from your actions as to how you felt, and we would like to know."

CHAPTER 25

MEMBERSHIP IN ORGANIZATIONS

INHERENT RIGHTS OF MEMBERS

When a member joins an organization, he establishes a contract between the organization and himself. By the act of joining, he acquires certain fundamental and inherent rights. An organization may, in its rules, give whatever additional rights it chooses to its members.

Each active or regular member of an organization has the following inherent rights, subject only to specific restrictions contained in the constitution, bylaws, or standing rules:

1. To receive notices
2. To attend meetings
3. To present motions, resolutions, or other business
4. To discuss
5. To vote
6. To nominate
7. To be a candidate for office
8. To inspect official records of the organization
9. To insist on the enforcement of the rules of the organization and the rules of parliamentary law
10. To resign, if all obligations to the organization have been fulfilled
11. To have a hearing before expulsion or other penalties are applied
12. To exercise any other rights given by the constitution, bylaws, or rules of the organization

The rights of members do not necessarily remain unchanged. The constitution or bylaws may be amended in the authorized manner, if the fundamental purposes of the organization are not altered. For example, fees or dues may be increased, and privileges which members formerly enjoyed may be extended or curtailed.

JOINING AN ORGANIZATION

Voluntary organizations have complete authority to grant or refuse membership in the organization, to make rules governing the admission of members, and to place restrictions on memberships. For example, an organization may require that any member, to be admitted, must receive the endorsement of the membership committee; or that membership in the organization shall be limited to twenty-five; or that only persons who own bulldogs may become members.

No particular procedure is necessary in joining an organization, so

long as a mutual understanding is reached as to membership. Organizations may require procedural steps for joining a group, such as signing the constitution and bylaws, securing the endorsement of the membership committee, or undergoing an initiation ceremony.

TERMINATION OF MEMBERSHIP

A member may sever his membership by resignation or withdrawal at his pleasure, unless there is a special rule to the contrary. If the rules of the organization provide a procedure for terminating membership, it must be followed. Some organizations, for example, have a rule that a member cannot resign until his dues and assessments are paid.

Every organization has inherent power to suspend or expel a member for cause, or to terminate his membership.

Before a member is expelled, he is entitled to a hearing before a fair and impartial committee who are acting in good faith. He must be given

LINES FOR JOINERS

Here is a thought about clubs
    That I'm sure you'll agree is a merry one:
It's better by far to belong
    To one than it is to carry one.

an opportunity to present his evidence and to refute evidence presented against him. The hearing cannot violate any rules of the organization, or any of the rights of the member under common law.

Practice Projects

1. Collect and compare the requirements of several organizations regarding the admission of members and the termination of membership.

2. Why are some unions exceptions to the general rule that voluntary organizations have complete authority to grant or refuse membership in the organization?

3. Ed Harris joined the Junior College Student Association, which included a free copy of the *Campus Daily* as one of the rights of each member. In the middle of the semester the Executive Council passed a rule that, from that date on, each student must pay a nickel for each copy of the *Daily,* because student funds were low. Ed Harris protested that he was being unlawfully deprived of one of his rights as a member. Discuss his contention.

CHAPTER 26

COMMITTEES AND THEIR WORK

RELATIONSHIP OF COMMITTEES TO AN ORGANIZATION

Most organizations are too large and their meetings too brief to do more than plan for work to be done, lay out general policies for doing it, and make final decisions. The work itself must be delegated to committees. Even in small organizations and in boards, it is advisable to divide up work among still smaller groups acting as subcommittees.

Committees are the working units of organizations. They actually do most of what the organization accomplishes. Every member needs a full understanding of their working methods and problems.

An organization delegates a share of its authority to a committee, but it does not at any time give up control over the matter that has been referred to the committee. Nor does it turn over to the committee the final decision on a problem. In theory, the final decision on the work, or investigation, or conclusions of a committee belongs to the organization. In actual practice, however, the reports and recommendations of a committee are usually adopted as the decision of the group as a whole. This fact emphasizes the power and value of committees.

ADVANTAGES OF COMMITTEES

A committee has many advantages which enable it to work more easily and effectively than its parent organization.

The first advantage is its size. Committees are seldom larger than twenty members and usually average about five in number. A small group can consider, plan, and carry out a piece of work more effectively than a large, unwieldy organization. A small number can meet oftener, deliberate more efficiently, and work more rapidly. The value of a committee is weakened if too many members are included. It is more important to have an efficient committee than to have "everybody on a committee."

The second advantage is that a committee can work more quietly and effectively because it is removed from the pressure of other business and from the prejudice of debate, and because it can devote more time to a subject. The committee members are in a position to think calmly and with the objective frame of mind that is necessary to formulate plans. This freedom enables the members to take up in a dispassionate way the matter referred to them. Thus a balanced judgment can be

arrived at, which would be more difficult to reach in a large meeting and in a limited time.

The third advantage is that a committee has greater freedom of discussion. Wide latitude is possible in talking over plans. The chairman, unlike the presiding officer, is an active participant in the discussion. During consideration of a problem, members may speak on a particular question as often as they wish. Questions may be asked while discussion is going on, and other related problems may be brought before the committee in the course of the discussion.

The fourth advantage is that of informal procedure. Fundamental requirements, such as limiting discussion to one main subject and allowing only one member to talk at a time, are necessarily observed, but small committees have little need for strict application of rules.

Large committees or committees which are holding public hearings must, of course, observe parliamentary rules with substantially the same strictness as an organization.

The fifth advantage is that many of the members of a committee are

DON'T LOOK AT ME,
I DIDN'T SAY ANYTHING

At meetings of clubs, by an effort of will,
I always contrive to keep perfectly still,
For it takes but a word of annoyance or pity
And wham! there I am on another committee.

experts in the problem being considered. Committee members are chosen for their ability and interest in a particular field. Through their training or through their service on a standing committee, they are usually specialists in the subject the committee is considering.

The sixth advantage is that delicate, troublesome, or embarrassing questions may be handled by a committee without publicity. In organizational work many problems arise which are best settled quietly and privately. Committees are ideal clearinghouses for these problems.

The seventh advantage is that a committee may hold hearings. This allows the committee to learn the opinions of members of the organization and of outside experts on the subject who may be called as consultants.

These advantages help to explain why the great bulk of organization work is carried on by committees.

COMMITTEES TRAIN MEMBERS

In addition to being the main working force of the organization, committees act as a training school. Members gain experience in working with others in committees, and their abilities are given a practical trial.

Since a committee is a miniature of the larger organization, most of the problems of the parent organization develop in committees. Members learn to solve these problems in a small group and gain confidence and experience for future broader leadership.

Chairmen of committees have excellent opportunities for developing the skills of leadership. Those heading important committees carry a volume of work and responsibility that is often equal to that of the president.

STANDING COMMITTEES

A standing committee is a semipermanent group, chosen to do work in a particular field which may be referred to it over a period of time. The life of a standing committee is usually the same as the term of office of the officers of the organization.

Standing committees and the method of their selection are provided for in the bylaws. Some standing committees are elected by the membership; others are appointed by the presiding officer, by the executive board, or by a combination of these methods. A standing committee is usually appointed to cover each important activity of an organization.

Standing committees constitute ever-ready, experienced groups to which questions in a particular field may be referred. They also handle routine duties which need to be carried out regularly.

Standing committees common to many organizations are membership, finance, public relations, minutes, and entertainment.

SPECIAL COMMITTEES

A special committee is selected to do a particular piece of work. As soon as the specific task assigned to the committee has been completed, and its report has been turned in, the committee automatically goes out of existence.

The organization may, however, vote to delegate additional work to the committee or to re-refer a matter to it. In this case the committee continues until the new assignment is completed and a final report is submitted.

Special committees are frequently appointed by the presiding officer or the executive committee, or are suggested or elected by the membership.

SELECTING SUITABLE COMMITTEES

Committees differ widely both as to the type of work they are called upon to do and the type of member they should include.

A committee chosen primarily for the purpose of investigating a subject or for studying a problem should be a representative committee. That is, it should include in its membership at least one representative of each different belief on the subject and of each important group or element of the organization.

If an investigating committee is composed largely or entirely of members who have the same ideas and belong to the same clique or group, it is not a representative committee and its report will not carry weight with the organization. If each group or different opinion is represented on such a committee, it is probable that the committee's report will be received with respect and confidence and that its recommendations will be followed.

A committee to hold hearings should be constituted similarly. If each group of the organization feels that it is represented at the hearings, there will be general satisfaction with the work of the committee.

A committee whose primary purpose is deliberation—thinking over and discussing a problem and coming to a conclusion on it—must also be a thoroughly representative committee.

When a congressional committee is selected to investigate a subject, its membership is carefully apportioned between Democrats and Republicans. Consideration is also given, in making appointments, to the part of the country that members come from, to their occupations, and to their stand on issues.

On the other hand, a committee which is created to carry out a certain project should be composed entirely of members who favor the project and have the ability to accomplish it. This principle was recognized early in American history. Thomas Jefferson wrote:

> "It is therefore a constant rule that no man is to be employed in any manner who has declared himself against it, and when any member who is against a bill hears himself named of its committee, he ought to ask to be excused."

Grey, the famous parliamentarian of the House of Commons, as early as 1680 expressed the principle that when work is to be done by a committee, only those in favor of the work should be appointed to the committee. He said:

> "The child is not to be put to a nurse who cares not for it."

Members should not be appointed to a committee "to get them interested." Committees are working units, and if they are burdened with uninterested members, they cannot be expected to function efficiently.

Some members do not like committee work, and there is a vast difference in the capacity of individuals for successful group relationships. Members who dislike committee work should not be included on committees.

It is a mistake to appoint committees when there is no work for them to do. Members who are put on such committees lose interest rapidly. The job to be done should precede the committee.

HOW COMMITTEES ARE CHOSEN

There are no fixed rules for selecting committees. The organization may choose any method it wishes. Usually the bylaws provide a method of choosing standing committees. The method of selecting special committees is often decided at the time the committee is created.

When the presiding officer appoints a special committee, it is wise for him to consult with members of the executive board and with other members before naming his appointees. Advisory boards, boards of directors, and executive committees usually have a wide knowledge of the abilities and experience of members of the organization. Consultation with these groups will enable the presiding officer to enlist the interest, support, and talents of members who might not be known to him personally.

When a committee to do a piece of work is appointed, it is a courteous and a common practice for the presiding officer to consult its chairman regarding the other members of his committee. Since the chairman is responsible for carrying out the committee assignments, it is only fair that he should have a voice in choosing his coworkers.

CHOOSING A COMMITTEE CHAIRMAN

"Let's make George Jenkins chairman of the committee. He always gets the job done and everybody likes him."

George probably heads every committee on which he serves. Why? What are the elusive qualities that make a good chairman? When the president appoints the chairman, or the members of the committee elect him, just what are the abilities they should look for?

A committee chairman should have the qualities of a leader—but it is a more intimate quality of leadership than is required of the presiding officer. The committee chairman does not always need the polish and ability to speak in public which a presiding officer should have. He does need a broad understanding of human nature and a love of working closely with people.

The chairman should be a person who understands that there is a real purpose in creating a committee—a purpose which cannot be served by any one of the individuals on that committee alone. If the parent organization had wanted an individual opinion, investigation, or execution of a piece of work, it would have assigned the task to an individual. The object of referring a matter to a committee is to obtain the considered opinion of the group and the cooperative thinking of the committee members.

The chairman should have a genuine understanding of the fact that although each member is working primarily toward the goal of the committee, he also hopes to satisfy some of his own needs and realize some of his own aims.

For example, Jane Hicks accepts an appointment on the "Get Out the Vote Committee" of the League of Women Voters, because she believes every citizen should vote. She also feels happy about serving on the committee because she wants a chance to become acquainted with her neighbors. She believes that the house-to-house canvassing will give her the opportunity she has been looking for. If the chairman of the committee, without talking to Mrs. Hicks, assigns her to stay in the office and keep records, she is not practicing good chairmanship. Mrs. Hicks will be unhappy and will work less effectively.

The chairman of a committee should be a coordinator of ideas. If he is unable to gather the ideas of the individual members into a working plan, hours may be wasted in fruitless discussion. It is the chairman's job to fuse the individuals of the committee into a group which can work and think as a cooperative unit.

To do this the chairman must have an open and seeking mind. He should consult with every member of the committee and ask questions individually and collectively. He should take every means to encourage statements of the different points of view and to draw out the best of each individual member. He must not be interested merely in his own opinion and in trying to force the group to accept it. No committee likes to be an audience, with the chairman as the star performer.

The chairman must be able to establish clearly in his own mind, and to explain explicitly to his members, the primary goal and the lesser goals of the committee's work. He must, in effect, say to them, "This is what we have to do." Throughout the life of the committee he must never lose sight of that ultimate purpose.

The chairman should guide but not direct discussion. He should summarize and present the problems which need decision, and whenever necessary he should repeat the summary. He should point out at intervals where the committee is in its thinking. Whenever there is a drift from the questions to be determined, he should courteously direct attention back to the points to be decided.

The chairman can serve as a conciliator between conflicts of attitude and be able to resolve them. He should also explain statements which are misunderstood.

The following situation illustrates the chairman's role as conciliator of conflicting attitudes and opinions:

The student-faculty committee was discussing censorship of the college newspaper. Bill Broom, student leader, felt that the student editor should have free rein in running his newspaper—all final decisions and acceptance or rejection of stories should be up to him. Mr. Jameson, faculty sponsor, believed that student editors too often overstep the bounds of school policy and that all stories, editorials, and columns should be submitted first to the paper's faculty sponsor for approval. This conflict of attitudes was resolved when the committee chairman suggested a short list of "don'ts" for the student paper. Any policy story, editorial, or column which dealt with one of these "don'ts" must first be approved by the faculty sponsor. All other material in the newspaper was to be left to the editor's own judgment.

The chairman should also strive to interpret statements when they are misunderstood. For instance, at this same meeting, Mary Thurber objected to limiting the students to certain topics. She understood that, on those topics, the faculty sponsor was to dictate any stories or editorials dealing with one of the "policy don'ts." The chairman resolved this misunderstanding by explaining that the students were to be free to write what they wished, and that the finished copy would be checked only for accuracy and adherence to school policy.

If no individual member is named as the chairman of a committee, the committee has the power to elect its own chairman from its membership. When no chairman is appointed, the member first named may call a committee meeting and preside during the election of a chairman. A mistaken notion persists that any member who proposes an idea should be made chairman of a committee to carry it out. A person is not debarred from becoming chairman because he proposes an idea, but the mere proposal does not necessarily endow him with the qualifications to be a good chairman.

TOOLS OF A COMMITTEE

Every workman must have his tools; a carpenter must have his saw, a seamstress her needle. So must every committee have its tools. Let us find out what these tools are.

The chairman should have the following material on hand at his first committee meeting:

1. List of committee members.
2. Copy of the motion or problem referred to the committee.
3. Special instructions to the committee, if any. These instructions should include a statement of exactly what the committee is expected to do, and whether the question is referred to it for discussion, study, hearings, investigation, recommendations, or action.
4. Statement of the powers and duties of the committee.
5. Copies of all papers or correspondence relating to the subject assigned the committee.
6. Copies of any rules, policies, or decisions of the organization relating to the subject.
7. Information on the type of report desired and the date set for its presentation.

SOURCES OF INFORMATION FOR COMMITTEES

Where does a committee get these tools? If the organization has an efficient secretary, he can furnish most of them. He will find the information in various records. The secretary can take the list of committee members and a copy of the motion or problem referred to the committee directly from the minutes.

Special instructions to the committee may be included in the motion creating the committee. Information to guide the committee may also be derived from ideas and understandings expressed during the discussion of the motion to refer the matter to a committee. For example, if the organization is discussing a motion to create a new class of memberships, it may become evident during the discussion that some members would like to appear before the committee and explain some of their ideas on the new membership extension. The presiding officer may have assured the members that they would be given this privilege. Such information should be included as a part of the special instructions.

The chairman of a committee appointed to carry out a project should be able to give the committee members a definition of the powers and duties of the committee. No standing or special committee has any powers or duties except those which are given to it by the organization.

Even an executive board or board of governors has only such powers and duties as are specifically assigned to it in the bylaws. The powers and duties of standing committees are similarly set forth. The powers and duties of special committees should be determined by the organization at the time the committee is created. Within limits, powers and duties can be inferred from the type of problem likely to confront the committee and from precedents in similar situations.

The president and secretary should assist committees by giving them any information from their records, or information or advice based on their knowledge of the organization and its policies. If the organization has an executive secretary, he can furnish all the materials which would be useful to a committee.

If the chairman has a clear understanding of what the committee is expected to do and what power it has to carry out the assignment, the committee will be able to work effectively. If either powers or duties are indefinite, or are not understood by the committee, confusion is inevitable. The chairman of a committee should understand that without specific authorization his committee does not have the power to represent the organization to outsiders, to enter into contracts, or to spend money.

The copies of all papers or correspondence relating to a subject assigned a committee can be obtained from the files or from the minutes. Copies of rules and policies relating to the subject may be found in precedents, in minutes, and in the bylaws of the organization. These may be difficult to collect, but the chairman must be sure that the plans and actions of a committee adhere to the policies of the organization. He must also be able to explain these policies to the members. No committee has the power to change a policy of the parent organization, and all committees should be careful to conform strictly to organization policies.

Information on the type of report desired may be drawn partly from a knowledge of the problem involved and partly from the discussion which took place on the motion. It is important that the committee understand what type of report the organization wishes and what points it should cover.

Obviously these tools are necessary, especially to a committee which is to carry out a project. Otherwise, lacking both information and direction, the committee will flounder about, overstep policies, make mistakes, or do unnecessary work and thus become discouraged.

EX-OFFICIO MEMBERS OF A COMMITTEE

Some organizations provide in their bylaws that the president or some other officer shall be a member of certain committees. Such a committeeman is called an ex-officio member.

Ex-officio members of committees are provided to correlate the work of the organization. The president and secretary are usually ex-officio members of the governing board. The treasurer is frequently an ex-officio member of the finance committee. This arrangement enables officers to keep in touch with the work of important committees and allows committees to profit by the experience and knowledge of the officers.

An ex-officio member of any committee has the same rights, duties, and responsibilities as any other member, unless the bylaws provide differently. When an ex-officio member ceases to hold office, his membership on a committee automatically terminates.

CALLING A COMMITTEE MEETING

In smoke-filled rooms or over Wedgwood teacups, around mahogany directors' tables or in the town meeting hall, thousands of committees are getting the business of America done. How do they go about it? Large or small, formal or informal, governmental or private, all committees follow certain fundamental procedures.

Meetings of committees are called by the committee chairman unless, as in the case of a standing committee, regular meeting dates have already been set. If the chairman is unable to act or fails to call a meeting, any two members of the committee may call the group together. No committee meeting is legal unless all members have been notified of it.

A quorum of any committee consists of a majority of the members, unless the organization has fixed a different number. A majority of the legal votes cast is necessary to take any action.

MINUTES OF COMMITTEE MEETINGS

Minutes of committee meetings are kept by the secretary, who is usually chosen by the committee members. These minutes are generally more complete than the minutes of an organization. There is a reason for this. Detailed and fairly complete minutes are needed as a source from which committee reports may be prepared. In meetings of an organization, members hear discussion and can follow the reasoning by which the assembly arrives at a decision. A committee report presents conclusions and decisions, and it is important to explain the steps by which these were reached. Detailed minutes will provide a record of these steps.

Suppose that the Executive Committee of the Portland Athletic Club has been instructed to bring in recommendations on a fitting way to acknowledge Mr. H. K. Daley's generous offer of a piece of land for a building site. The committee reports that it recommends that Mr. Daley be thanked most graciously for his offer, but that the offer be refused.

This unexpected recommendation is vigorously protested, and immediately a spirited argument starts. The chairman of the committee explains that there is a possible cloud upon the title to the land, which might involve the club in future litigation, and that, even if this problem were overcome, there is another difficulty. The site is on filled ground, reclaimed from tidelands, and test borings indicate that the foundations necessary to support a five-story steel building would be so expensive as to be almost prohibitive. As the various steps leading to the committee's conclusions are explained, the members begin to agree with the committee. The recommendation alone would be misleading without a presentation of the facts on which it is based.

Committee minutes include a record of opinions expressed, information gathered, and actions taken. The minutes remain the property of the committee and are not open to inspection by anyone except a member of the committee.

SUBCOMMITTEES

A committee has the right to appoint subcommittees. For example, the committee on arrangements for the annual meeting might appoint subcommittees on program, banquet, invitations, and awards. These subcommittees are chosen by the committee members or by the chairman, and are responsible only to the committee appointing them. Subcommittees have only such powers and duties as are given them by the parent committee.

PROCEDURE IN COMMITTEE MEETINGS

The procedure of committees should be as simple as possible. Since one of the objects of appointing a committee is to permit informal discussion, only enough formal procedure to serve the purpose of the committee should be used.

Large committees of thirty or forty members considering controversial subjects may find it necessary to apply parliamentary rules as strictly as the organization itself. Smaller committees can follow very informal procedure. In such committees it is not necessary to second a motion, to wait for recognition by the chairman, or to rise when presenting a motion or discussing a subject.

During discussion in a committee, the chairman should not be overly technical in applying parliamentary rules. He must, however, apply all the rules that are necessary to maintain order, to keep the subject clearly before the group, and to confine the discussion to the pending subject.

The final report of any committee must always be voted upon formally, and all recommendations or resolutions to be presented to the organization must be agreed upon by formal vote at a meeting of the committee.

The chairman has a different relationship to the committee than has a presiding officer to his organization. A presiding officer makes no motions, does not take part in discussion, and usually does not vote except in case of a tie. The chairman of a committee has all the rights of any other member, including the right to propose motions, to discuss them, and to vote. In small governmental bodies, such as boards of supervisors and city councils, each member represents a different district. If the chairman were not permitted to propose motions, discuss them, and vote, his district would be without representation.

The chairman of a committee takes part in discussion, just as any other member does, and may actively advocate his own beliefs. However, he should remember that his primary duty is to obtain the opinions of all the members of the committee and to blend these into a working agreement.

Committees have the task of carrying out the program of our voluntary organizations. They are the agents who plan and administer this phase of our American self-government. Each one—local or international—is important to our democracy. A knowledge of good committee procedure helps to get committee work done—easily, swiftly, and with accord.

Practice Projects

1. Divide the group into smaller groups of about five to nine members. Assign each group a different type of committee project—standing committee, investigating committee, committee to hold hearings and submit recommendations, committee to solve a problem, committee to recommend a plan, and other types. Let these committees hold several meetings, discuss their assignment and plan their work.

2. One committee may hold its meeting in front of the class so that, at the end of the committee meeting, criticisms and comments may be made by the observers.

3. Choose two members to prepare the materials for a committee about to begin a project.

CHAPTER 27

COMMITTEE REPORTS

ONE COMMITTEE PLANS A REPORT

"We've worked so hard investigating this question of adding a children's wing to the library! I do hope we can write a good enough report to make the project go over," said Chairman Phillips anxiously as he glanced about the committee table.

"Who's going to write it?" queried Mrs. Moore. "I'm no good at writing."

"I think we can all work on it," the chairman answered. "I'll write the introduction about how we planned our work and what steps we took.

"Ed, you supervised the survey on the need for a separate wing for children, and you have all the figures. That section comes second, and you should write it.

"Jim, you worked on the architectural end. Suppose you write the section on the cooperation of the local architects, and the plans which were submitted. Attach a copy of each plan to it.

"As for you, Pete, you write the part about costs and estimates, and attach the contractors' estimates that you collected.

"You're our lawyer, Cliff. So you're the logical one to draw up the explanation of the reasons for the proposed bond issue. That part will be especially helpful for our city council to use when they submit the bond issue to a vote of the people. You should phrase our resolutions, too, which will be attached to our report.

"Bob, here, has worked out all the plans for the publicity campaign. We have an important job convincing the voters that we need a wing for the children and persuading everybody to get behind the bond issue.

"Of course, what each of us writes won't be final. But at our next meeting, we can put all these parts of the report together, read them aloud, and everybody can make corrections and suggestions on the whole report.

259

REPORT CARD

Committee reports
    Can be nasty or nice,
And breezy or stuffy,
    And vague or precise.

Committee reports
    Can be weak or strong,
And a little too short
    Or a lot too long.

"Then, Mrs. Moore, if you'll type the corrected report, we can read and vote on it at our next meeting. We'll follow the same plan with our resolutions."

Thanks to the knowledge and evident experience of its chairman, this committee seems to be laying an excellent foundation for the preparation of a good report.

Proof of the effective planning that went into the report of this committee may be found in the following newspaper item which appeared six weeks later:

"NEWTONVILLE, Wis., June 8 (A.P.). The bond issue of $50,000 to add a new wing to the Public Library for the exclusive use of the children of Newtonville was carried yesterday by a decisive majority. Mayor W. E. Stillman and the Board of Library Trustees credit the work done by the Library Committee of the Newtonville Civic Association with being largely responsible for the victory of the bond issue. This committee of nine members, headed by Chairman Harold Phillips, conceived the idea for the wing, secured plans and estimates, and directed the publicity campaign."

Good committee work deserves an equally good report. The members of an organization may fail to understand or appreciate the accomplishments of a committee unless its plans and work are clearly explained in its report.

PREPARING A COMMITTEE REPORT

A committee report is usually supervised by the chairman of the committee and worked out cooperatively by the members. The general character of the report is necessarily determined by the kind of work the committee has done. Some committees which prepare important and lengthy reports print or duplicate copies for every member. If reports are printed, they are usually not read in full at the meeting. A brief summary of the report is read, or a copy of the printed report is handed to the secretary, when the committee's report is called for. A notation is included in the minutes that a printed copy of the report was presented and that copies are to be given or sent to each member.

The length of reports varies widely. All reports should be as brief as is consistent with the information which is being presented. A committee which has made an important investigation or held hearings may submit a report of several hundred pages. On the other hand, the report of a nominating committee or a committee to revise a resolution may be only a few lines long.

WHAT A COMMITTEE REPORT SHOULD CONTAIN

Committee reports usually cover the following main points:

1. A statement of the motion, subject, or piece of work which was referred to the committee, and why it was referred; that is, whether the subject was referred for action, clarification, investigation, study, or to obtain recommendations upon it.

2. A brief summary of the methods followed by the committee. If a study or investigation was made, the general plan that was followed should be explained.

3. The information gathered by the committee, if it was an investigating or fact-finding group, or a summary of the work accomplished by a committee assigned a particular task.

4. The conclusions or findings of the committee, and its recommendations. Some committees include recommendations as a part of the report, but the resolutions or motions which implement or enforce the recommendations should never be included in the body of the report. These motions or resolutions should be attached on a separate sheet. They should be numbered and prepared so that each one can be considered and voted upon separately.

The report should also include any other material which the committee believes will be of interest to the organization. A committee report should give credit to anyone not a member of the committee who has made a special contribution or has rendered particular service to the committee. It should not mention individual members of the committee unless they have performed some outstanding service.

AGREEING ON A COMMITTEE REPORT

The report should represent the collective judgment of the majority of the committee, after the members have deliberated together and have had the opportunity to discuss the report freely with each other. Therefore, it is necessary that the report be agreed upon at a meeting of the committee, and that the motion approving it as the report of the committee be voted upon formally.

It is sometimes impossible for the members of a committee to meet because they live too far apart. In such instances, provision should be made in the bylaws for consideration of the report by each member separately and for individual agreement on it. Unless such provision is made in the bylaws or in the motion creating the committee, a committee report agreed upon by each member separately is not valid.

When a committee report in its final form has been considered and

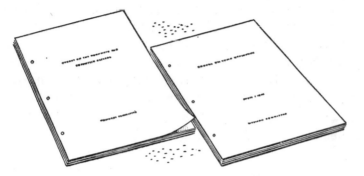

formally approved by a majority of the members at a committee meeting, it should be signed by the chairman of the committee.

If any member or group of members of the committee wishes to prepare a report which is different from or disagrees with the proposals or recommendations of the majority of the members, they have a right to prepare a minority report. This report is prepared in the same manner as a majority report, except that it is signed by all the members who agree with it. A minority report may agree with the report of the majority as to facts assembled or work done, but may advocate different solutions and recommendations.

DISPOSING OF COMMITTEE REPORTS

"The special committee to investigate property values in this district will now present its report."

This announcement, or one similar to it, by the presiding officer introduces the report of a committee.

Since most committees have worked diligently on the problem assigned to them, it is only courteous that the organization take the time to give adequate consideration to the committee's report and to its recommendations.

When a committee report has been read and considered by the organization, the assembly has several alternative ways of disposing of it.

1. A committee report may be filed. This is the most usual method of disposing of the bulk of committee reports. To move that a report be filed means that the organization has received the report and is including it in its records without expressing an opinion on it. When a report is filed, the organization is not bound by it.

If the organization wishes to commend, or congratulate, or thank the committee, this action may be included in the motion to file the report. It is better practice, however, to thank the committee by a separate motion, which is proposed after the report is disposed of.

If the report is routine, or consists of a brief summary of the progress made by a committee, it is not necessary for the assembly to vote on it. The presiding officer may state, "The report will be filed," and continue with the business of the meeting.

If the report is a final one, the member presenting the report, or any other member, may propose the motion that the report be filed.

2. Final decision on a committee report may be postponed until a more convenient time. This action is logical and wise if there is insufficient time to examine the report properly.

3. A report may be returned to the committee. If an assembly feels that a report is incomplete, or if it wishes more information, or desires a committee to do more work on the subject, it may re-refer the report to the committee, with a request for additional facts or with added instructions.

4. A committee report may be adopted. If a committee report is adopted, the assembly binds itself to any opinions, conclusions, recommendations, or resolutions which are contained in the body of the report. Adoption of a committee report does not, however, bind the organization to any recommendations or resolutions which are submitted separately from the report.

An assembly should be cautious about adopting committee reports. Use of the word "adopt" or "accept" in the motion which disposes of the report commits the assembly to anything contained in the body of the report. Unless there has been opportunity to study a report thoroughly, and unless there is complete agreement about its contents, it is usually wiser to receive or to file it.

5. A committee report may be rejected.

The motion disposing of a committee report is usually stated in an affirmative form.

"I move that the committee report be adopted (or filed, or referred to the committee, or postponed)."

However, a negative vote on a motion to adopt a committee report has the effect of rejecting the report. A report which is rejected is filed, and a notation of its rejection is made in the minutes.

If the organization likes portions of a committee report but disapproves of others, it may vote to divide the report, adopt certain parts of it, and reject the remainder.

A committee report cannot be changed or amended by the assembly because it lacks the power to make a committee say what it did not say or to write into a committee report something the committee did not include. The assembly, however, may decline to accept all or any part of the report.

6. A committee report may be referred to an officer, a board, or another committee for study. For example, important final reports are sometimes checked by the executive committee or board of directors before action is taken on them by the organization.

7. Financial reports from a treasurer, board, or committee are usually referred automatically to the auditing committee or the auditors. It is their duty to certify the correctness or incorrectness of such reports. A financial report which concerns only proposed or future expenditures is treated as any other report or recommendation and not as a financial report.

8. A minority report may be substituted for the majority report. If there is a minority report, one of the members signing it informs the chairman that such a report has been prepared. He should do this immediately after the majority report has been presented to the assembly, and before any action is taken on it. A minority always has the right to present its report, even though a motion has been proposed to adopt the report of the majority.

When the minority report has been read, it is not considered or discussed unless someone moves to substitute it for the report of the majority. If the motion substituting the minority report for that of the majority carries, the minority report becomes the report of the committee and is the only one considered. The majority report is then filed for reference.

A Committee in Action

Perhaps the whole subject of committees may be made clearer by a simple, concrete example of the way committees are created and function.

Let us suppose that the Junior Chamber of Commerce of Centerville is holding its June 14 meeting. When new business is called for, Mr. Jackson is recognized.

MR. JACKSON: "Some of us think it is time we began planning our annual Fourth of July picnic. I move that the Jaycees hold a picnic on the Fourth of July at Tilden Park for the members and their families, and that the president appoint a committee of five members with full authority to make arrangements for the picnic, that expenditures be kept within the sum of seven hundred dollars, and that the committee report at our next meeting on June 28."

PRESIDENT (after discussion and a favorable vote): "The motion is carried. Your chairman appoints Alfred Ellis as chairman of the Picnic Committee. Al, have you any suggestions as to other members of the committee to work with you?"

MR. ELLIS: "Ray Moore and Jack Turnbow were both on the committee last year, and I think their experience will be helpful."

ANOTHER MEMBER: "Mr. Chairman, I suggest Danny Brown. He's in the food business and can help with the eats."

PRESIDENT: "Thank you, Bill. The secretary will please prepare the instructions for this committee. . . ."

The next day the secretary mails the chairman of the committee a copy of the instructions:

Instructions to the Committee on Arranging the Fourth of July Picnic for the Junior Chamber of Commerce of Centerville

1. Members of Committee:

Alfred Ellis, Chairman	Daniel Brown
Ray Moore	Martin Jackson
Jack Turnbow	

2. Expenditures of the committee are limited to a total of seven hundred dollars. All bills for contracted expenditures are to be sent to the treasurer for payment, after they have been okayed by you as chairman of the Picnic Committee.

3. The committee has full power to make arrangements for all details of the picnic.

A final report on the plans is to be given at the meeting on June 28. Enclosed are reports of the picnic committees for the two preceding years, which may be helpful to your committee in working out details.

A letter from the Police Department offering the services of the well-known Centerville Happy Harmony Quartet, without charge, for the picnic, is also included.

The executive committee estimates that there will be approximately 400 persons present, including children.

(signed) JOSEPH DAVENPORT, *Secretary*

At the next meeting, when called upon for a report, Alfred Ellis, chairman of the Picnic Committee, arose and read the following:

Progress Report of the Committee Appointed for the Fourth of July Picnic, Junior Chamber of Commerce of Centerville

The committee reports as follows:

The committee met on seven different evenings at the home of the chairman. A subcommittee on special guests was appointed, consisting of Martin Jackson; another subcommittee on refreshments, consisting of Danny Brown, chairman, Jack Turnbow, and Ray Moore; and a subcommittee on entertainment, consisting of Alfred Ellis.

Every member of the picnic committee devoted considerable time to interviewing merchants and finding out costs, and to the various arrangements that we hope will make the picnic a success.

The committee reports that all arrangements have been completed for what we believe will be our most outstanding picnic.

Some form of entertainment has been provided for everybody—members, wives, and sweethearts, teen-agers, and children. The affair will begin at ten o'clock when we assemble at the speaker's platform for the salute to the flag and all join in singing "The Star Spangled Banner." After a brief greeting from our president, the day's festivities will begin.

The program subcommittee has scheduled plenty of events throughout the day to keep the young people active and the older ones happy. There will be swimming contests, diving exhibitions, a baseball game, lifesaving demonstrations, a raffle for a live pig, singing, a folk-dance festival, sack races, a watermelon-eating contest, a tug of war between fathers and sons, and for the youngsters, there will be pony rides. The program subcommittee has also made arrangements for baby sitters—three mothers of members will handle that job.

The refreshment subcommittee, under Danny Brown, will dispense the best eats we have ever had. Through the courtesy of the Acorn Grill we are able to have a feast of barbecued lamb and beef. This will be accompanied by hot dogs and rolls, plenty of potato salad, and ice cream.

This subcommittee has asked each of the wives to bake a cake, and these will be judged by the mayor and councilmen of Centerville, and prizes awarded the winners. As soon as the cakes have been judged, they will be passed out as an additional dessert. Coffee will be served with the lunch, and a beer and soft-drink stand will be open all day.

Martin Johnson of the special guests subcommittee has invited Lieutenant Governor Knight to be the honored guest at the picnic.

There will be no charge for the picnic to members of the Junior Chamber and their families, and you are all invited.

The work of our publicity chairman is evident in the Centerville *Gazette,* and a special notice will be sent to each member.

Respectfully submitted,

(signed) ALFRED ELLIS, *Chairman*

MR. ELLIS: "Mr. President, I move that the report be filed."

PRESIDENT (after a "second" and discussion): "It has been moved and seconded that the report of the picnic committee be filed. Those in favor, say 'Aye.' . . . Those opposed, 'No.' . . . The motion is carried, and the report will be filed."

MEMBER: "I move a rising vote of thanks to the picnic committee for the fine work they have done. If the picnic proves half as good as their report indicates, we'll give them a stag dinner later."

At the next regular meeting the following report was read.

Final Report of the Committee Appointed for the Fourth of July Picnic

Your committee is glad to report that our picnic on the Fourth of July was even more of a success than the committee had expected. Four hundred and eighty-two people attended, and everyone said they really enjoyed the day.

A summary of expenditures shows the following:

Food	$468.82
Telegrams	4.93
Rent on dishes and silverware	12.60
Programs	9.80
Total expenditures	$496.15

A detailed financial report, with receipts, is attached, showing all expenditures and donations.

The committee all worked hard, but special recognition should go to Jack Turnbow, who secured all of the prizes at no cost to the Chamber, and who took movies of the picnic, which he will show at our next meeting.

Respectfully submitted,

(signed) ALFRED ELLIS, *Chairman*

Recommendations

The committee for the Fourth of July picnic respectfully suggests the adoption of the following recommendations:

1. That a letter of thanks be sent to the manager of the Golden State Market for his contribution of six hundred rolls.

2. That a letter of thanks be sent to the Alvarado County Meat Dealers' Association for their very generous contribution of four beefs and eight lambs.

3. That letters of thanks be sent to the Happy Harmony Quartet, Habermann's Stables, Acorn Grill, and to the Acme Moving Company.

4. That Lieutenant Governor Paul Knight be formally thanked for his excellent talk and for the flags which he gave to the children as souvenirs.

(signed) ALFRED ELLIS, *Chairman*

MEMBER: "I move that we file this report, adopt the resolutions of the committee, and give Alfred Ellis and members of his committee a hearty vote of thanks."

PRESIDENT (after vote is taken): "The Picnic Committee will be our honored guests at the Stag Dinner to be held on August 19, when we'll see Jack Turnbow's movies of the picnic."

Practice Projects

1. Let the class hold an annual meeting of the Good Government League. Select various students as chairmen or members of the following standing committees which will present reports to the organization, covering the past year:

1. Committee on finance
2. Committee on new projects
3. Committee on membership
4. Committee on program

Select other students, in groups of threes, to present reports as special committees on the following:

1. A committee to investigate the enforcement of local laws against gambling
2. A committee to attend the November session of the town meeting and report on the events of the meeting
3. A committee to prepare a plan for raising funds to establish a circulating library for the members

All of these reports should be judged as to their form, brevity, completeness, clearness, and originality. As each report is presented to the meeting of the Good Government League, make final disposition of it.

At least one minority report should be submitted.

2. Appoint five students to conduct a model committee meeting before the class. The other students may act as observers and critics. They should take notes and be prepared, at the conclusion of the committee meeting, to offer comments on the good and bad points of the conduct of the meeting and on the participation of the members.

3. Several students could bring a committee report of some organization, board, club, or society, and read the report to the group, for study and criticism.

CHAPTER 28

MEETINGS

MEETINGS AND CONVENTIONS DEFINED

A meeting is an assemblage of the members of an organization for any length of time during which there is no separation of members except for a recess. A meeting covers the period between the time when the organization convenes and when it adjourns. An adjournment terminates a meeting, but a recess is only an interruption or an interlude in a meeting.

A convention is a group of meetings spoken of collectively or as a unit. The term "convention" or "conference" usually refers to the gathering of a group of people for a series of meetings which follow in close succession.

There is another term which has caused considerable confusion in parliamentary procedure. "Session" sometimes refers to a single meeting such as an "evening session," or it may refer to a series of meetings such as a "session of Congress." Because of this confusion in the use of the term "session," it is best to avoid its use entirely and to refer to "meetings" or "conventions" instead.

271

OPEN AND SHUT PROPOSITION

At many a meeting
This problem is posed:
The discussion is open,
The minds are closed.

KINDS OF MEETINGS

There are three kinds of meetings: regular meetings, special meetings, and adjourned meetings. Each has different requirements, rules, and regulations which govern it.

Perhaps the most important legal requirement of any type of meeting is proper notice. The courts hold that all requirements for notice of meetings, as stated in the bylaws, must be met if the meeting, whatever its kind, is to be legal.

The other important legal requirement for meetings is that a quorum must be present. The quorum of an organization is usually the same for all its meetings, regardless of the type.

Regular Meetings

Organizations usually have a fixed time and place for holding meetings, and these are stated in the bylaws or standing rules. Meetings held in compliance with these requirements are usually referred to as regular meetings.

Members are presumed to be familiar with the bylaws and standing rules, and consequently many organizations provide no specific notice for regular meetings. However, if any change is made in the established or customary or generally understood time or place of regular meetings, it is imperative that notice of that change be given to every member. Unless this is done, the proceedings of the meeting will not be legal.

A regular meeting cannot be convened unless a quorum is present, except to vote to adjourn after fixing the time for the next, or adjourned, meeting. A regular meeting follows the established order of business.

When the motion to adjourn a regular meeting is voted upon, the chairman should state explicitly whether the next meeting is a regular meeting, an adjourned meeting, a special meeting.

Special Meetings

A special meeting is a meeting which is not regularly scheduled and which is called to transact definite and specified business. The bylaws or rules of an organization should provide the method for calling special meetings. Usually there is some provision for the presiding officer or executive board to call a special meeting if he feels that it is necessary

Another customary provision is that if some of the members of an organization wish a special meeting, they may present a written request, signed by a specified number of members, and a special meeting must then be called by the presiding officer or executive board.

A special meeting does not follow the regular order of business. It is subject to the following restrictions:

1. Every member of the organization must be notified of the meeting. If it is proved that any member was omitted from the list of those notified, the transactions of the meeting are not valid.

2. The call or notice for a special meeting must state all items of business which the meeting is to consider. This statement of the items to be considered cannot be phrased in general language, such as "any other proper business" or "other business for the good of the order."

If an item of business is stated, such as a proposal "that we levy an assessment of five dollars per member to raise funds for our library," this specific proposal may be amended at the special meeting. For example, it may be amended by substituting for it the motion "that the dues be increased fifty cents a month to raise funds for our library." Notice to each member of a proposal to raise money for the new library would also be notice that the question of exactly how the money was to be raised might be discussed and that amendments might be proposed. An amendment which would change the effect of the motion radically, however, cannot be proposed. For example, an amendment "that the library be closed because of lack of sufficient funds," would not be in order.

3. When the special meeting convenes, it cannot consider any business not specified in the call for the meeting.

The list of items of business to be considered, as stated in the call, constitutes the order of business for the special meeting. A copy of the call should be inserted in the minutes of the meeting.

Adjourned Meeting

An adjourned meeting is legally a continuation of the previous regular or special meeting. The interval between the adjournment and the reconvening of the adjourned meeting is, in effect, a recess.

An adjourned meeting begins at the point where the original meeting terminated, and any business which was pending when the original meeting ended is still pending when the adjourned meeting convenes.

An organization can transact any business at an adjourned meeting which might have been transacted if there had been no adjournment. Any limitations on the organization at the original meeting remain in force for the adjourned meeting, and an adjourned special meeting can transact only such business as could have been transacted at the special meeting.

Adjourned meetings may themselves adjourn to later adjourned meetings.

No adjourned meeting may be set for a time which is later than the time of convening the next regular meeting.

When it is desirable to continue a regular or special meeting at a later time, a motion to adjourn or recess the meeting to that time makes the second meeting an adjourned meeting of the first. Frequently there is not enough time to transact all business at a regular or special meeting. It is more convenient to complete the unfinished business at an adjourned meeting than at a special meeting, because an adjourned meeting usually does not have the rigid requirements regarding notice that apply to a special meeting.

Practice Projects

1. Discuss the particular usefulness of each of the three main types of meetings.

2. In your opinion, which is the more important safeguard of an organization's actions—to observe strict standards as to notice of a meeting, or to require a high vote to pass measures? Defend your opinion.

3. Contrast the rules governing special and adjourned meetings.

4. Prepare the notice of a special meeting. Conduct the meeting according to the specifications of the notice.

CHAPTER 29

MINUTES

WHAT MINUTES CONTAIN

Minutes vary all the way from the brief, handwritten page in the minutes book of a small organization to the printed verbatim minutes of a large organization.

Minutes are a record of motions introduced, reports made, actions taken, and votes cast. Every motion and the name of its proposer should be recorded, whether it was passed or lost. It is also good practice to record the name of the seconder. No record of discussion is kept.

When a vote is taken by roll call, by ballot, or by division which is counted, the number voting on each side is recorded. When a vote is taken by roll call, the original record is inserted as a part of the minutes.

Written reports of officers and committees are not generally included in full in the minutes. They are summarized, and a page reference or file number is given which refers to the complete report. Oral reports are summarized.

Minutes should not contain personal opinions, interpretations, or comments of the secretary. It is his duty to record business transactions and not to interpret sentiments or feelings. Such phrases as "an outstanding speech," "a persuasive argument," or "a brilliant report," are out of place in the minutes.

Where gratitude or appreciation is to be expressed, it should be in the form of a vote of thanks or a resolution of appreciation.

FORM OF MINUTES

In ordinary organizations, the secretary takes notes which are sufficiently detailed, complete, and accurate so that he can prepare the minutes correctly. When the minutes have been prepared, they should be written in the official minutes book of the organization, and the record of the proceedings of each meeting should be signed by the secretary.

This record book is the property of the organization and remains in the custody of the secretary, but it is open to inspection by any member.

The minutes of organizations naturally vary greatly according to their particular needs, but there are certain forms which all organizations follow. The opening sentence or paragraph should contain the following facts:

1. Kind of meeting (regular, special, adjourned)
2. Name of organization
3. Time, place, and date when the meeting was called to order
4. Name of presiding officer

The body of the minutes is made up of a brief chronological record of the business transacted. The minutes usually close with the phrase "Respectfully submitted," followed by the signature of the secretary.

CORRECTING AND APPROVING MINUTES

The presiding officer calls upon the secretary to read the minutes at the proper point in the order of business. If a motion is proposed to postpone the reading, this may be done by a majority vote. Otherwise the secretary reads the minutes slowly and clearly, and at the conclusion of the reading, the presiding officer asks:

"Are there any corrections to the minutes?" He pauses a moment, and if no corrections are suggested, he says:

"The minutes will stand approved as read."

If an error is pointed out and the error is disputed, it is the duty of the presiding officer to determine, either by questions or by taking a vote, whether a mistake has been made in the minutes and to correct that mistake. He may say:

"Those who consider the paragraph on new members correct as read, say 'Aye.' . . . Those opposed, 'No.' " . . . Or "Those who are in favor of making the correction proposed by Mr. L. say 'Aye.' . . . Opposed, 'No.' . . ."

After the corrections have been completed, the chairman may say:

JUST A MINUTE

To takers of minutes
  I bow very humbly.
I know how they've labored,
  And shouldn't be grumbly.

But still I'm entitled,
  I think, to some glowers
At the ones who read minutes
  Not in minutes, but hours.

"If there are no further corrections, the minutes will stand approved as corrected."

Or a member may move that the minutes be approved as corrected.

Corrections are noted at the end of the minutes of each meeting. After the minutes have been approved, the secretary writes the word "approved," with the date, and signs his name.

In some large organizations, it is the practice to reproduce or print copies of the minutes shortly after the meeting, and to send copies to each member for his information and to give him an opportunity to correct any errors. When this method is followed, corrections are made at the next meeting in the same manner as though the minutes had been read at that meeting. Organizations should not make a practice of postponing or deferring the reading of the minutes. It is difficult to correct minutes a week or a month after they were prepared, and even more difficult when minutes have been postponed for several meetings.

MINUTES COMMITTEE

In order to save valuable time in meetings, an increasing number of organizations are handling their minutes in the same way that they do their financial reports. Financial reports are made up by the chairman or the treasurer and are submitted to an auditing committee which certifies their correctness. When an organization has a minutes committee, minutes are similarly reviewed.

The members of the minutes committee take notes just as does the secretary. The secretary then writes the minutes and gives them to the minutes committee, which checks, examines, and, if necessary, corrects them.

At the next meeting, instead of listening to a reading of the minutes of the previous meeting, the assembly receives a brief statement from the minutes committee that the minutes have been corrected and approved. This method saves considerable time and results in more carefully checked and more nearly correct minutes.

Practice Projects

Rewrite the following minutes in good parliamentary form, retaining the facts, and supplying the necessary data where it is missing:

YOU TAKE MINUTES, I'LL TAKE MINUETS

Minutes of previous meetings,
Greetings!

And secretaries who think I need you
And therefore read you
Without fail,
Hail!

Minutes typed and dressy
Or messy,
Hello!
But frankly, do I listen
With eyes a-glisten?
No!

(Except—and this an utter shame is—
At places where my name is.)

Minutes of Eastside Improvement Club

"A very enthusiastic monthly meeting of the Eastside Improvement Club opened the year's work. Everybody has been feeling tired of the Christmas holiday vacation and was glad to get back to work. I read the minutes as usual.

"Our president talked on the need for uniform planting of trees in the parking strips bordering Western Boulevard, and his sentiments were warmly approved by all, and it was decided by a motion to take this matter before the City Council as soon as possible.

"A very delightful and friendly letter was received from the president of the Sunnyvale Improvement Club, suggesting that we join with their club in buying wild flower seed to be sown along the highways this spring. We gave this letter to Mr. Morse because he is chairman of the Committee on Preservation of Native Shrubs and Flowers. Just then the mayor came in. Imagine our surprise!

"One of the members, Mrs. Sampson, suggested that we suspend things so that we could hear Mayor Taft talk in the middle of the meeting. Mr. Thomas agreed with her, and this motion went over by a large vote. Our chairman, Mr. Lawrence, introduced the mayor and his talk was highly inspirational. He complimented our club and he pledged himself to do all he could to carry out our plan for relandscaping the municipal rose garden.

"We all stood up and voted to thank him when he finished. I was pleased to note that even our most outspoken Republican member, Mr. Stewart, joined in the vote.

"The committee on new setback restrictions gave an excellent report, saying that the building inspector had agreed not to permit any more violations of the setback restrictions in residential districts.

"There was a long and disagreeable discussion about the motion to forbid billboards in the Park Hills area. Everybody was immensely relieved when the motion about the billboards passed. One of the members suggested that if we stopped so much talking and got down to voting immediately, things would be better, and this idea carried.

"Miss Young thought it would be a wonderful idea to buy benches for people to sit on while waiting for our buses, which operate so efficiently. Personally I have always been convinced that there was a tendency to graft among certain officials in the bus company.

"Mr. Jeffrey didn't like the idea of the benches and he felt we should put off talking about them until the next meeting, which we did.

"Mr. Levere made a motion about weed control but, much to the disappointment of some of the group, he withdrew it.

"The fifty cents a year raise in dues met with hearty approval. I have long felt such a move was desirable myself.

"The members broke up the meeting on time because they could smell the delightful fragrance of Mrs. Elwood's coffee and doughnuts coming from the kitchen."

(signed) ALFRED JAY BROWN, *Secretary*

CHAPTER 30

NOMINATIONS AND ELECTIONS

NOMINATIONS DEFINED

A nomination is the formal presentation to the assembly of the name of the candidate for the office to be filled. Nominations may be made by a member from the floor or the nominees may be named in a report by a nominating committee.

If the constitution or bylaws do not state the method of nominating officers, any member may offer a motion determining how the nominations are to be presented. This is an incidental motion.

Regardless of how nominations are made, members are not limited to voting for the candidates nominated. Except when voting by voice vote, they may vote for any person who is eligible, regardless of whether he has been nominated. Anyone who receives the required number of votes is elected. A nomination, therefore, serves only to focus attention upon certain members as nominees, and no member is barred from election by the fact that he has not been nominated.

NOMINATIONS FROM THE FLOOR

Nominations from the floor are in order as soon as the chairman calls for them. He may say:

"Nominations for the office of president are now in order."

Any member may rise and nominate another member:

"I nominate Mr. Morris for president."

A nomination does not require a second, although a second is permissible if a member wishes to express his approval of the candidate. In many organizations it is customary to preface the formal nomination by a nominating speech describing the fitness of the nominee for the office. Such speeches serve a real purpose in large organizations where nominees are frequently unknown to many of the members.

ELECTION FORMULA

To be elected, one must cry
That one is simply not the guy,
But quite unworthy, ill-prepared,
Unwell, unbalanced, plenty scared.
One must decline to run, and say
That one will run the other way
And will not serve if, unexpected,
One is, by outside chance, elected.
One must seem woeful, weak, and daft,
Then bare one's neck to feel the draft.

As each name is presented for nomination, the secretary records it. If possible, another member writes the name on a blackboard or screen which the members can see.

NOMINATIONS BY NOMINATING COMMITTEE

MR. JONES: "I nominate Mr. Davis for secretary."

MR. DAVIS: "I decline the nomination. I'm going to be away for several months this winter, and therefore I can't serve. Besides I don't know anything about writing minutes."

This exchange illustrates one reason why many organizations prefer to have candidates for office proposed by a nominating committee. The presentation of nominations by a committee has several advantages.

The first is that a nominating committee is able to make as thorough an investigation of the nominee's qualifications as the members wish. Thus a more considered choice of nominees is possible.

A second advantage is that a nominating committee can interview prospective nominees and make sure that they are willing to serve if nominated and elected. Frequently nominees will turn down a nomination from the floor because they do not have time to weigh the pros and cons of acceptance. If consulted earlier by a nominating committee, they will often be willing to accept the responsibility of office.

The third advantage is that a nominating committee can study the needs of the organization and can apportion representation among different groups equitably. Various groups or opinions of the organization are entitled to representation in the list of nominees. Nominations from the floor seldom permit time to consider this proportional problem.

A fourth advantage is that a nominating committee can prepare a list of officers who can work harmoniously with each other. It is usually good practice, for example, for a nominating committee, after agreeing upon a candidate for president, to consult with him regarding his choice for secretary.

There are several methods of choosing a nominating committee. There is a persistent belief that a nominating committee is not "democratic," and that all nominations should be made from the floor. Actually a nominating committee is a thoroughly democratic way of selecting candidates, provided it is chosen by a democratic method.

If an organization permits the president or board of directors to appoint a nominating committee, it will not be democratic, because it will have been chosen undemocratically and will probably not be representative of all the members. Such a method of selecting a committee frequently results in self-perpetuation in office of the president, or board of directors, or of a faction which they represent.

A nominating committee should usually be elected by the members of the organization by means of a nominating ballot or by nominations from the floor. The president should have no part in the selection of a nominating committee; nor should he be an ex-officio member of the committee or attend committee meetings.

REPORT OF NOMINATING COMMITTEE

Some organizations believe that officers and members of the organization should be permitted to offer suggestions freely to members of the nominating committee. Others believe that the members of the nominating committee should be left completely alone to follow their own judgment.

Some organizations insist that the name of more than one nominee be presented for each office. Others believe it is unnecessary to present more than one nominee for each office, because additional nominees can always be added from the floor at the time the nominating committee's report is presented. There is nothing particularly "democratic" about putting up the names of nominees only to have them rejected. Such procedure often hurts people needlessly. It would seem sensible for a nominating committee to pick the best candidate for each office and not to pad the report with additional names.

There is a common misconception that a member of a nominating committee may not be nominated for office by the committee. Of course, it is possible for the committee to nominate its own members for office. If this were not true, election to the nominating committee would be equivalent to disbarment as a candidate for election. Nevertheless, it is unethical for a nominating committee to present the names of any considerable proportion of its members as candidates. If the committee submits a list of nominees which includes several of its members, competing nominees should certainly be presented from the floor.

The final report of a nominating committee must be formally voted upon at a meeting of the committee and signed by all the members of the committee who agree with it. A minority report may be presented.

The report of the nominating committee is usually made at a meeting previous to the date of the election. Another procedure is to mail a printed report to each member in time for consideration before the election.

When the report of the nominating committee is called for, it is read by the chairman of the committee and is handed to the recording secretary. The committee's report is treated as though the nominations in it had been made from the floor. The presiding officer reads the title of the first office and the name of the nominee presented by the committee for that office, and asks, "Are there any further nominations?" He then reads, in turn, the titles of the other offices and the names of the other nominees presented by the committee and, in each instance, asks if there are any further nominations. He waits a reasonable time to see whether there are nominations from the floor.

CLOSING NOMINATIONS

When all nominations have been presented, a motion is sometimes made "to close nominations." Such a motion is superfluous. The vote may be taken whenever there are no further nominations. Any person receiving the required vote will be elected.

A motion to close nominations cannot be proposed until a reasonable time has been given for the presentation of additional names. Nominations may be reopened by a motion to that effect.

In elections by ballot, members may, in effect, nominate any person they choose by writing the name on the ballot.

VOTING ON CANDIDATES

When there are no further nominations, the assembly proceeds to vote upon the names of candidates by the method laid down in the constitution or bylaws. If no method is provided, any member may propose a motion determining the method of voting.

Irregularities which could not affect the result in an election do not invalidate the election, but any substantial violation of the rules does invalidate an election.

When the voting is done by voice vote or by rising, a vote may be taken on each office as soon as the candidates for that particular office have been nominated; or it may be delayed until nominations for all offices have been made. When the election is by ballot, nominations for all offices are completed before the balloting, so that only one ballot is necessary.

The report of the nominating committee is not voted upon as a whole, unless there is only one nominee for each office and no nominations from the floor, and unless this method of voting upon the report is authorized in the bylaws.

VOTE NECESSARY TO ELECT

Usually the vote necessary to elect a member to office is provided in the constitution or bylaws. A majority vote is required to elect any officer, unless there is a special provision in the bylaws for election by plurality or some other vote.

If the bylaws require a vote by ballot, the rather common belief that a motion authorizing the secretary "to cast a ballot" meets this requirement is not true. The so-called "casting of a vote" by proxy through the secretary is not legal, unless there is special provision for it in the bylaws. Ballot voting is provided to ensure secrecy, and, since no one can oppose the casting of a vote by the secretary without revealing his opinion, this requirement of secrecy is violated by such a motion.

Some organizations require that when no candidate receives a majority vote, the next vote is taken only on the two candidates who received the highest vote. Other organizations provide that the candidate with the lowest vote be dropped as each successive ballot is taken. Some organizations provide for proportional voting.

MOTION TO MAKE A VOTE UNANIMOUS

A vote cannot be made unanimous by passing a motion to that effect. A unanimous vote means all of the legal votes cast. The motion to make a vote unanimous has no legal effect and does not change the legal vote in any particular unless the motion itself receives a unanimous vote.

INSTALLATION OF OFFICERS

An election becomes effective immediately, if the candidate is present and does not decline, or if he is absent and has already consented to his candidacy. If he is absent, and has not consented to his nomination, his election becomes effective as soon as he is notified, unless he declines immediately.

Unless some other time is specified in the bylaws, an officer assumes his office as soon as he has been declared elected. Frequently bylaws provide for the installation of officers at a later meeting.

Unless the bylaws contain specific methods for conducting installations, members may follow any plan that seems suitable. Installation of officers, however, cannot be delayed beyond the date of election, without specific authorization from the bylaws.

FILLING VACANCIES

The regular time for holding elections of officers is determined in the constitution or bylaws. Elections to fill vacancies or to elect delegates or committees may be held at any regular or special meeting, unless the bylaws provide differently. A vacancy in an office should be filled as soon as possible.

Practice Projects

1. Elect a nominating committee to prepare a report. Vote on these nominations and any others that may be made from the floor.

2. Discuss the advantages and disadvantages of nomination by committee.

3. Elect delegates to a national convention from the floor, and choose several students to make nominating speeches.

CHAPTER 31

CONFERENCES

WHAT IS A CONFERENCE?

"You say we ought to hold a conference. What do you mean when you say 'conference,' anyhow?" queried Austin Phillips of the little knot of people who lingered on the steps of the Alumni building.

Elsa Metcalf answered promptly, "Well, to me it means about forty people getting together to listen to someone talk and then to ask questions, the way we do at the League of Women Voters. It's really just a meeting."

"That's not my idea of it," put in Bill Warner. "I think of a conference as a big affair—like the Congregational Conference of about 5,000 people, or the Youth Conference. It's more of a convention, I'd say."

"You'd be surprised at *my* idea of a conference," chuckled Joe Johnson. "It's small. I have a conference with myself lots of mornings when I'm shaving. Talk right back to myself in the mirror and settle a lot of things."

"I think you're all wrong," said Edith Frisbee. "To me a conference is just another name for a committee meeting. You know, maybe five to fifteen people."

The term conference means different things to different people. The most usual conception of the term, however, is a face-to-face meeting of a relatively small group of people who come together to explore a problem and to work out a solution. In fact, a conference often is a committee meeting.

A conference has a distinctive purpose—it seeks to solve a problem. On the other hand, if a group of people meet to listen to a lecture, that group is not a conference.

A conference operates through free discussion. A meeting where someone makes a speech and other persons ask questions is, therefore, not a conference.

SHAPE OF THINGS TO COME

Round-table discussions are sound,
  Round-table discussions are fair,
So long as the table is round
  And the people around it are square.

If the Cadillac salesmen of New Jersey meet to hear the sales manager describe the next year's model, they are not holding a conference but a sales meeting. If, however, the same salesmen meet to discuss the problem of "overcoming sales resistance," and each salesman contributes his own experiences and ideas in the hope of reaching some solution, that is a sales conference.

A conference, then, is a group of people meeting together to solve a problem by free discussion. An old saying gives us this definition: "A conference is a meeting of representatives who sit until they settle."

SPIRIT OF A CONFERENCE

Though people may disagree on the size of a conference, they usually agree on the spirit or atmosphere which is necessary for a good conference. This spirit pervades and dominates a conference and is probably more important than the exact techniques of its operation. It is an atmosphere of warm and friendly cooperation.

The basic idea underlying all conferences is that many minds working voluntarily and cooperatively can achieve far more than the same individual minds working separately. Implicit in this conviction are certain indispensable elements.

The first element is a faith in the ability of individuals to contribute to a common solution. Thus the opinion of every individual in the group must be sought, welcomed, and considered.

Another element is a belief in the process of free discussion. Each individual has equal rights to discuss and to ask questions, to hear and to be heard.

A third element is an open-mindedness on the part of the members, a willingness to try to reach agreement on a solution—even to the extent of honest compromise. A member who goes to a conference with one fixed idea in mind, who is deaf to the ideas of every other member, who will not listen to fact or weigh argument, who will not concede any detail in order to reach a group solution—such a member lacks this necessary element.

People will express their ideas freely if they are treated with courtesy, dignity, and encouragement, and if the spirit of the group is friendly and warm. Members wither and "clam up" under a sarcastic barb, a bored yawn, or an air of superiority. On the other hand, the gates of their minds swing open, unlocked by cordial understanding and appreciation, and they are impelled to speak.

PREPARATION FOR A CONFERENCE

Many conferences fail because the members are expected to start from scratch and to handle problems they have not had time to consider. Adequate preparation is the first step toward ensuring a good conference.

Choosing the members who are to attend the conference requires thought and judgment. The membership should represent differing interests and opinions. A representative membership will lend weight to the decision of the group. Members will abide by the solutions if they feel that their point of view was represented in making the decision.

A conference is more likely to be successful if the members have had an opportunity to think over the problems and come to the conference with some formulated ideas. Information furnished to the members in advance, concerning the problem to be discussed, will be of help. The participants should be given a precise definition of what the powers of the conference are, what it is expected to do, and what the range of its authority is.

When the members come together, they should first of all be made acquainted with each other, if they are strangers, for acquaintance fosters a desire to agree. It is also helpful if each member is informed concerning the experience and background of the other members.

Either the leader or a committee should prepare a preliminary statement of the problem to be solved by the conference and assemble any material which will help the group in deciding the problem.

These preparatory steps help to get a conference off to a good start.

PRINCIPLES OF CONFERENCE DISCUSSION

In any group seeking to reach an agreement—a meeting of minds—certain principles of discussion should be observed.

1. The subject under discussion needs to be kept clearly before the group, to prevent digression and consequent confusion.

2. At any given time, consideration should be confined, chiefly, to the particular point under discussion. The relationship of this point to the whole problem may be discussed, but the main consideration should be given to the immediate point.

3. Questions should be taken up in a logical sequence, to avoid wasting time on matters not necessary to the decisions to be made.

4. An equality of opportunity to participate in discussion should be maintained. No one should be permitted to monopolize discussion. Everyone should be encouraged to contribute.

5. Each factor of the problem should be taken up and considered in the light of the whole problem.

6. When an analysis of the problem is completed, the conclusion should be stated and its accuracy tested.

7. The final decision of the conference should be clearly stated—first to determine whether there is actual agreement, and second to place it on record.

THE CONFERENCE LEADER

To be successful, a conference leader needs varied qualities. He needs a deep-seated belief in the ability of a group of individuals to reach a constructive solution. If he has this belief, he will do everything possible to stimulate and encourage members to express their own opinions. If the leader, within himself, doubts the ability of the group to work out a solution, and instead seeks to steer them toward his solution, the purpose of the conference will not be accomplished.

He also needs a fundamental respect for individuals and their opinions—a love of people, which is reflected in the tones of his voice, his responses, and his attitudes.

A conference leader should be an artist in handling human relations. His chief concern, after all, is how to guide the members so that they will work together effectively and happily.

Ordway Tead explains that the good leader seeks a power *with* people and not a power *over* people. He is a mobilizer of the best efforts, ideas, and judgments of the individuals and an expert in bringing them to bear upon the problem under consideration. His is the task of summoning, focusing, and releasing the ideas and desires of the persons who make up the group. He is a catalyst and not a driver.

A good leader needs sincerity, imagination, patience, understanding, self-confidence, modesty, tact. He should also be able to understand the point of view, feelings, and attitudes of others, to stimulate members to offer suggestions; to clarify and restate ideas; and to unify divergent opinions.

LEADING COOPERATIVE THINKING

During the conference, the leader should be alert to the need for co-ordinating and advancing cooperative thinking. Some members are slow to think, others jump too rapidly to conclusions. Some allow their ideas to wander, others want to plunge ahead before points are settled. Some become confused, others are too direct. Some are shy and hesitate to tell what they know, others want to talk all the time. If the group is to think as a team, the leader must be able to unify all these divergent tendencies.

It is his responsibility to open discussion and to get members started talking. Likewise he is the one who closes the discussion and summarizes it.

During the discussion he should be ready to serve and assist the group in many ways. If speakers stray from the subject, he must guide them back to it by gentle and courteous reminders. He may curb meandering discussion by a question. He may summarize the discussion frequently, to let the members see where they are on the road to their goal. He may point out areas or ideas where there is substantial agreement and lead discussion on to unsettled points. He may restate differences and try to open doors for compromise or agreement. He may correct misunderstanding of terms or ideas that are blocking progress. He may set up standards for use in measuring ideas. He may suggest brief pauses for rest or to relax tension. All of these aids are tools of the leader and often of the members, for guiding cooperative thinking.

ATTITUDE OF CONFERENCE MEMBERS

We are sometimes told that a member of a conference should go prepared to see how many of his own ideas he can give up in order to agree with others. This advice may suit Mr. Milquetoast, but it is not an attitude which is likely to contribute to constructive solutions.

The phrase "an open and seeking mind" more nearly expresses the desirable attitude for a conference member.

Many people go to conferences holding firm convictions. There is no reason why one cannot have both firm convictions and an open mind. Sometimes one's convictions are strengthened during the conference. Sometimes one person holding a strong conviction will in the end find the other members in agreement with him.

Over a period of years, Chief Justice Holmes of the Supreme Court of the United States was frequently the lone dissenter. His dissent was based on a few fundamental principles. However, toward the end of his years of service, the Court swung toward his beliefs, and in that later period history shows a majority of the justices in substantial agreement with the opinion of the "Great Dissenter."

A firm conviction and a closed mind, however, make a conference member virtually useless.

Experience has shown that many conferences result in honest compromise. Such compromises represent the best thought and effort of the whole group and are arrived at through an attitude of listening and learning. There is considerable difference between yielding on a principle and yielding on a detail. Most good conferences arrive at a conclusion which is a composite of the ideas of many members. Each member offers a small contribution which is fitted into the whole plan and cemented together like a mosaic by the wisdom of the whole group. Such conferences end with satisfied members. They go away feeling that the solution is satisfactory and the problem clarified. "It is not just what I had hoped for," they say, "but it is good. We got someplace."

STATING THE PROBLEM

Before we find the answer, we must know the problems. If a problem is clearly presented to the group, there is a good chance of finding a satisfactory solution.

The members of a conference should begin their deliberations by agreeing upon an accurate and appropriate statement of the problem to be solved. The person in charge of the conference may present the problem himself or he may arrange for its presentation by another member or by a committee. The presentation of a problem for solution usually involves most of the following points:

   a. What is the nature of the problem?
   b. How did it arise?
   c. What is its scope?
   d. How does it relate to other factors?
   e. What is the exact point requiring solution?
   f. What are the factors and forces underlying it?

In stating the problem, members are sometimes startled to find that the solution becomes evident. This means that the true nature of the problem had not been fully comprehended before.

CLARIFYING IDEAS INVOLVED

Once the problem has been clearly stated, the next important step is to be sure that each member of the group understands it. Otherwise he cannot aid in its solution. Each member should feel entirely free to question the statement of the problem and every pertinent fact relating to it.

Usually the terms used in stating the problem need clarification, to be sure that there is agreement upon them. If the World Affairs Council has set a conference to consider the problem of "socialistic trends in democratic countries," several questions must be settled. Just what is meant by "socialistic"? Does the term refer to political beliefs or to economic practices? Just what is a "trend"? Does it include a few unconnected events or is it limited to a long-term policy? And which countries should be listed as "democratic countries"? All these and other questions must be clarified and defined before progress can be made in seeking a solution.

STATING GROUP OBJECTIVES

With the problem clearly drawn and the meaning of its terms and ideas clarified, the group may turn to stating its objectives. What is its immediate goal? What is its future goal? What are its motives and desires? To what end is it working? Sometimes these answers are so clear as to be self-evident.

Just as frequently, the answers are vague because the individuals of the group have not analyzed the objectives, are not openly revealing their motives, or are themselves confused as to where they want to go.

The Oakdale City Council, let us say, has called a conference to consider the problem of garbage disposal. Some members believe that garbage disposal should be a private enterprise and not a city project. Their approach is governed by their goal of maintaining the status quo in private enterprise. Other members are convinced that garbage disposal is primarily a health problem, and their thinking is centered upon civic health. Still others hold that garbage disposal is a matter of city revenue, and their reasoning concerns a goal of adequate charges for garbage collection, revenue from the sale of some of it to hog farms, and converting the remainder into salable fertilizer.

These divergent goals and motives must be clarified, and a primary goal selected, if the conference is to accomplish anything constructive. Each must be examined and then either eliminated or fused into the agreed-upon goal.

STATING SOLUTIONS

With the problems and the goals of the group clearly before them, the members are in a position to seek the best possible solution. First, list all the solutions which appear reasonable. Don't overlook those which have already been tried. They are probably the most logical and may have failed only because they were not properly applied.

What new solutions can be added? Do not shy away from unorthodox solutions. Sometimes the future proves them to be the best ones. If all solutions can be listed where they can be seen, it will help the members of the group to keep them in mind.

While these solutions are being listed, the leader should be careful that members do not start to appraise and evaluate them. This work is to be done later. The purpose of this period of the conference is merely to collect all the possibilities which are worth discussion, and it does not matter at this point whether some members of the group approve or disapprove of the suggestions offered.

ANALYSIS AND EVALUATION OF SOLUTIONS

With all the potential solutions to the problem listed, the group is ready to analyze and evaluate each solution and to eliminate the undesirable. In this process all the steps taken so far serve a purpose. The goals which the group have set up provide a standard of measurement against which each solution can be checked.

The reasoning and analytical ability of the members come into play particularly during this portion of the conference. Each solution can be taken up in turn, studied, questioned, and, if found unworthy, eliminated.

A preliminary analysis of the suggested solutions will usually enable the group to eliminate at once those which give no promise of usefulness.

When the proposals have been narrowed to two or three, then concentrate on these and question every detail about them. Study their relationship to the whole problem. Consider their probable result. Will any of them actually solve the problem? Test each solution against all known facts. Test them as to anticipated results. Test them against experience.

Effective group thinking is a trial-and-error method of testing the proposed solution against the facts. In certain instances an actual test of the proposal can be made—a kind of "trial run." In some instances a full-scale trial may be feasible.

STATING THE FINAL SOLUTION AND PLANNING ACTION

Before the work of a conference is completed, the results should usually be put into the form of a statement. This is necessary in order to be certain that it is an agreed-upon solution. It is good procedure, in most instances, to put this statement of the results of the deliberation into final form before a last recheck on the solution is made.

If the group cannot agree quickly to the statement of the solution, there probably has not been full agreement on the problem and its solution.

Now that the best plan has been selected, can it be improved? Have any of the other proposals some elements which will improve the solution accepted as best? Often the better parts of several solutions that have been offered will make up the solution finally accepted.

When the best solution has been agreed upon, it should be applied to the problem it is intended to solve, and as far as possible its result should be rechecked.

If the conference group has the right or duty of planning action to be taken on the solution to the problem, the plan for action can be added to the statement of the solution.

When the group is a committee, acting on assignment from the parent body, the statement of the solution and the recommendations for action become an important part of the committee report. Any proposed solution should be presented as a motion or resolution.

CONSERVING CONFERENCE TIME

Too frequently the word "conference" is thought of synonymously with "gab fest." It is painful to see the time of capable and high-salaried men and women wasted at conferences because such meetings are improperly run. People shy away from conferences that waste their time, but get great personal satisfaction from those that are well run and effective.

Most conferences are too long. There is no reason why they should not be compact, with every minute put to good use.

The first way to make a conference effective is to plan it carefully. The more thorough the planning, the more productive the results will be. If the group is a large one, much of the preconference planning can be done by one or more committees that submit reports as a basis for discussion. If the group is small, the chairman or some member can take over this study and planning. Without planning, a conference can be as ridiculous and as unproductive as the following notes show this one to have been.

Conference Notes

Chairman Miller presented need for raising funds for a new headquarters.

Mr. Kestler and Mr. Frederickson argued as to how the problem should be discussed. Mr. Kestler wanted everybody limited to one speech.

Mrs. Brown took thirty-five minutes to describe a new type of conference she had read about. It sounded unique but was too complicated for most of the members to understand.

Mr. Mills made a sarcastic remark about how women's groups train their members to talk too much. Chairman Miller told a joke to try to restore harmony.

Mrs. Edmonds pointed out that, "We've got to do *something* about raising funds."

Mr. Grant asked the group whether they had thought about possible profits from renting the proposed headquarters to other organizations. This started a long argument about the difficulties of other organizations in town.

Mr. Donald objected to a reference made to the mayor's campaign fund. Mr. McCrea tried to defend the mayor.

Several of the members had to leave.

The meeting adjourned to meet one week later.

Another method of saving time at conferences is to fix a definite hour for closing. The experience of many groups shows that, after about an hour of concentrated thought, most members become fatigued and their attention wanders. If it is necessary for the conference to continue for longer than an hour, it is wise to have a brief recess before going on.

One way to make conferences progress is to move along rapidly at points where general agreement is evident, it being necessary only to be sure that there is agreement. Ideas and facts about which everyone has the same opinion need not be discussed. A nod of approval is as effective as a detailed explanation. "O.K." or "I agree" says as much as a speech.

Similarly, when there is agreement before the conference on the problem to be solved and on the probable best solution, it is foolish for a conference that is considering difficult problems to waste time going through any of the initial steps outlined.

The techniques for conducting any conference must be completely flexible. They are intended only as a pattern for the meeting and not as fixed and irremovable hurdles to be overcome. Use those which are needed and discard those which seem unnecessary in the particular instance.

The leader has the chief responsibility for conserving conference time. He may summarize points of view and move on promptly to another issue. He may courteously request speakers to keep on the subject. He may discourage members who monopolize the discussion, and he may ask questions to shorten explanations. He may remind members of time limitations. Important as it is for everyone in a conference to play his part, it is the leader who sets the pace of group thinking.

In conferences, by the light of many minds, we see and solve our problems.

Practice Projects

1. Divide the group into small subgroups of four or five members. Let each subgroup choose a problem of genuine interest to its members. At convenient times, meet as a conference and submit a written report to the whole group.

2. Choose one small group to conduct a conference before the whole class. Members of the class may act as observers. Give each observer an opportunity to comment later on his evaluation of the conference.

3. Give a report on some conference leader whom you have observed. In your report, include comments on the leader's ability and techniques.

CHAPTER 32

CONVENTIONS

THE NATURE OF CONVENTIONS

The impulse that leads men and women to band together and converge on an agreed meeting place, for the furtherance of a common cause, is too deep to be new. When Chaucer, writing of that long ago "Aprille with his shoures sote" reminded that then "longen folk to goon on pilgrimages," he was, in effect, telling us of a fourteenth-century convention.

Since Chaucer's time, the urge to congregate for a common cause has strengthened. Woven permanently and prominently into the pattern of this nation's social and economic life is that characteristically American institution, the convention. Each year in the United States more than ten million people set forth on migrations to attend conventions of their choice. Who goes to conventions? What are the purposes of conventions? What do they accomplish?

Everybody goes to conventions. At nine, little Mary packs her T-shirts and shorts and sets off with the Brownies. Meanwhile her big sister is attending the National Conference of Student Councils. Mother plans to take in the State Convention of the PTA, and Dad is going to the convention of the Elks and, soon afterwards, to the International Association of Machinists. Grandfather has just come back from the biggest convention of them all, the annual gathering of the American Medical Association.

Conventions are not just meetings on a grand scale. There are important differences. Meetings are attended by members—conventions by representatives of members. Meetings transact local business, while conventions deal largely with matters on the regional, national, or international level. Meetings are composed of people who know each other because they meet at frequent intervals. Conventions assemble delegates, representing widely distributed groups of members, who rarely meet oftener than annually.

303

CONVENTIONAL REMARKS

One thing we shouldn't fail to mention,
For good or bad, is the convention,
Where men (the ones without their wives)
Lead dangerous, exciting lives,
And women, leaving dusty houses,
Have fun, with or without their spouses,
Where chairmen rap and rap repeatedly
And call for order rather heatedly,
Where suddenly the new loudspeaker
Goes off, or anyhow grows weaker,
Where many people get acquainted
And someone in the back has fainted,
Where motions and emotions blend
And it is midnight at the end.*

* Convention experts (to whom, greetings)
Have lately jet-propelled such meetings.

CONVENTION BONDS VARY

Conventions vary widely in the strength and homogeneity of the bonds which unite their members. Some organizations, such as trade and professional groups, are built around a field of common competence as their group interest. Examples of closely knit groups are The American Institute of Physics, The American Bee Keeping Federation, The American Book Publisher's Council, Inc., and the Patent, Trademark, and Copyright Law Section of the American Bar Association. Such groups have cohesion and solidarity because the major interests of their members are identical, and because these interests represent the lifework, or skills, or vital concerns of every member.

Thus, if you are an orthopedic surgeon, your interest centers instinctively in The American Academy of Orthopedic Surgeons. It is the group which largely determines the standards of orthopedic surgery, disseminates knowledge of new techniques and progress, educates the public about the problems of your field of surgery—and its members think and talk your language.

Many organizations are more loosely knit, because their interests are more widespread. The American Legion, for example, is composed of men who have shared a common, though often widely differing, experience. The Federation of Women's Clubs is made up of members who belong to various types of women's clubs which have joined the Federation. The Elks are associated primarily for fellowship and charity but represent otherwise divergent interests. Yet these groups have a solidarity and a loyalty which create strong bonds. They achieve miracles, and their conventions are of world-wide interest and their resolutions front-page news.

CHARACTERISTICS OF CONVENTIONS

Conventions are characterized by certain psychological group traits. Many of them are massive and unwieldy and cannot be expected to operate as quickly and effectively as a small group such as a committee. They are swayed by sentiment and oratory. They yield to sudden impulses. They dart in the most unexpected directions. They can become almost intoxicated with enthusiasm, and they can rise to the heights of idealism.

Despite their handicap of numbers and their unpredictability, conventions are the mass mind in orderly action as distinguished from the senseless violence of the mob.

Usually conventions are packed with action and emotion. They generally have too little time and too much business. Their members are torn by conflicting problems and interests: the local problems of the community which the delegate represents; the general problems of the whole organization; the social events which are an important and valuable element of every convention; the competing sections or attractions which are scheduled at the same hour; and the sightseeing and shopping which always accompany convention attendance.

Delegates move in a swiftly shifting kaleidoscope of cooperative experience and accomplishment. It is imperative that conventions be planned so that they progress rapidly, effectively, and surely toward maximum achievement.

CONVENTIONS ARE BIG BUSINESS

Conventions have changed unbelievably since the turn of the century. They have developed from inadequately financed meetings, which were a burden upon the local members, into self-supporting institutions.

In 1912, Mr. John Smith, Chairman of the Board of Deacons of the First Methodist Church of Kansas City, attended the Methodist General Conference in Minneapolis. He was met at the railroad station by several of the local church members, who served as a hospitality committee. He drove in a carriage to the home of the superintendent of the Sunday School. Here he shared the spare room with another delegate from Dallas, Texas. His hostess got up every morning at six to prepare his breakfast. Then she hurried through her housework so that she could help the Ladies' Aid cook the delegates' luncheon and dinner in the church basement. Mr. Smith paid his own expenses.

In 1952, Mr. John Smith, Jr., was a delegate to the Methodist General Conference in San Francisco. At the airport he took a taxi to a good hotel. The clerk greeted him and gave him the key to his room, which had been reserved for him several weeks earlier by the Convention Bureau. On the desk in his room he found mail, invitations, convention material, and flowers awaiting him. The hotel was within walking distance of the convention hall, and many of the section meetings were held in the hotel itself.

Mr. Smith, Jr., enjoyed an expertly planned program, enabling him to make the most of his time. The business sessions were well spaced and compact, entertainment included excellent meals and banquets where he was able to talk business and to enjoy himself at the same time, discussion sections were informal and stimulated him to take part, and the sightseeing and shopping tours gave him a comprehensive idea of the San Francisco Bay region. His expenses were paid by the organization he represented as an official delegate.

An hour after the convention adjourned, Mr. Smith settled himself in his seat and waited for the plane to take off. He was a little tired as he reflected happily on the effective business sessions, the problems solved and the work accomplished, the good times, the old friends he had seen, and the new friendships he had made. As the plane gained altitude, he took a regretful and affectionate look at the community he had learned to know—at the two bridges spanning the San Francisco Bay, the red sunset just beyond the Golden Gate, and the millions of lights twinkling from the surrounding hills. Then he pulled out his notebook and started to jot down some of the inspiration he had absorbed during the convention, to pass on to the folks at home.

In the span of a single lifetime, conventions have become big business. They have become self-supporting institutions. *Every year, in the United States, more than ten million people spend more than two billion dollars on twenty thousand conventions,* at the state, national, and international level.

THE CONVENTION BUREAUS

Almost all the large cities of Canada and the United States have a convention bureau with a staff of experts.

These executives have a triple task: they educate the businessmen of the community in the advantages and profits to be gained from conventions and thus raise the funds for the operation of the bureau; they sell the advantages of their particular locality to organizations which plan to hold conventions; and most important of all, they offer sound, experienced, and expert help to every convention that seeks it.

Each bureau is a nonprofit organization, each has its own budget, and each is an independent unit. Each bureau represents the businessmen of the community and is supported by them.

These local bureaus are all united by membership in the International

Association of Convention Bureaus. This organization exists principally to promote exchange of convention data and general convention information which will be valuable either to the bureau members or to conventions. The announced purpose of the Association is to foster the best practices of civic salesmanship, within the bounds of competitive possibility, and to encourage sound convention practices among organizations.

In recent years another organization to promote better conventions has been formed—the American Convention Institute, Inc. It is primarily a research and educational organization. Its membership includes all those executives whose businesses are involved in conventions—the heads of the convention bureaus, hotel managers, auditorium managers, and the presidents of railroads, bus companies, and airlines. The Institute has numerous sections, which meet annually in convention to study how conventions can be made more effective. Here we have a convention of convention experts.

The convention bureaus correlate the interests of conventions and communities. When conventions are successful, the community as well as the organizations benefit. The bureau employees are impresarios whose behind-the-scenes directions make the conventions run smoothly and on schedule. They give attention to all the multitudinous variety of details which require the advice and management of experts.

The convention bureau is of particular help in handling the three most important problems of a convention, which are the time and location of the convention, its financing, and its management.

The help which different bureaus can give varies, since they are limited by their individual budgets. But if the national representatives of the organization planning the convention call upon the local manager, they will receive all the help the bureau can give. Each manager understands the resources of his bureau, is familiar with climatic conditions and the convention resources of his community, and knows the services provided by individual hotels and agencies.

The bureau manager and his staff will provide competent assistance on most matters pertinent to conventions—budgeting, costs, auditorium and general hotel arrangements, registration, promotion of attendance, publicity, radio, entertainment possibilities, local speakers, exhibit arrangements and services, and contacts with city officials and other leaders.

The bureau is a friendly agency ready to supply information and advice on the convention resources of the city; through it the organization can clear most of the detailed arrangements. The bureaus assist with registration, publicity, and the promotion of convention attendance. They furnish pictures and cuts of local points of interest, and suitable stories and copy for trade publications and membership journals. They facilitate promotion through the mail, press, and radio. They usually assume responsibility for housing the delegates and cooperate in planning both the budget and the registration fees. The bureau's advice is free. Many of its services are performed without charge.

TIMING AND LOCATIONS OF CONVENTIONS

The date and meeting place of a convention are of paramount importance to the organization concerned. The convention bureaus, in spite of their rivalry in securing the more important conventions, realize that the choice of a wrong location, or the choice of an inadequately equipped city or an unsuitable time of the year for the particular locality, can ruin a convention. Cooperation between the bureaus is stronger than their rivalry.

If a convention is held in San Francisco, the merchants and hotels in San Diego, Los Angeles, Portland, and Seattle will all share the profits. Delegates usually plan stopovers and visit cities en route. Consequently, the rivalry to secure a convention is tempered by this knowledge, as well as by the fact that no convention going to a city that cannot suitably care for it will be successful.

Too often decisions on a time and place are made on the floor of a convention as a final item of business. The delegates are likely to be worn out, the rules of procedure for agreeing on a meeting place are often poorly defined, and the decision made on the basis of politics or sentiment. The sensible method of selecting a time and place for a convention is to give this responsibility to the board of directors or the executive committee of the organization. If desirable, the decision of the board may be checked by a vote of the convention.

If the decision on the time and place of future convention is left to the executive committee, representatives of the inviting cities can be interviewed and questioned, pertinent data can be checked, agreements can be confirmed, and the cities under consideration can sometimes be visited and inspected.

Larger organizations frequently decide the time and place of a convention as much as five years in advance. This ensures them priority over other organizations in the city selected, and allows time for careful planning. Few cities can accommodate more than one large convention at a time. It is therefore important that the time and place chosen for the future convention fit into the national schedule of conventions.

FINANCING A CONVENTION

All convention expenditures fall into two general classifications: those that are inherently essential and those that are optional.

The *essential* expenses of staging a convention are those expenses which are absolutely necessary if the convention is to be held. These include the cost of presenting the program, compensation of speakers, special equipment and services, expenses of the staff, transportation of records to the convention city, printing of promotion forms, programs, notices of the convention and of the convention proceedings, as well as the cost of noncommercial exhibits and similar expenses which are essential to the convention. The essential expenses of a convention should be paid for by the whole organization, either from its treasury or from a per capita tax on every member, whether or not he attends the convention.

Optional expenses include convention entertainment and other expenses not altogether essential, although usually desirable. Few organizations can afford to finance all the optional expenses. Such expense should be prorated among the delegates in attendance. This is usually done by means of a registration fee, payable at the time of registration, which entitles the delegate to participate in all the events of the convention and to receive a badge, program, and other convention material. Authority to assess such a fee should be included in the bylaws of the organization. Some organizations vary the amount of the registration fee according to the amount of entertainment which the delegate wishes to purchase. This plan, or the sale of separate tickets for each event, leaves the entertainment committee uncertain as to how much money it will have available to spend.

The registration fee should be computed carefully and its intended use explained to the members. Above all else it should be adequate.

The simplest procedure for deciding on a registration fee is to estimate the total amount needed, make a liberal allowance for contingencies, and divide it by the expected attendance, estimated on a conservative basis. It is well to set the fee at an amount which can remain the same for several years. The delegates can then anticipate this fee as a normal expense.

The plan of adequate self-financing, which spreads the essential convention costs over the entire membership equally, and divides the optional expense equally among those who attend the convention, is a satisfactory arrangement. The convention bureaus estimate that twenty thousand members of a national organization can carry the essential expense of a convention at a per capita cost of one dollar. The two thousand of those twenty thousand members who attend the convention can carry the optional entertainment expense at a per capita cost of a ten-dollar registration fee.

When a convention is on a completely self-financing basis, an organization is independent in selecting its location and in planning the convention, and is welcome wherever it goes.

MINUTES OF CONVENTIONS

There are three ways in which proceedings of conventions are usually recorded:

1. Verbatim reports by a reporter
2. Minutes prepared and approved by the secretary or a minutes committee
3. Abstract of minutes prepared for publication

The reporter keeps a record of everything that is said. The secretary keeps a complete record of every action taken. This record of the convention proceedings, prepared by the secretary and approved by the organization, constitutes the official minutes of the convention. The abstract of the minutes is a résumé of important actions taken, and is intended for publication as a report for those members who did not attend, or as a basis for publicity.

SEATING OF DELEGATES

No person should be admitted to any meeting of a convention without presenting his credential card. Confusion is avoided if carefully drawn and rigidly enforced rules for the seating of delegates, alternates, observers, visitors, and others, are strictly adhered to. In taking votes and recognizing speakers, it is important that the presiding officer be able to tell which persons are the accredited delegates, by the location in which they are seated. Alternates should not be seated with delegates unless the delegate whom the alternate represents is absent. Visitors, members who are not delegates, and observers should all be assigned separate seating locations.

Many conventions, although efficient in most respects, are lax in restricting voting to persons who are entitled to vote. One student of conventions, as an experiment, found that he was able to walk unchallenged into the national conventions of many organizations. Although he was not a member of any of them, his vote was never questioned.

Ushers should require all persons to show their credentials before taking their seats. If pages for carrying messages are provided, it is unnecessary for delegates or members to walk about the convention floor while the meetings are in progress.

SAVING TIME IN CONVENTIONS

Since the time of a large convention is valuable, every means should be utilized to streamline procedures. The chief responsibility for seeing that things move along on schedule rests with the presiding officer. It is his duty to see that the adopted order of business is followed, that motions and reports are offered promptly, that discussion is confined to the matter before the assembly, that speakers do not exceed their time, and that votes are taken promptly.

In large organizations, one method of conserving time is to vote by delegations. The chairman of the delegation is able to take and report a vote quickly. He polls his delegation and reports the results when his name is called.

Committees conserve convention time by submitting printed reports, or by offering only a brief oral summary of the report before it is filed.

Roll-call votes are sometimes necessary, even though they are time consumers. They will, however, require less time if entrance to the convention hall is restricted to two doors, where delegates are required to sign their names on entering or leaving the hall. This method will provide a correct list of all those in the meeting at any given moment and the names of those present will always be available for calling the roll. This plan shortens the time needed to call the roll since absentees are eliminated.

It is impossible for a huge group of people to correct minutes accurately, and they waste time trying to do so. Instead of having the minutes read and corrected at each meeting, a minutes committee can prepare and certify the minutes, and thus save valuable time for more important work.

Announcements can be less time-consuming if a rule is adopted requiring that they be written out and handed to an announcement committee. This committee can make all announcements at one time, post them on a bulletin board, or flash them on a screen.

REFERENCE AND SCREENING COMMITTEES

In some large conventions, the actual expense of operating the convention brings the cost of business sessions to from five hundred dollars to a thousand dollars per minute. Time saved is money saved. It is important to channel and screen motions or resolutions, to conserve time and to make it possible for the convention to close at the appointed hour.

Inexperienced delegates often fail to realize that the purpose of a convention is largely to discuss and decide upon important policies which have been proposed and considered previously by local units. Conventions are not like town meetings, where there is time for everyone to speak on every subject and where each contribution of a new idea is welcomed. Since a convention has a very limited time in which to work and a large amount of work to do, it cannot give its attention to small details or to unconsidered new ideas. If any delegate who has an idea could get up and present it from the floor, and go romping off on a speech in support of it, the necessary convention business would never get done.

To meet this situation, most conventions channel all motions and resolutions through a screening committee and various standing reference committees. The screening committee is the hopper into which new business is poured and through which it is filtered. Most large organizations require that new proposals be submitted to this committee a considerable time in advance of the convention. If a member does introduce a motion embodying a new idea on the floor of the convention, it is automatically referred to the screening committee.

Any member or unit may submit a motion or resolution to the screening committee. If the committee feels that the proposal is a suitable one for consideration of the convention, it refers the motion or resolution to the appropriate standing committee.

The American Medical Association has pioneered in the development of such committees and has used them very effectively.

Anyone who understands how complex modern conventions are must appreciate the wisdom of such a reference system. This device is not a curb on democratic processes. Rather, it is an orderly delegation of work for the benefit of the group as a whole.

This procedure is also a safeguard against the sudden introduction of new ideas which local groups and delegates have had no opportunity to investigate or discuss.

ACCREDITING OF DELEGATES

When the number of delegates to which each local district is entitled is determined, the head office usually sends two delegate cards to the local secretary for each allotted delegate. Each card certifies that the person whose signature appears on it is the duly elected delegate from that unit. The card is signed by the local president or secretary, or both. One of the cards is returned to the national or state registration committee, and the other is given to the delegate. Credentials for alternates are handled in the same manner. Time is saved if the necessary registration fees accompany the credential card. Before the convention, each delegate reports to the registration committee desk, presents his credential card, fills out a registration blank, and receives his badge and other convention material.

CREDENTIALS COMMITTEE

After the opening ceremonies, which may consist of an invocation, an address of welcome, and a response, the credentials committee usually presents its preliminary report. It is important that this report be presented as early as possible so that members will know who is entitled to vote. The committee report usually consists of a list of the delegates and their alternates and the ex-officio members of the convention who are present. Ex-officio members usually include the officers of the convention, the chairmen of the convention committees, and the members of the executive board.

When the report of the credentials committee has been adopted, the list of the accredited delegates which it contains becomes the official roll of those who are entitled to vote. Supplementary reports by this committee may be given later in the convention if necessary.

REPORT OF THE RULES COMMITTEE

Usually the report of the rules committee follows that of the credentials committee. Sometimes it is the first report given. This report should be presented early so that the delegates may have rules under which to work. Ordinarily, the rules of a convention differ very little from those of the previous convention.

Rules are adopted by a majority vote, and can be suspended at any time by a two-thirds vote. Convention rules differ widely, but usually cover such subjects as registration of delegates, seating of delegates, alternates, and guests, limitation on length of speeches, how motions and resolutions may be introduced, the privileges of nonvoting members and visitors, and any other special rules peculiar to the convention.

CONVENTIONS ARE ORGANIZED SOCIETY

Perhaps because of expert and careful planning and a widening knowledge of how to work well in groups, conventions are becoming increasingly efficient, smooth-running, and effective. The harassed officers and committeemen of a few years back are now leaders who have their jobs well in hand, and have time to participate in convention activities and to enjoy them.

Conventions have come to be complex mechanisms which have lost many of the characteristics of a town meeting. They reflect instead the intricate and far-flung civilization of the twentieth century. We could not do without them.

These great cooperative gatherings are making significant contributions to the development and unity of American life and, indeed, to the whole world. They exhibit an astounding intelligence and an amazing capacity to work under pressure, a deep sincerity of purpose, and a wisdom of decision.

Conventions are highly efficient bodies, capable of acting upon many diverse ideas. They are the best means yet discovered for accomplishing a vast amount of necessary work. Despite all their distractions, they manage to end their sessions with a stimulated, informed, and rededicated group of delegates, who return to their homes to pass on their strengthened convictions to the members of their organization. Conventions are *representative* democracy at its best.

They are the means by which voluntary organizations like our churches, our fraternal and business groups, and our educational groups are kept alive. With their widespread representation from many parts of the world, they constitute the greatest integrating force of our day. Conventions are organized society in America. They concentrate and stimulate and give voice to the faith and loyalty which make this nation strong.

Practice Projects

Select a committee to visit the nearest convention bureau and to report on the assistance and ideas which the bureau can furnish.

If time permits, plan a convention for some organization the class may select. Conduct the opening business session of the convention.

CHAPTER 33

PROCEDURAL TRENDS AND THE FUTURE OF ORGANIZATIONS

PROCEDURE CHANGES

It is clear that the fundamental principles of procedure by which democratic organizations function will remain essentially the same. They have developed through centuries of experience in democratic countries and are basic to democratic assemblages. Procedural rules, however, are not static. They change with changing conditions. Certain definite trends are evident.

SIMPLIFICATION

There is a strong demand for simplification of procedures and for the subordination of ritualism and technicalities to fundamental principles. An instance of the trend toward simpler terminology is the use of such easily understood terms as "vote immediately" and "postpone temporarily" in place of such misleading terms as "the previous question" and the "motion to lay on the table." Likewise, some of the older manuals devote several pages to complicated discussions of insignificant rules regarding amendments which have already been acted upon. More recently, it has been found possible to replace all these complications by the single principle that when an amendment is adopted or rejected, the same amendment, even though expressed in different words, cannot be proposed again at the same meeting.

ELIMINATION OF TECHNICALITIES

Groups show a determination to increase their efficiency by the use of new and streamlined methods. They tend to disregard minor technicalities—the small, dogmatic, and entangling devices which, in the post-

317

SOMETHING TO MOON ABOUT

Be it late or be it soon,
The first arrival at the moon,
  The first to be a resident,
Will take a hasty look around
And then, of course, proceed to found
    A club, and be its president.

He'll build, before he builds a home,
A clubhouse bright with glass and chrome
    And fire that's warm with embers,
Then search the craters all about
With eager eye and friendly shout
    And start a drive for members.

Civil War period, were laid down as rules. They seek to return, rather, to the principles and essentials of orderly democratic procedures as developed by their own experience, and as interpreted by the many decisions of our courts.

The courts themselves have underwritten this trend by repeated emphasis on principles rather than technicalities. Organizations are pursuing a steady course toward simplicity in all procedures and emphasis on essentials rather than on useless and hampering details.

MAJORITY CONTROL

Groups tend, increasingly, to place more trust in the decisions of the majority. This belief in the wisdom of majority rule is the keystone of democracy and of democratic procedures. Legislative bodies have never required more than a majority vote for any procedural motion. There is a long line of court decisions which hold that there are no rules of parliamentary law which require more than a majority vote on any motion.

This principle is likely to be followed in the not too far distant future by voluntary organizations. In fact, there are already some organizations that require no more than a majority for procedural votes, such as the motions to vote immediately and to suspend rules, which, since the Victorian period, have required a two-thirds vote. As yet, however, most organizations still follow the rule requiring a two-thirds vote for certain procedural motions.

Organizations are becoming generally aware that every vote which is higher than a majority takes power away *from* the majority and gives it to a minority—and organizations resent being ruled by minorities.

DELEGATION OF AUTHORITY

Since the days of our early town meetings, when it was thought that all the work must be done in the meeting itself by all the members, there has been a gradual change in the concept of how democratic organizations operate. With no loss of the voice or rights of the individual, there has been a gain in efficiency. We now see that we can trust small groups to represent the larger body in the accomplishment of the ever more complex tasks of our organizations. Within organizations the increasing delegation of work to committees is an example of what Franklyn S. Haiman calls "authority derived in a democratic way and subject to democratic review." We may anticipate a further expansion of the activity of committees.

TIMESAVING METHODS

Procedures which save time in meetings are being rapidly adopted. The use of a minutes committee to correct the minutes, instead of the time-consuming and inefficient method of correcting minutes by the whole meeting, is one device that is proving effective. The limitation of a committee report to a brief oral summary, with the longer written report placed in the file, or the substitution of printed reports which members may read at their leisure is another widely used technique that has saved many meeting hours. It is insisted that routine reports be as concise as possible and be called for only when necessary. A group is unwilling to listen to the repetition of a long, detailed financial report at every weekly meeting.

Time is also being saved by the elimination of roll-call votes and votes by ballot where secrecy is not important, by the grouping of announcements, by proceeding by unanimous consent in noncontroversial matters, and by increased understanding on the part of presiding officers that they must keep the meeting moving and confine discussion to the subject before the assembly.

Groups will no longer listen to lengthy speeches during the discussion of a motion. They are impatient with a member who prepares an oration and interjects it into discussion. This insistence on confining discussion to short, pertinent presentations conserves the time of the group.

BETTER-TRAINED MEMBERS

Another significant trend is a realization of the importance of educating all members of organizations in meeting procedures and in methods of working together in groups. The results achieved by an informed group so far exceed those of a group where only a few leaders are trained, that the wisdom of educating every member in group skills is evident.

When important decisions are to be made, many organizations now provide that the members shall be informed of the question ahead of time, so that they will have an opportunity to study and to consider the problem. This is particularly true of conventions and annual meetings. The time necessary for discussion and decision on a motion about which members have had time to think is thus noticeably shortened.

Simplicity in procedure, reliance on majority decisions, emphasis on timesaving devices, delegation of work and authority to committees, and a more universal training of the membership in group skills are the obvious trends in procedure characterizing the immediate future.

THE PIONEER PERIOD

We are coming to the end of what might be called the pioneer period of voluntary organizations. It has been a time of phenomenal, mushrooming growth. Like all pioneer periods, it has often been wasteful—wasteful of the money, time, and effort of individual members.

Because of this waste, the generous outpouring of energy and interest by millions of individuals has fallen short of achieving its maximum. Much has been done the hard way. The borrowed bylaws which worked well for one group but which were unsuited to another, the lack of adequate sources of information on how to write such simple things as committee reports or minutes, the inability to profit by the experience of other workers because records had not been kept, the entangling technicalities of unnecessary procedures, all have made working in groups difficult and wasteful.

Organizations have been too busy getting things done to give careful thought to their methods or to the lessons of experience. Each group has worked largely within itself with little knowledge of what other organizations were doing. Rivalry has flourished. In one state, for example, nine organizations to aid the blind expended strength in jealous competition which, if coordinated, might have gone much farther toward achieving their common purpose.

There have been few standards or criteria of judgment—few yardsticks to measure the success or failure of an organization. Much of the potential strength of organizations has therefore been unrealized and their actual strength undirected or misdirected.

Members of organizations have not had an adequate knowledge of the groups to which they belong. Even though joining an organization sets up a relationship similar to that of a contract, members have joined a group with only a vague idea of its purpose and nature. They have continued as members without any real understanding or knowledge of what the group was doing or how it was doing it. They have sometimes found that they were lending aid and prestige to an organization with whose policies they did not agree. Good citizens have sometimes been shocked to learn that they belonged to subversive organizations.

Because of these weaknesses, elements subversive to democracy have been able to dominate some of our groups. These infiltrations are often unrecognized. This same lack of knowledge has made it possible for a few power-grasping individuals to gain control and to thwart the majority will, even in some of our larger national organizations.

Happily, difficulties characteristic of a pioneer period disappear with growth. The over-all picture of our voluntary organizations is one of astounding achievement—of the establishment, in little over a century, of an informal government which stems from the voluntary group activity of our private citizens and is sometimes more important in our lives than our formal government. When Jefferson said of the nation, "So we shall go on, puzzled and prospering beyond example in the history of man," he described the development of voluntary organizations during this pioneer period.

AS MATURITY COMES

As modern transportation makes distances dwindle, and as life becomes more complex, the role of our voluntary organizations increases. The need likewise increases for careful analysis of how groups function most effectively. This need has yet to be met.

In an article in *Fortune,* Russell Davenport says of the field of voluntary organizations, "One element of American self-government which plays a role so vast as to be virtually immeasurable has been relatively neglected by students of this country. . . . It has been so little explored, indeed, that it is difficult to find a name for it."

WE ARE LEARNING

But explorers are beginning to dig busily in this area. Historians are compiling data on the growth of this new phenomenon. Political scientists are studying the effects of organizations upon formal government and upon legislation. Lawyers are interpreting the hundreds of cases concerning voluntary groups that have been decided by the courts, and are devising bylaws to meet the individual needs of new organizations. Teachers of speech and of English are busy improving the only method of communication which groups have—their speech—and are training students to participate in group discussions. Parliamentarians are concerned with group principles, procedures, and methods. They are interested in simplifying, clarifying, and stating them in conformity with the law. Social psychologists are digging deep into the motivations, behavior patterns, and human dynamics which control the actions of the individuals in the group. Sociologists are analyzing the effects of groups on individuals and the place of organizations in our culture pattern. Educators are training teachers to supervise participation of students in organizations, from the grade school through college.

In the fields of education and the social sciences particularly, there is recognition of the fact that adult lives are largely lived in organizations, and students are not only being instructed in ways to work effectively within campus groups, but are being prepared for skillful participation in organizations that will be of lifelong value.

COOPERATIVE SOLUTIONS

Most significant of all is the fact that the voluntary organizations *themselves* are showing a realization of their own weaknesses and a vigorous determination to do something about them. The more farseeing groups are expending money and effort to train their members in parliamentary procedure, in taking part in discussion, and in the art of working successfully in conferences and committees. Outstanding in these achievements of membership training are the labor unions, the PTA, and the American Farm Bureau Federation.

Voluntary organizations are beginning to realize that they can profit from studying problems which are common to all groups. Recent research with national organizations proves that almost every competent group has worked out a distinctively original and highly successful solution to at least one problem. This solution would be valuable to other organizations, if they but knew about it. For instance, one group has found ways to cut its meeting time from three hours to one. Another has worked out a truly democratic way to permit individual members to share in the formulation of national policies. Still another group has developed a remarkable plan for assuring that every member is almost as well informed regarding policies and specific aims as the national president of the organization. Solutions evolved by these organizations should be made available to other groups. Associations are coming to realize that cooperation among groups with similar interests pays dividends, while rivalry is destructive.

They are also gaining a deeper understanding of what democratic leadership is. The more they appreciate its potentialities the more willing they are to put their trust in the leaders, who can learn with and from the group, and who grow stronger in the give-and-take of opinions.

Students of voluntary organizations are glimpsing the unlimited possibilities of intelligent, cooperative effort. They see that there are many problems common to all organizations. One of these is the problem of determining specific and well-thought-out purposes which are correlated with those of similar groups and of the community; another is the creation of an individualized bylaw structure which will serve these purposes; yet another is the formulation of suitable policies, and maintenance of a continuity of these policies despite an annual change in leadership; and difficulties posed by new members, programs, finances, expansion, trained leadership, apportionment of work, and reorganization. These are only a few of the problems shared in common by organizations large and small.

THE FUTURE

Out of this period of study by organizational specialists, as well as by leaders and active participants in group effort, will come valuable contributions to the future of voluntary organizations. This study will help to develop standards for the evaluation of an organization—its ethics, administration, finances, and general achievement. The establishment of standards will tend to eliminate the weak and the undesirables among organizations, for example, those who collect ten dollars to accomplish a dollar's worth of work.

Likewise, out of this study of group effort will come solutions for those problems which most organizations share in common. New ideas, new methods, and improved ways of working together in groups will heighten the contributions which voluntary organizations can make.

The priceless rights of free speech, free assemblage, and freedom to participate in voluntary groups is denied millions of human beings in the world today. In America, however, these freedoms are flourishing. They will continue to exist and to grow stronger only if we exercise them. Our voluntary groups are our "greatest phenomenon." They are also our greatest talking point in selling democracy to others.

Every man, woman, and child who is an active member of a voluntary organization is not only furthering the immediate intent of the group but contributing directly to our democratic self-government. As a member, you are more important than you think.

We of America must so strengthen our self-government through voluntary organizations that we shall fulfill the promise and prophecy of Abraham Lincoln when he said:

"Our forefathers planted the germ which has vegetated, and still is to grow and expand into the universal liberty of mankind."

PARLIAMENTARY CONTESTS

1. *Conducting a Meeting*

Students are divided into two or more groups. The first competing group is given fifteen minutes during which it is to conduct a meeting, beginning with the call to order and ending with adjournment, omitting only the reading of minutes. The meeting should be one which is remote in character from the type of organization to which the students usually belong. For example, Group 1 might be assigned a meeting of Local 2021 of the Carpenters' Union.

A second competing group is given the same length of time to conduct a meeting of (for example) the faculty of Southern University. Each competing group is rated on the ability of its members to:

1. Follow a correct meeting plan
2. Demonstrate facility in the use of parliamentary procedure
3. Show knowledge of motions and their uses
4. Prove ability to speak briefly and well
5. Display aptitude and imagination for participating in a meeting under unfamiliar circumstances

Humor, ability to detect errors, and general adaptability should all count in scoring.

2. *Conducting a Committee Meeting*

Each contesting group is assigned a different imaginary committee project. The group will then work out its project in a committee meeting held in front of the audience. The project is not announced until each group is ready to give its demonstration. Each project is different. Each contesting group will be judged on the speed and efficiency with which its members organize the committee, agree upon its purposes, duties,

326

and powers, and plan how the work assigned it is to be accomplished. Contest time—fifteen minutes.

3. *Preparing a Committee Report*

Each contesting team is supplied with identical instructions, outlining a problem which is assigned to it as a committee. Each team will meet separately and prepare a written report, to be read by the committee chairman at the end of a half hour. While the committees are writing their reports, other types of contests may continue. This contest is designed to test the student's ability to work out a plan of cooperative effort and to write an imaginary report of the committee's accomplishments.

4. *Picking the Best Presiding Officer*

Students are divided evenly into two groups, one on each side of the room. Each student is given a number. One group acts as a challenging group, the other as the answering group. Student Challenger No. 1 addresses a question or a motion to Student No. 1 in the answering group. The answering student replies to it as he would reply if he were presiding over a meeting. Student Challenger No. 2 presents a question or a motion (good or bad) to Student No. 2, the answerer. This process continues until each student on one side has been challenged. The roles of the groups are then reversed. Scoring: one point for each correct answer.

5. *Definitions*

This contest is similar to the old-fashioned spelling bee, except that instead of spelling a word, each student must define a parliamentary term. One person announces the term to be defined. If a student misses a definition, he takes his seat. Any term connected with parliamentary procedure may be presented for definition. This continues until only one student remains standing.

DEFINITIONS OF
PARLIAMENTARY TERMS

Accept an amendment: Informal agreement by proposer of a motion to include a proposed amendment; mover may say, "I accept the amendment."

Adhere: When a motion is pending, and other motions, like the motion to amend, are applied to it, these motions are said to *adhere* to the original motion; and when this motion is postponed or referred to a committee, these *adhering* motions go with it.

Adjourn: To terminate a meeting officially.

Adjourn sine die (without day): An adjournment which terminates a convention or conference.

Adjourned meeting: A meeting which is a continuation of a regular or special meeting and which is legally a part of the same meeting.

Adopt: To approve, to give effect to.

Adopt a report: The formal acceptance of a report. Adoption commits the organization to everything included in the report.

Affirmative vote: A "yes" vote to a question before an assembly; an agreement to its acceptance.

Agenda: The official list of business to be considered at a meeting or convention.

Amend: To change, by adding, deleting, or substituting words or provisions.

Annul: To void or cancel an action previously taken.

Appeal: A decision of the presiding officer may be *appealed* from. An *appeal* requires that the decision be referred to the assembly for its determination by a vote.

Apply: One motion is said to *apply* to another motion when it is used to alter, dispose of, or affect the first motion.

328

Assembly: A group of persons gathered together for some common purpose, whether an organized body or not. Includes mass meetings as well as organized associations.

Assessment: Authorized levy of a fee made upon members of an organization.

Ballot: A paper, or a mechanical device, by which votes are recorded. Used to ensure secrecy in voting.

Bylaw: A rule of an organization, ranking immediately below the constitution in authority and above the standing rules. May often include the usual provisions of a constitution.

Candidate: One who is nominated or offers himself as a contestant for an office.

Carried: Approved by the necessary affirmative vote of the group.

Chair: The chairman or presiding officer.

Change in parliamentary situation: Phrase used in determining when a motion may be renewed. A *change in the parliamentary situation* means that motions have been proposed or disposed of, there has been progress in debate, or other changes have occurred to create a new situation so that the assembly might reasonably take a different position on the question.

Changing a vote: Request to alter one's own vote which has already been taken.

Charter: Written grant of authority, usually from a state to a corporation, guaranteeing rights, franchises, or privileges.

Classification of motions: Division of motions into groups, usually according to their purpose or precedence.

Close debate: To stop all discussion on a motion and to take a vote on it immediately.

Common law: Law developed by court decisions. Judge-made law.

Conference: A group meeting informally for consultation, discussion, and sometimes decision.

Consideration: Deliberation on a subject and examination of it before taking a vote.

Constitution: Document containing fundamental law and principles of government adopted by an organized body.

Convene: To open a meeting formally.

Convention: Assembly of delegates or representatives of allied groups met for a common purpose.

Credentials: Certificate or testimonial indicating right of a person to represent a certain group.

Debatable: Capable of being discussed.

Debate: Discussion or presentation of opinion on a matter pending before a deliberative body.

Delegate: Member sent to represent an organized group and empowered to act for it.

Deliberative body: Body which proceeds by discussion and consideration of questions and makes decisions by vote.

Demand: The assertion of a parliamentary right.

Dilatory tactics: Strategy used to delay action; use of motions and discussion to delay a vote.

Disappearing quorum: Required number of persons present at beginning of meeting but subsequently diminishing in size as persons leave.

Discussion: Consideration of a question by oral presentation of views of different persons.

Dispose of motion: To remove it from the consideration of the assembly.

Dissolve an organization: To terminate its official life.

Division of assembly: A vote taken by counting members, either by rising or by show of hands. Often taken to verify a voice vote.

Division of question: Separation of a main motion into two or more independent parts, each of which is capable of standing alone.

Ex-officio: To hold an office, or position, because of holding another office; e.g., a president may be an *ex-officio* member of the finance committee.

Executive board: Chief committee of an organization. Usually conducts organization business during intervals between meetings.

Expel a member: To remove someone from membership in an organization by group action.

Expunge: To strike out or cancel the record of a previous action.

Filibuster: To obstruct or prevent action in an assembly by dilatory tactics, such as speaking merely to consume time.

Floor: When recognized formally by the chairman, one is said to have the *floor*. He is the only person allowed to speak.

Gavel: Mallet used by presiding officer of a deliberative body to open and close meetings and to maintain order.

General consent: An informal method of disposing of routine and generally favored proposals by the chairman assuming the group's approval, unless objection is raised. Also called "unanimous consent."

Germane: Pertaining or relating directly to, having definite bearing upon. Applied to the relationship of amendments to motions.

Hearing: Meeting to listen to ideas or arguments with a view to making a decision or recommendation.

Honorary member or officer: One who is given membership or office by reason of his eminence or position.

Illegal vote: A vote which cannot be counted because it does not comply with the rules of the organization.

Immediately pending question: When several questions are pending before the assembly, the one last proposed, which the assembly must decide first, is the *immediately pending question*.

In order: Correct from a parliamentary standpoint at a given time.

Incidental motions: Motions relating to questions which arise incidentally out of the business, or order or manner of considering the business, of an assembly.

Incorporate: To form a group of people into a legal entity recognized by law and with special rights, duties, functions, and liabilities distinct from its members.

Informal consideration: A method of considering a question without observing the rules governing formal debate.

Inquiry: Question directed to the presiding officer by a member.

Instructions to committee: Directions specifying the powers and duties of the committee, the work desired, the type and date of report or similar matters.

Invariable form: A motion is said to have an *invariable form* when it can be stated in only one way and when it is, therefore, not subject to change or amendment.

Irrelevant: Not related to, not pertinent, not applicable.

Lay on the table: To postpone a motion until a later but as yet undetermined time.

Legal vote: A valid vote, one which conforms to all legal requirements.

Legislative body: A representative body having the power to make laws.

Limit debate: To place restrictions on the time to be devoted to debate on a question or the number of speakers or the time allotted each.

Logrolling: Agreeing with other members to assist them with motions in which they are interested in return for a promise of assistance from them.

Main motion: A motion presenting a subject to an assembly for discussion and decision.

Majority vote: More than half of the total number legally voting, or if by ballot, more than half of the legal votes cast, unless otherwise defined.

Mass meeting: Large or general assembly which is open to anyone.

Meeting: An assemblage of the members of an organization during which there is no separation of the members except for a recess. A meeting is terminated by an adjournment.

Member in good standing: Member who has fulfilled all the obligations required of him by the organization.

Minority: Less than half of members or votes. Group having fewer than the number of votes necessary to control the decision.

Minutes: Official record of motions presented and actions taken by an organization.

Motion: A proposal submitted to an assembly for its consideration and introduced by the words "I move."

Negative vote: Adverse vote; vote against a proposition.

New Business: Any business other than unfinished or "old business" which may properly be brought before an assembly.

Nomination: The formal proposal of a person as a candidate for an office.

Object to consideration: To oppose discussion and decision on a main motion.

Oppose: To work actively against a measure or candidate.

Order of business: The formal program or sequence of different items or classes of business arranged in the order in which they are to be considered by an assembly.

Out of order: Not correct from a parliamentary standpoint at the particular time.

Parliamentarian: An adviser to the presiding officer; one who is skilled in parliamentary practice.

Parliamentary authority: The manual or code adopted by an organization as its official parliamentary guide, which governs in all matters not covered in the constitution, bylaws, and rules of the organization.

Pending question: A question, or motion, before the assembly which has not yet been voted upon.

Personal interest: Private financial gain which would result from the decision of the organization on a proposition.

Personal privilege: Request by a member for consideration of some matter of concern to himself and related to himself as a member.

Plurality: More votes than the number received by any other of three or more opposing candidates or measures. May be less than a majority.

Point of order: An assertion amounting to a demand addressed to the presiding officer that a mistake should be corrected or a rule enforced.

Postpone definitely: To defer consideration of a motion or report until a specific time.

Postpone indefinitely: To kill a motion or report by deferring consideration of it indefinitely.

Postpone temporarily: To defer consideration of a report or motion until the assembly chooses to take it up again. The old form of the motion was "lay on the table."

Preamble: An introduction preceding a constitution or a resolution, stating its purpose or the reason for its proposal.

Precedence: The right of prior proposal and consideration of one motion over another, or the order or priority of consideration.

Precedent: Something previously done or decided which serves as a guide in similar circumstances. An authoritative example.

Prefer charges: To accuse formally an officer or member of some offense, ordinarily for disciplinary purposes.

Presiding officer: Chairman who conducts a meeting.

Previous question: Motion to close debate and force immediate vote. Old form of motion to vote immediately.

Privilege of assembly: Request for a favor or privilege to be extended to the group.

Privileged motions: The class of motions having the highest priority.

Procedural motion: A motion which presents a question of procedure as distinguished from a substantive proposition.

Progress in debate: Such developments during the consideration of a question as might reasonably justify the renewal of a motion.

Proposition: A proposal submitting a question of any kind for consideration and action. Includes motions, resolutions, reports, and other kinds of proposals.

Proxy: A signed statement transferring one's right to vote (or to participate in a meeting) to another person.

Putting the question: Submitting a question to vote; taking a vote on a question.

Question: Any proposition submitted to an assembly for a decision.

Question of privilege: Request or motion affecting the comfort or convenience of the assembly or one of its members.

Quorum: Number or proportion of members which must be present at a meeting to enable the assembly to act legally on business.

Recess: A short interval or break in a meeting.

Recognition: The formal acknowledgment by the chairman indicating that a member has the right to speak.

Reconsider: Motion to cancel the effect of a vote so that the question may be reviewed and redecided.

Refer to committee: Motion to delegate work to a small group of members for study, decision, or action.

Reference committee: Standing committee of a convention to which all motions dealing with a certain subject are referred.

Regular meeting: A meeting scheduled in the bylaws and held at definite intervals.

Renew a motion: To present the same motion a second or subsequent time at the same meeting.

Repeal: To annul or void.

Repeal by implication: When two measures are passed which conflict with each other, the portions of the last which conflict with the first repeal them by implication.

Rescind: To repeal, to nullify.

Resolution: A formal proposal submitted in writing for action by an assembly. Introduced by the word "Resolved."

Restricted debate: Debate which is restricted to the propriety or advisability of a motion in relation to a main motion but which does not open the latter to debate.

Resume consideration: To take up for consideration a motion which has been postponed temporarily. The old form of the motion was "take from the table."

Rising vote: Vote taken by having members stand.

Ritual: A form or ceremony observed by an organization; a verbal formula.

Roll call: Calling names of members in a fixed order as each answers "present" or votes.

Ruling: Decision of presiding officer on a question or point of order.

Second: An indication of approval of the consideration of a proposed motion.

Sergeant at arms: Officer who maintains order in an assembly, under the direction of the presiding officer.

Seriatim: Manner of considering any document by sections or paragraphs.

Special committee: A committee appointed to accomplish a particular task and to submit a special report. It ceases to exist when its task is completed.

Special meeting: A meeting called to consider certain specific business which must be set forth in the call.

Specific main motion: A main motion which has a name, a specific form, and is subject to special rules, as opposed to a general main motion. Examples of specific main motions are to rescind, to reconsider, and to resume consideration.

Standing committee: A committee to handle all business on a certain subject which may be referred to it, and usually having a term of service corresponding to the term of office of the officers of the organization.

Standing rules: Rules formulated and adopted by an organization to meet its own particular needs, and remaining in force until repealed.

Statute: A law made by a legislative body.

Steam-roller: To force a measure through to vote by ruthlessly or arbitrarily overcoming the opposition.

Substantive motion: A motion which presents a concrete proposal of business, not a procedural motion.

Suppress a motion: To kill it without letting it come to a vote.

Suspend: Motion to set aside a rule or make it temporarily inoperative.

Teller: Member appointed to assist in conducting a vote by ballot.

Tie vote: A vote in which the positive and negative are equal, as a 20-to-20 vote. A tie vote is not sufficient to take any action.

Two-thirds vote: Two-thirds of all legal votes cast.

Unanimous: Without any dissenting vote. One adverse vote prevents *unanimous* approval.

Unanimous consent: An informal method of disposing of routine and generally favored motions by the chairman assuming approval of a request for *unanimous consent.* Is defeated by one objection.

Unfinished business: Any business deferred by a motion to postpone to a definite time, or any business which was incomplete when the previous meeting adjourned. *Unfinished business* has a preferred status at the following meeting.

Viva voce vote: A vote taken by calling for "ayes" and "noes" and judged by volume of voice response. Sometimes called "voice vote."

Voluntary organization: Nongovernmental organization which members join by choice.

Vote immediately: Motion to close debate, shut off subsidiary motion, and take a vote at once.

Well taken: A point of order with which the presiding officer agrees is said to be *well taken.*

Withdraw: Motion by a member to remove his motion from consideration by the assembly.

Write in: To cast a ballot for a person who has not been nominated by writing in his name.

Yeas and nays: Roll-call vote during which each member answers "yea" or "nay" when his name is called.

BIBLIOGRAPHY OF LEGAL
DECISIONS

CHAPTER 2. *What Is Parliamentary Law?*

Witherspoon v. State (1925) 138 Miss. 310, 103 So. 134; *Nevins v. Springfield* (1917) 227 Mass. 538, 116 N.E. 881; *Landes v. State* (1903) 160 Ind. 479, 67 N.E. 189.

CHAPTER 3. *Fundamental Principles*

Briggs v. MacKellar (1855) 2 Abb. Pr. (N.Y.) 30.

CHAPTER 4. *Pattern of a Meeting*

Terre Haute Gas Corp. v. Johnson (1943) 221 Ind. 499, 48 N.E. 2d 455.

CHAPTER 5. *How Motions Are Handled*

In re Sawyer (1888) 124 U.S. 200, 31 Law Ed. 402; *Cockran v. McCleary* (1867) 22 Iowa 75.

CHAPTER 7. *Discussion*

People v. American Institute (1873) 44 How. Pr. (N.Y.) 468.

CHAPTER 8. *Quorum*

People v. Wright (1902) 30 Colo. 439, 71 Pac. 365; *Shugars v. Hamilton* (1906) 122 Ky. 606, 92 S.W. 564; *U.S. v. Ballin* (1888) 12 Sup. Ct. 507, 144 U.S. 1; *Kimball v. Marshall* (1863) 44 N.H. 465; *In re Gunn* (1893) 50 Kan. 155, 32 Pac. 470; *Madison Avenue Baptist Church v. Oliver St. Baptist Church* (1867) 28 N.Y., Super. 649, 2 Abb. Pr. N.S. 254, 32 How. Pr. (N.Y.) 335; *Stone v. Small* (1882) 54 Vt. 498.

CHAPTER 9. *Vote Required*

State v. Reichmann (1911) 239 Mo. 81, 142 S.W. 304; *Commonwealth v. Fleming* (1913) 23 Pa. Sup. Ct. 404; *State v. Vanosdal* (1892) 131 Ind. 388, 31 N.E. 79; *Cram v. Bangor House Proprietary* (1835) 12 Me. 354; *Murdock v. Strange* (1904) 99 Md. 89, 57 Atl. 628.

337

CHAPTER 10. *Methods of Voting*

Richardson v. Francistown Union Congregational Society (1877) 58 N.H. 187; *O'Neil v. Tyler* (1892) 3 N.D. 47, 53 N.W. 434; *State v. Ellington* (1895) 117 N.C. 158, 23 S.E. 250; *Landers v. Frank Street Methodist etc. Church* (1899) 114 N.Y. 626, 21 N.E. 420.

CHAPTER 13. *Motions to Change Motions*

State v. Cox (1920) 105 Neb. 175, 178 N.W. 913; *Hood v. City of Wheeling* (1920) 85 W.Va. 578, 102 S.E. 259; *Casler v. Tanzer* (1929) 234 N.Y. Supp. 571; *Drake v. Callison* (1930) 122 Fed. 722.

CHAPTER 14. *Motions to Control Debate*

Terre Haute Gas Corp. v. Johnson (1943) 221 Ind. 499, 48 N.E. 2d 455.

CHAPTER 15. *Motions to Defer Actions*

People v. Davis (1918) 284 Ill. 439, 120 N.E. 326; *Wright v. Wiles* (1938) 173 Tenn. 334, 17 S.W. 2d 736.

CHAPTER 16. *Motion to Refer to a Committee*

In re Holman (1917) 270 Mo. 696, 195 S.W. 711; *Dancer v. Mannington* (1901) 50 W.Va. 322, 40 S.E. 475; *State v. Buckley* (1875) 54 Ala. 599.

CHAPTER 17. *Motions to Suppress Motions*

Wood v. Milton (1908) 197 Mass. 531, 84 N.E. 332; *Zeiler v. Central Railway Co.* (1896) 84 Md. 304, 35 Atl. 932.

CHAPTER 18. *Motions to Terminate Meetings*

Tevey v. Aylward (1910) 203 Mass. 102, 91 N.E. 315; *Hill v. Goodwin* (1876) 56 N.H. 441; *Pollard v. Gregg* (1914) 77 N.H. 190, 90 Atl. 176.

CHAPTER 19. *Motions to Meet Emergencies*

French v. Senate (1905) 146 Cal. 604, 80 Pac. 1031; *Tayloe v. Davis* (1924) 212 Ala. 282, 102 So. 433; *State v. Alt* (1887) 26 Mo. App. 673.

CHAPTER 20. *Motions Affecting Previous Actions*

Crawford v. Gilchrist (1912) 64 Fla. 41, 59 So. 963; *Kay Jewelry Co. v. Board* (1940) 305 Mass. 581, 27 N.E. 2d 1; *Neill v. Ward* (1930) 163 Vt. 117, 153 Atl. 219; *Whitney v. Van Buskirk* (1878) 40 N.J.L. 463.

CHAPTER 22. *Creating an Organization*

Branagan v. Buckman (1910) 122 N.Y. Supp. 610; *Ostrom v. Greene* (1897) 45 N.Y. Supp. 852; *American Basketball Club v. Johnson* (1920) 179 N.Y. Supp. 498.

CHAPTER 23. *Constitution, Bylaws, and Standing Rules*

French v. Senate (1905) 146 Cal. 604, 80 Pac. 1031; *Tayloe v. Davis* (1924) 212 Ala. 282, 102 So. 433; *Higgins v. Curtis* (1888) 39 Kan. 283, 18 Pac. 207.

CHAPTER 24. *Officers*

State v. Hoyt (1867) 2 Ore. 246; *Ostrom v. Greene* (1897) 45 N.Y. Supp. 852; *Tandy v. Hopkinsville* (1917) 174 Ky. 189, 192 S.W. 46; *Budd v. Walla Walla Publishing etc. Co.* (1885) 2 Wash. 347, 7 Pac. 896; *Commonwealth v. Vandegrift* (1911) 232 Pa. 63, 81 Atl. 153.

CHAPTER 25. *Membership*

Simons v. Berry (1924) 205 N.Y. Supp. 442, 210 App. Div. 90; *Brotherhood of Railway Trainmen v. Williams* (1925) 211 Ky. 638, 277 S.W. 500; *Marshall v. Pilots' Assn.* (1902) 18 Pn. Sup. Ct. 644; *Hall v. Morrin* (1927) Mo. App. 293 S.W., 435; *Evans v. Brown* (1919) 134 Md. 519, 107 Atl. 535.

CHAPTER 26. *Committees and Their Work*

Whitney v. New Haven (1890) 58 Conn. 450, 20 Atl. 666; *State v. Milwaukee* (1914) 157 Wis. 505, 147 N.W. 50; *Salmon v. Haynes* (1897) 50 N.J.L. 97, 11 Atl. 151.

CHAPTER 27. *Committee Reports*

Whitney v. New Haven (1890) 58 Conn. 450, 20 Atl. 666; *Reitzammer v. Desha Road Improvement District* (1919) 139 Ark. 168, 213 S.W. 773.

CHAPTER 28. *Meetings*

Lisbon Lund Company v. Town of Lake (1907) 134 Wis. 470, 113 N.W. 1099; *Ex parte Mirande* (1887) 73 Cal. 365, 14 Pac. 888; *Strain v. Mims* (1937) 123 Conn. 275, 193 Atl. 754.

CHAPTER 29. *Minutes*

Turnbull v. Giddings (1893) 95 Mich. 314, 54 N.W. 887; *Anniston v. Davis* (1893) 98 Ala. 629, 13 So. 331; *Wheat v. Van Tine* (1907) 149 Mich. 314, 112 N.W. 933.

CHAPTER 30. *Nominations and Elections*

State v. Tyrrell (1914) 158 Wis. 425, 149 N.W. 280; *Attorney General v. Oakman* (1901) 126 Mich. 717, 86 N.W. 151; *State v. Starr* (1906) 78 Conn. 636, 63 Atl. 512; *Witherspoon v. State* (1925) 138 Miss. 310, 103 So. 134; *State v. Reichmann* (1911) 239 Mo. 881, 142 S.W. 304.

READING BIBLIOGRAPHY

Armstrong, James William, *Public Speaking for Everyone; a Practical Handbook*. New York, Harper & Brothers, 1947. 246 pp.

Auer, John Jeffery, and Henry Lee Ewbank, *Handbook for Discussion Leaders*. New York, Harper & Brothers, 1947. 118 pp.

Baird, Albert Craig, *Argumentation, Discussion, and Debate*. New York, McGraw-Hill Book Company, Inc., 1950. 422 pp.

———, *Discussion; Principles and Types*. New York, McGraw-Hill Book Company, Inc., 1943. 348 pp.

Baird, Albert Craig, and Franklin H. Knower, *General Speech; an Introduction*. New York, McGraw-Hill Book Company, Inc., 1949. 500 pp.

Barnard, Chester Irving, *The Functions of the Executive*. Cambridge, Mass., Harvard University Press, 1938. 334 pp.

Beard, Charles Austin, with the collaboration of William Beard, *American Government and Politics*, 10th ed. New York, The Macmillan Company, 1949. 832 pp.

Bradford, Leland P., and John R. P. French, Jr. (ed.), "The Dynamics of the Discussion Group," *Journal of Social Issues*, Vol. 4, No. 2, Spring, 1948. Contains articles by different authors.

Brigance, William Norwood, *Speech: Its Techniques and Disciplines in a Free Society*. New York, Appleton-Century-Crofts, Inc., 1952. 582 pp.

Brown, Alvin, *Organization; a Formulation of Principle*. New York, Hibbert Printing Co., 1945. 308 pp.

Cannon, Clarence, *Cannon's Procedure in the House of Representatives*, 6th ed. Washington, D.C., Government Printing Office, 1951. 498 pp. (81st. Cong. 2d sess. House doc. 741).

Channing, William Ellery, *The Works of William E. Channing*, 17th complete ed. Boston, American Unitarian Asociation, 1867. 6 vols. in 3. Or any other edition.

Chase, Stuart, *Roads to Agreement; Successful Methods in the Science of Human Relations*. New York, Harper & Brothers, 1951. 250 pp.

Commons, John Rogers, and others, *History of Labor in the United States*.

New York, The Macmillan Company, 1918-35. 4 vols. There are various editions of this work.

"Conducting Union Meetings," *The Ammunition,* 6:6-13, February, 1948. Published by United Automobile Workers of America.

Cooper, Alfred M., *How to Conduct Conferences,* 2d ed. New York, McGraw-Hill Book Company, Inc., 1946. 207 pp.

Corwin, Edward Samuel, *The Constitution and What It Means Today,* 10th ed. Princeton, N.J., Princeton University Press, 1948. 273 pp.

Coyle, Grace Longwell, ed., *Studies in Group Behavior.* New York, Harper & Brothers, 1937. 258 pp.

————, *Group Experience and Democratic Values.* New York, Woman's Press, 1947. 185 pp.

Crocker, Lionel, *Business and Professional Speech.* New York, The Ronald Press Company, 1951. 463 pp.

Curti, Merle, "The Changing Pattern of Certain Humanitarian Organizations," *Annals of the American Academy of Political and Social Science,* 179:59-67, May, 1935.

Cushing, Luther Stearns, *Lex Parliamentaria Americana: Elements of the Law and Practice of Legislative Assemblies in the United States of America.* Boston, Little, Brown & Company, 1856. 1063 pp. A second edition was issued in 1863 and reissued in 1866.

————, *Manual of Parliamentary Practice: Rules of Proceedings and Debate in Deliberative Assemblies.* Boston, W. J. Reynolds, 1845 (copyright 1844). 173 pp.

————, *Rules of Proceeding and Debate in Deliberative Assemblies, with Additional Notes by the Publisher.* New York, Chiswick Publishing Co., 1899. 226 pp.

Davis, Joseph Stancliffe, *Essays in the Earlier History of American Corporations.* Cambridge, Mass., Harvard University Press, 1917. 2 vols.

Elliott, Harrison Sacket, *The Process of Group Thinking.* New York, Association Press, 1928. 229 pp.

Eurich, Alvin Christian, and Elmo Chamberlin Wilson, *Cooperative Contemporary Affairs Test.* Issued annually. Originally issued by the American Council on Education Cooperative Test Service; now issued by the Educational Testing Service Cooperative Test Division, Princeton, N.J.

Ferguson, John Henry, and Dean E. McHenry, *The American Federal Government.* New York, McGraw-Hill Book Company, Inc., 1947. 818 pp.

————, *Elements of American Government.* New York, McGraw-Hill Book Company, Inc., 1950. 803 pp.

Findlay, Bruce Allyn, and Esther Blair Findlay, *Your Rugged Constitution: How America's House of Freedom Is Planned and Built*. Stanford, Stanford University Press, 1950. 281 pp.

Foster, J. M., "Secret Societies and the State," *Arena*, 19:229-239, February, 1898.

Garland, Jasper Vanderbilt, *Discussion Methods, Explained and Illustrated*, rev. ed. New York, The H. W. Wilson Company, 1951. 376 pp.

Gilman, Wilbur E., Bower Aly, and Loren D. Reid, *Fundamentals of Speaking*. New York, The Macmillan Company, 1951. 608 pp.

Given, William Barns, *Bottom-up Management: People Working Together*. New York, Harper & Brothers, 1949. 171 pp.

Gray, Giles Wilkeson, "A Philosophy of Parliamentary Law," *The Quarterly Journal of Speech*, 27:437-441, October, 1941.

Gray, Giles Wilkeson, and Waldo Braden, *Public Speaking: Principles and Practice*. New York, Harper & Brothers, 1951. 581 pp.

Haiman, Franklyn Saul, *Group Leadership and Democratic Action*. Boston, Houghton Mifflin Company, 1951. 309 pp.

Handbook of Trade Union Methods. New York, International Ladies' Garment Workers' Union, Educational Department, 1937. 96 pp.

Hannaford, Earle S., *Conference Leadership in Business and Industry*. New York, McGraw-Hill Book Company, Inc., 1945. 289 pp.

Hatsell, John, *Precedents of Proceedings in the House of Commons, with Observations*. London, Printed by H. Hughes, for J. Dodsley, 1781. 247 pp. There have been other editions of this volume. The last one was issued in 1818, printed by L. Hansard.

Hayakawa, Samuel I., *Language in Action; a Guide to Accurate Thinking, Reading and Writing*. New York, Harcourt, Brace and Company, Inc., 1941. 243 pp.

Hegarty, Edward J., *How to Write a Speech*. New York, McGraw-Hill Book Company, Inc., 1951. 226 pp.

Herring, Edward Pendleton, *Group Representation Before Congress*. Baltimore, Md., Johns Hopkins Press, 1929. 309 pp.

Hill, Walter B., "The Great American Safety-Valve." *Century*, 44:383-84, July, 1892.

Hoffman, Paul Gray, *Peace Can Be Won*. Garden City, N.Y., Doubleday and Company, Inc., 1951. 188 pp.

Hoffman, William G., *Public Speaking for Businessmen*. New York, McGraw-Hill Book Company, Inc., 1949. 419 pp.

Homans, George Casper, *The Human Group*. New York, Harcourt, Brace and Company, Inc., 1950. 484 pp.

Jefferson, Thomas, *A Manual of Parliamentary Practice*. Washington City.

Printed by Samuel Harrison Smith, 1801. 99 pp. Second ed., Washington, Joseph Milligan and William Cooper, 1812. 188 pp. There have been many later editions of this.

Jennings, Helen Hall, *Leadership and Isolation; a Study of Personality in Interpersonal Relations,* 2d ed. Longmans, Green & Co., Inc., 1950. 349 pp.

Keltner, John, "Committee Dynamics: Leadership Aspects," *The Gavel,* 22:59-63, March, 1950.

Knowles, Malcolm S., *Informal Adult Education; a Guide for Administrators, Leaders and Teachers.* New York, Association Press, 1950. 272 pp.

LaPiere, Richard Tracy, *Collective Behavior.* New York, McGraw-Hill Book Company, Inc., 1938. 577 pp.

LaPiere, Richard Tracy, and Paul R. Farnsworth, *Social Psychology,* 3d ed. New York, McGraw-Hill Book Company, Inc., 1949. 626 pp.

MacIver, Robert Morrison, and Charles H. Page, *Society: an Introductory Analysis.* New York, Rinehart & Company, Inc., 1949. 697 pp.

Mason, Paul, *Manual of Legislative Procedure.* New York, McGraw-Hill Book Company, Inc., 1953. 640 pp.

McBurney, James Howard, and Kenneth G. Hance, *Discussion in Human Affairs.* New York, Harper & Brothers, 1950. 432 pp.

———, *The Principles and Methods of Discussion.* New York, Harper & Brothers, 1939. 452 pp.

McKown, Harry Charles, *The Student Council.* New York, McGraw-Hill Book Company, Inc., 1944. 352 pp.

Merriam, Charles Edward, *Public and Private Government.* New Haven, Yale University Press, 1944. 78 pp.

Morgan, Edmund Morris, and Francis X. Dwyer, *Introduction to the Study of Law,* 2d ed. Chicago, Callaghan & Company, 1948. 357 pp.

Ogg, Frederic Austin, and Perley Orman Ray, *Essentials of American Government,* 7th ed. New York, Appleton-Century-Crofts, Inc., 1952. 774 pp.

———, *Introduction to American Government,* 10th ed. New York, Appleton-Century-Crofts, Inc., 1951. 1063 pp.

Overstreet, Harry Allen, and Bonaro Wilkinson Overstreet, *Leaders for Adult Education.* New York, American Association for Adult Education, 1941. 202 pp.

Pierson, George Wilson, *Tocqueville and Beaumont in America.* New York, Oxford University Press, 1938. 852 pp.

Powers, David Guy, *Fundamentals of Speech.* New York, McGraw-Hill Book Company, Inc., 1951. 380 pp.

Roethlisberger, Fritz Jules, *Management and Morale*. Cambridge, Mass., Harvard University Press, 1941. 194 pp.

Sandford, William P., and Willard Hayes Yeager. *Practical Business Speaking*. New York, McGraw-Hill Book Company, Inc., 1937. 316 pp.

Schlesinger, Arthur Meier, *Paths to the Present*. New York, The Macmillan Company, 1949. 317 pp.

Schriber, Julius, *It Pays to Talk It Over; Some Notes and Suggestions for Group Discussion Leaders*. Washington, D.C., National Institute of Social Relations, 1947. 48 pp.

Simpson, Ray Hamill, *A Study of Those Who Influence and Those Who Are Influenced in Discussion*. New York, Columbia University Press, 1938. 89 pp.

Smith, Thomas Vernor, *The Democratic Way of Life*. Chicago, University of Chicago Press, 1926. 210 pp.

Stern, Renée Bernd, *Clubs, Making and Management*. Chicago, Rand McNally & Company, 1925. 250 pp.

Stigers, Marquis Fay, *Making Conference Programs Work*. New York, McGraw-Hill Book Company, Inc., 1949. 256 pp.

Sturgis, Alice Fleenor, *Sturgis Standard Code of Parliamentary Procedure*. New York, McGraw-Hill Book Company, Inc., 1951. 268 pp. A manual for adoption by organizations.

Swisher, Carl Brent, *Growth of Constitutional Power in the United States*. Chicago, University of Chicago Press, 1946. 261 pp.

Tead, Ordway, and Henry C. Metcalf, *Personnel Administration; Its Principles and Practice,* 3d ed. New York, McGraw-Hill Book Company, Inc., 1933. 519 pp.

———, *The Art of Leadership*. New York, McGraw-Hill Book Company, Inc., 1935. 308 pp.

To Secure These Rights. Washington, D.C., Government Printing Office, 1947. 178 pp.

Tocqueville, Alexis Charles Henri Maurice Clérel de, *Democracy in America*. The Henry Reeve text as revised by Francis Bowen, now further corrected and edited with introduction, editorial notes, and bibliographies by Phillips Bradley; foreword by Harold J. Laski. New York, Alfred A. Knopf, Inc., 1946. 2 vols. This work was first published in France in 1835, in England 1835-1840.

Trecker, Harleigh, and Audrey R. Trecker, *How to Work with Groups*. New York, Woman's Press, 1952. 167 pp.

———, *Social Group Work; Principles and Practice*. New York, Woman's Press, 1948. 313 pp.

Tyler, Alice Felt, *Freedom's Ferment: Phases of American Social History to 1860.* Minneapolis, University of Minnesota Press, 1944. 608 pp.

U.S.A., the Permanent Revolution, by the editors of *Fortune* in collaboration with Russell W. Davenport. New York, Prentice-Hall, Inc., 1951. 267 pp.

University Debaters' Annual: Reports of Debates and Other Forensic Activities of American Colleges and Universities During the Academic Year, Vols. 1-37. 1914-1915 to 1950-1951. The H. W. Wilson Company.

Utterback, William Emil, *Decision Through Discussion: a Manual for Group Leaders,* 3d ed. New York, Rinehart & Company, 1950. 51 pp.

————, *Group Thinking and Conference Leadership: Techniques of Discussion.* New York, Rinehart & Company, 1950. 248 pp.

Van Doren, Carl Clinton, *Great Rehearsal: the Story of the Making and Ratifying of the Constitution of the United States.* New York, The Viking Press, Inc., 1948. 338 pp.

Waples, Rufus, *A Handbook on Parliamentary Practice.* Chicago, Callaghan & Company, 1883. 275 pp. Second edition enlarged, Chicago, Callaghan and Company, 1901. 306 pp.

Wright, Milton, *Getting Along with People.* New York, McGraw-Hill Book Company, Inc., 1935. 310 pp.

Wilson, Gertrude, *Social Group Work Practice: the Creative Use of the Social Process.* Boston, Houghton Mifflin Company, 1949. 687 pp.

INDEX

347